The Evolution of Psychoanalysis

The Evolution of Psychoanalysis
CONTEMPORARY THEORY AND PRACTICE

John E. Gedo

Other Press
New York

Production Editor: Robert D. Hack

This book was set in 11 pt. Apollo by Alpha Graphics of Pittsfield, NH.

Library of Congress Cataloging-in-Publication Data

Gedo, John E.
   The evolution of psychoanalysis : contemporary theory and practice
/ by John Gedo.
     p.   cm.
   Includes bibliographical references and index.
   ISBN 1-892746-27-1
   1. Psychoanalysis—History. 2. Psychoanalysis—Philosophy.
I. Title.
   [DNLM: 1. Psychoanalytic Theory. 2. Psychoanalysis—trends. WM
460 G296e 1999]
RC503.G433 1999
616.89'17—dc21
DNLM/DLC
for Library of Congress
                                                     99-17458

I dedicate this book to Fred Levin and Arnold Wilson, whose work carries on in original ways what mine has aimed for.

Contents

Part II
Historical Summary

Introduction:
The Plan and Aims of
this Guide to the Literature

The current profusion of psychoanalytic publications—even if one confines attention to the literature available in English—would seem to make futile any efforts to master the intellectual history of our recent past. To reduce the material to manageable proportions, it is necessary, first of all, to establish some firm *terminus* after which one's account will begin. In other words, the date of first publication of the monographs to be surveyed will be one factor to dictate my choices. Because I expected to complete this work by the end of 1998, it seemed reasonable to focus on the twenty-five year period that would then terminate—that is, to consider only books published since 1973. This decision is less arbitrary than it may appear to be, for I published my first book (Gedo and Goldberg 1973) in that year; as an active contributor to the literature, I believe I have had to do so much reading that I am particularly well prepared to serve as guide to the significant works of the period in which I labored.

Although the books I have selected range in their date of publication from 1974 to 1997, this circumstance does not mean that I have surveyed the production of that quarter century in its entirety. This volume has been in preparation for several years, and I have pursued my reading for it topic by topic. As a result, the terminal point of my review is somewhat different in every chapter. To put this another way:

it is conceivable that I have overlooked works that will prove to be greatly influential if they have appeared in the last two or three years. I am confident that this possibility has been avoided for books published earlier, for I have given serious consideration to every work that received a favorable review in the most widely read English-language psychoanalytic journals.

In order neither to overburden myself nor to present developments in psychoanalysis in excessive detail, I have arbitrarily chosen to limit the number of monographs to be reviewed *in extenso* to sixty. This limitation has resulted in the exclusion of perhaps a dozen volumes that have considerable merit; I have tried, however, to refer to these works more briefly at appropriate junctures. I have also limited the number of books by a single author to be featured (to no more than two); in the case of some prolific contributors, I may have selected a work that might not prove to have the most lasting influence. I have confined my review of several works to particular portions of the book that I judged to have special merit. In a few instances, various aspects of one monograph have been considered in more than one chapter.

Every history reflects the subjectivity of the historian; I cannot possibly avoid reading the books of my colleagues (and competitors!) through my own bias. In other words, my present convictions and past writings will exert an inevitable distorting influence on my historical map of contemporary psychoanalysis. Wherever I became aware of this pull, I have tagged it by providing specific references to my published work. At the same time, I cannot serve as a critic of my own books, no matter how relevant they may be to a topic under consideration; consequently, I have not included them among the works featured in this guide. I must confess my hope that it is this omission that will prove to be the most significant lacuna in this volume.

In order to avoid cluttering my text with repeated references to my past work, it may be advantageous at the outset to spell out which of my attempted contributions I consider to be relevant to more than one issue to be discussed in this history. I do not claim priority in all these matters, but I have been one of the most persistent advocates of the following viewpoints:

1) a consistent commitment to psychoanalysis as a natural science, specifically one of the life sciences (Gedo 1991, 1993a, 1997a);

2) a hierarchical view of mental functions, determined by the hierarchical arrangement of the central nervous system (Gedo 1979a, 1981b, 1988; Gedo and Goldberg 1973; Wilson and Gedo 1993);

3) the centrality of the concept of self-organization for a clinically and epistemologically valid psychoanalytic theory (Gedo 1981b, 1988, 1996a);

4) a view of psychoanalytic treatment as an effort to correct dyspraxic patterns of behavior and to fill in apraxic deficits (Gedo 1988, 1991, 1993a, 1995a, b);

5) a technical algorithm that goes beyond interpretation (Gedo and Goldberg 1973; Gedo 1979a, 1981a, b, 1984, 1991, 1995a, b, 1996a; Gedo and Gehrie 1993);

6) the conclusion that, in terms of adaptation, mental contents are epiphenomenal; it is mental processing (that is, the biology of mind) that matters (Gedo 1991, 1993a, 1995a, b, 1996a).

I continue to believe that the foregoing viewpoints are valid and important.

Beyond omitting my own works, the most stringent limitation I have placed on this survey is that of dealing only with books focused on one (or at most a few) specific topic(s). Thus I have excluded heterogeneous collections of papers, however distinguished, such as the works of Anna Freud or Melanie Klein. Unfortunately, a few influential contributors have published only books of this type. Regrettably, I have also had to leave out multi-author edited volumes, even those that do maintain a focus on a single topic, for the heterogeneous views presented in such books defy this reviewer's integrative capacities. I believe, moreover, that authors who have made important contributions through such publications or through journal articles have for the most part also presented their ideas in book form. Several volumes in which previously published articles have been recast into a monograph are, in fact, represented in this survey. By including them, I have brought some of the most important contributions of the years just before 1973 into the history of the period on which I focus.

The Evolution of Psychoanalysis is meant to be a guide to those psychoanalytic books of the recent past that I look upon as *significant*. By this I do not mean that each of these books is necessarily one of the best of the era; very flawed works may, unfortunately, become quite influential. And some excellent works may lack significance for intellectual history—for instance, books that popularize the ideas of previous contributors. Still others do a fine job in dealing with a narrow topic, but that topic as such does not have sufficient importance for psychoanalysis as a whole to merit inclusion here. (Some fine books on specific aspects of psychopathology, such as Krystal's [1988] volume on alexithymia, provide the most cogent examples of such a narrow focus.) In a few cases, an author has published a series of books containing many of the same ideas; I have generally tried to include the most recent of such sequential position statements, not necessarily the one I consider most meritorious. I must confess, however, that I have not been entirely consistent about such a chronological choice among one author's works.

Finally, I came to the reluctant conclusion that the vast literature on the interdisciplinary uses of psychoanalytic scholarship merits a separate guide of its own, although its omission here means that some of the most interesting works of the period will go unmentioned. Perhaps I may be permitted to claim, in this connection, that my own books on creativity (Gedo 1983, 1996b; Gedo and Gedo 1992) are probably the best work I have done. But this volume is bulky enough, without venturing beyond the boundaries of "psychoanalysis proper."

I should also specify that significance does not necessarily imply popular success: some of the books I regard as quite important have not become widely known. Conversely, many works that have had wide distribution in the mental health community are, in my judgment, unworthy of consideration for a history of psychoanalytic ideas. Some of these are merely pastiche, borrowings from hither and yon; others digest previous work competently enough but introduce little or no novelty; a few may have become popular precisely because they (over)simplify complex issues. No doubt, however, nobody will be in complete agreement with my selections, and it is possible that I have inadvertently overlooked books I would have appreciated if they had come to my attention. On the topics covered in this guide, however, I did give serious consideration to every book that appeared in the reference list of the works I have featured. About certain topics, such as sexuality and gender issues, I have been unable to find any monographs that met my criteria for inclusion. (For a similar assessment of that literature, see S. Mitchell 1997.) Thus I cannot claim that this work is comprehensive; it is confined to those matters about which the past generation has made significant progress.

I must also address an issue of a different kind about this history: I have undoubtedly been more thorough in surveying the earlier years of the past generation than the more recent ones. This outcome is, in part, the natural result of my greater familiarity with the products of the period when I was myself most active in the field. Yet I do have a better reason for having skewed my sample in that direction: I believe that only with the passage of time does it become apparent which of the books published in a given era have had real significance for the discipline. Hence choices among the monographs of the most recent years are much more difficult to make. In this regard, I have probably erred on the side of excessive skepticism.

As a consequence, the most novel intellectual fashions within psychoanalysis are under-represented in this book. Admittedly, I am out of sympathy with most "post-modern" developments, so that I may well look upon important innovations as mere fads. At any rate, the latest novelties I even consider in this survey are hermeneutics, narratology, social constructivism, and intersubjectivity. (For a detailed assessment of these developments from my own perspective, see Gedo 1997a.) Beyond that "new wave," psychoanalysis has need for a younger historian. Needless to say, I have decided not to deal with those psychoanalytic fashions of the past that have in the interval become passé.

This volume consists of two (unequal) parts. In the first, which consists of five essays, I present reviews of the sixty featured monographs, arranged topic by topic, forming an annotated bibliography of the core psychoanalytic contributions of the past generation. The second part is a synoptic history of these intellectual developments, both theoretical and clinical, followed by a brief Conclusion. This organizational scheme will permit readers either to follow my thesis sequentially or to use this book as a work of reference in which the principal contributions on various topics produced from 1974 to 1997 are critically assessed. To facilitate both ways of using this guide, I have supplemented my reviews of the featured monographs, wherever necessary, with information about other pertinent works. Within my text, I have made an attempt to provide cross-references to related issues covered under different headings.

The first essay deals with the fundamental philosophical issues that underlie psychoanalytic conceptualization (chapters 1–2). The second is concerned with the principal theoretical and pragmatic problems that faced the discipline about twenty-five years ago—challenges that constituted a turning point in the intellectual history of the discipline (chapters 3–7). The third essay presents information relevant to those problematic issues that has come to light in the past generation, either through investigations in cognate disciplines or through psychoanalytic scholarship (chapters 8–10). In the fourth, I review the positions of the principal schools within psychoanalysis as they have evolved during this period, or (in the case of French psychoanalysis) as they have made their impact on the American psychoanalytic community (chapters 11–15). The fifth essay deals with the work of would-be ecumenicists that, in my judgment, lays the groundwork for future progress in psychoanalysis (chapters 16–18).

The single essay of the historical part of the book consists of chapters 19 and 20.

To orient readers for what follows, permit me to present a brief précis:

As it has concluded the first century of its existence, psychoanalysis as a domain of knowledge faced a number of interrelated crises. The challenge that perhaps proved most urgent was provided by a series of follow-up studies that called into question the efficacy of the traditional treatment methods most psychoanalysts utilized. Almost simultaneously, the consensus about the metapsychology Freud devised at the birth of psychoanalysis collapsed under rigorous scrutiny from theoreticians and methodologists. One corollary of this development was the necessity to reexamine the theory of motivation, which had suffered relative neglect since Freud last revised it in 1920. The important changes within the philosophy of science that characterize the Zeitgeist of the late twentieth century have called into question the epistemic foundations of psychoanalysis and raised doubts about the position of the discipline among the sciences. One of the alternatives suggested to resolve this issue was that psychoanalysis is primarily (or even exclusively) a hermeneutic enterprise, outside of natural science. Another possible solution, based on a dualistic position on the mind/body question, is that of a science of pure psychology, represented within psychoanalysis mostly by the proponents of a "relational perspective."

The past twenty-five years have yielded a vast amount of new information that must be taken into consideration to meet the challenges I have listed. Within clinical psychoanalysis, refinements in therapeutic procedures have led to new observations. The rapid expansion of the field of infant observation (started within psychoanalysis but now spread beyond its boundaries) has provided data against which developmental hypotheses have to be measured. The domains of cognitive science and of semiotics have also brought to psychoanalytic attention vital information about the development of crucial functions that these developmental hypotheses must take into account. Probably most important in this regard is the explosion of new knowledge about the early development of the central nervous system.

Psychoanalysis faces the second century of its existence in considerable intellectual disarray. Judging by its literature, most of its writers belong to one or another inward-looking school of thought, isolated from the others; each of these traditions has its own evolutionary path, but all too often this is merely a grudging retreat from the indefensible positions each school espoused in the past. Such parochialism can be found among ego psychologists, self psychologists, object relations theorists, Kleinians, and Lacanians, and no doubt in schools of lesser renown as well. Throughout my career, I have opposed such isolationism; I am sure the essay in which I review the various schools reflects my distaste for their cultishness. It should be understood, however, that many contributors who have more or less adhered to each of these viewpoints have been able to transcend them. In the fifth essay of this volume, I consider the new consensus such contributors seem to be forging, in both theory and technique.

It is to this future consensus that my concluding historical overview will, I trust, make some contribution.

I make no apology for restricting the purview of this book to psychoanalysis as a body of knowledge (internal affairs, if you will), despite the fact that the last twenty-five years have been marked by dramatic developments in its relations with society at large. Like that of interdisciplinary endeavors, the topic of psychoanalysis and its social matrix deserves separate treatment. Excellent works have dealt with many aspects of this matter, which are truly of vital importance for the future of psychoanalysis as a profession. Take, for instance, Juliet Mitchell's (1974) *Psychoanalysis and Feminism*, arguably the best defense of the discipline against any of its detractors. As a contribution to psychoanalysis itself, this scholarly work by Mitchell's own estimate merely reviews the conclusions of past authors: advances in the psychoanalytic view of the psychology of women made in a previous generation.

A historian is like a passionate voyager, ever tempted to go on to the next golden city, just over the horizon. To complete a successful journey, however, requires the renunciation of boundlessness.

Chicago
November 1998

I

TOPICAL REVIEWS
OF THE LITERATURE

THE CONCEPTUAL BACKGROUND

I
Epistemology

Michael Polányi came to the philosophy of science from physical chemistry; his writings allude to psychoanalysis only tangentially. Nevertheless, Polányi's brilliant, historically informed defense of science as a social institution offers psychoanalysis the intellectual tools it needs to affirm the scientific legitimacy of its observational methods and of its theory construction. As a contribution to the history of ideas, Polányi's work is a stunning attack on logical positivism, the epistemological view that demands empirical proof for all scientific propositions.

In a beautifully argued analysis of the evolution of scientific method, Polányi demonstrates that inductivism (inference from observational data to form hypotheses) is not the sole pathway to truth; he shows that the contemporary tendency of scientists to minimize the role of speculation in making discoveries is itself irrational. The fact that no theory can be proven through induction was long ago demonstrated by David Hume. Moreover, only the greatest scientists possess the rare ability to develop abstractions from observational data. Polányi stresses that

5

the history of science has been obscured by the emphasis it has placed on the process of validation at the expense of studying the process of discovery—a point well illustrated by the prevalent tenor of the books of Edelson and Grünbaum to be reviewed here. In Polányi's judgment, discoveries are generally based on conviction and self-confidence on the part of the scientist, and on the force exerted by the beauty, elegance, profundity, and grandeur of ideas, not on passionless or pseudo-objective procedures.

The foregoing characteristics of scientific work suggest that it can be propagated only by direct personal contact. This scientific tradition of mentoring has been continuous from the days of Galileo through those of Freud, and (one might add) it is still explicitly perpetuated within psychoanalysis. In this view, practicing science is an art mastered by a tiny elite, and it remains viable only if it succeeds in impressing a wider public and eliciting its support. In the last analysis, attacks on science as well as outsiders' efforts to control it are akin to wars of religion. Such opposition has grown in the contemporary world, which (in Polányi's opinion), is characterized by barren skepticism on the one hand and fervent reformist programs on the other. Modern societies thus tend to subvert science into a merely utilitarian enterprise. Polányi sees these attempts to bend knowledge to practical uses as disastrous obstacles to scientific progress, a point well exemplified, in my judgment, by the pragmatic tilt of psychoanalysis as a profession, in response to a hostile society.

Polányi frankly labels science as a system of beliefs; hence he defines scientific innovation as the replacement of one set of normative beliefs by another that has aroused greater credence. In these belief systems, facts that cannot be accounted for are simply disregarded, or they are dismissed as anomalies. Modern empiricists find these conditions embarrassing and therefore tend to deny or rationalize them. I believe that Polányi's description fits the history of psychoanalysis particularly well, a fact that the intellectual discourse of the past twenty-five years (which I shall attempt to map out in this volume) will substantiate.

Recent efforts to study human behavior scientifically have given rise to particularly sharp controversies. The positivists have condemned psychoanalysis and espouse the doctrine of behaviorism, for two reasons. First, behaviorism evades the problem of values, which they wish to exclude from consideration; second, it seemingly conforms to their shibboleth that scientific propositions must be stated in a manner that can, in principle, be disproved—what they call falsifiability. Polányi shows that splitting the factual from the moral aspects of human affairs is necessarily invalid: one can deal with such matters only from the personal perspective of a sentient and responsible being who is participating in scientific activities. In other words, science is always person-bound, albeit comparatively less so in the so-called exact disciplines.

It follows from these considerations that science has to discover exact standards for extended uses of personal knowing. Although Polányi does not say so, this is clearly a crucial task psychoanalysis could perform in the development of science. Through such efforts, it might help to correct the tendency of modern positivism and rationalism to deny that knowledge is forever uncertain and that the current, tentative version of knowledge can be based only on faith in one's predecessors, empathy, and the appreciation of others' purposes and meanings.

Along these lines, the epistemologist Adolf Grünbaum has correctly discerned that Freud intended to develop psychoanalysis into a branch of natural science. He devotes a considerable portion of *The Foundations of Psychoanalysis* (1984) to a rebuttal of the views of those of his philosophical colleagues who believe Freud's position on this fundamental issue to have been a misunderstanding of his own achievements. I shall discuss this matter further in chapter 6, where I consider the issue of hermeneutics; suffice it to say here that I found Grünbaum's lucid arguments to be persuasive; in my judgment, he demonstrates that the hermeneuticists have missed the essence of psychoanalysis and have also mischaracterized all of natural science. The philosopher/analyst Carlo Strenger (1991) also finds that Grünbaum has the better of this argument.

Grünbaum next addresses the problem of an admitted prerequisite of scientificity: the empirical testability of psychoanalytic propositions. The positivist philosopher Karl Popper had made the claim that analytic hypotheses are not falsifiable (and hence do not qualify as natural science), but Grünbaum shows that numerous analytic tenets have, in fact, been disproved; on occasion, Freud himself changed his theories as a result of such disproof—witness his abandonment of the seduction hypothesis of neurotic etiology. In Grünbaum's view, the problem is not that psychoanalytic propositions are unfalsifiable; it is that they have not been properly validated. Although he is on solid ground in calling attention to this unsatisfactory state of affairs, the prospective and extra-clinical validation studies he calls for are so complex and costly that in the foreseeable future there is no chance whatsoever of carrying them out. For the moment, psychoanalysts will have to continue to lend credence to one or another set of normative beliefs, without validation. As Strenger (1991) puts this, psychoanalysis at its core is a fruitful research program, not a set of specific propositions that urgently call for validation.

Grünbaum devotes much of his 1984 book to an examination of the feasibility of validating analytic propositions on the basis of clinical evidence collected in the analytic situation. He argues, convincingly, that therapeutic success is not probative for such propositions because the possibility of placebo effects can never be ruled out. This is the reason for Grünbaum's insistence on the need for *extraclinical* validation studies. I find it odd that Grünbaum, who is thoroughly familiar with the history of Freud's abandonment of his seduction hypothesis, fails to acknowledge that psychoanalytic hypotheses have repeatedly been found to be invalid because they led to therapeutic *failures*. Nor does he discuss the fact that the discipline does not lend credence to any belief on the basis of the report of a single case but, as the material in the chapter on the Challenge to Therapeutics will demonstrate, only on that of collective experiences. This is a point cogently discussed by Rubinstein (1997, chapter 6).

In *Psychoanalysis: A Theory in Crisis*, Marshall Edelson (1988) takes up most of the issues Grünbaum covered in 1984. He emphatically agrees with the latter that psychoanalysis is a natural science; Edelson rightly argues that psychoanalysis must be regarded as such because of its postulation of *causal* explanations. He points out that hermeneuticists consistently overlook these causal claims of psychoanalysis about actual (intrapsychic) events that, according to psychoanalytic theories, propagate their influence through a system with enduring properties. Thus Edelson defines psychoanalysis as a discipline that studies a world of psychological *facts*. The propositions of such a discipline must possess truth value and be subject to scientific canons, which are uniform for all scientific domains. Scientific discovery should therefore be followed by scientific justification, by means of empirical testing. Contrary to the view of hermeneuticists, such validation studies are all the more important for psychoanalysis precisely because (as they have stressed) its primary data are skewed by the observer's subjectivity, and the entities it studies are non-material.

Edelson believes that Grünbaum's caveats about the lack of validation of psychoanalytic hypotheses should be taken very seriously, but he disagrees with the latter's skepticism about the possibility of validation through case-study methods. One prerequisite for successful employment of such methods is consistently to assess the cogency of several rival hypotheses for a given clinical contingency; such a research design may render even the study of a single case useful. Edelson rightly points out that a hypothesis gains support if it is able to predict events generally regarded as unlikely. In any case, clinical tests can certainly subject analytic hypotheses to refutation; Edelson stresses that, for scientific validation, it is always negative instances that are most telling. He concedes, however, that most clinical inferences remain unproved, merely gaining credibility as a result of possessing associative links. Decisive confirmation is provided only when conditions are reexperienced as conscious states. (Edelson does not say so, but this may occur without prior interpretation by the analyst.) Finally, Edelson concedes Grünbaum's cogent point that mere detection of a particular set of mental contents does not in itself validate any causal proposition within psychoanalytic theory: correlation does not prove causality.

One reason for Grünbaum's excessive pessimism about the probative value of clinical data is his unwarranted assumption that the causal connections central for analytic theory are those linking current data to the childhood past—matters truly extremely difficult to establish. Both Edelson and Strenger (1991, Chapter 4) fault Grünbaum for having misrepresented psychoanalytic theory on this score. I would add that Grünbaum's refusal to acknowledge that, at present, there are a number of analytic theories as worthy of serious consideration as the 100-year-old Freudian propositions on which his discussion is focused also limits the relevance of his thesis; as this review of the principal psychoanalytic books of the past twenty-five years will demonstrate, many analytic propositions have recently been invalidated, and some have even been validated, both through clinical and through extraclinical methods. Grünbaum's habit of dismissing the ideas of those who disagree with Freud by labeling their work as "not analysis" is unacceptable.

Grünbaum's inquisitorial stance is particularly ill fitting in view of the fact that, despite his extensive reading of its literature, his understanding of psychoanalysis (both as treatment and as an assembly of theoretical propositions) betrays some weaknesses. For instance, he fails to realize that if he dispenses with Freud's metapsychology, as he has chosen to do because of the controversies to be considered in the chapter on the Challenge to Metapsychology, his continuing focus on the concept of repression becomes a solecism, for repression is not the purely clinical construct he believes it to be. Similarly, he does not grasp that the reason analysts insist that observational data obtained in the analytic situation are uniquely relevant is that, beyond the bounds of the basic rule of free association, one cannot witness how the mind of another person operates when it is free of the constraints of social requirements. Edelson has given appropriate emphasis to the fact that psychoanalytic theory is focused on explaining how the mind works in these circumstances, and that it is in that regard that psychoanalysis and neuroscience are convergent (see the chapter on Toward a Biological Metatheory).

In *Validation in the Clinical Theory of Psychoanalysis*, Grünbaum amplifies his arguments and responds to the numerous reactions provoked by his 1984 book, including those of Edelson and Strenger. In the 1993 volume, Grünbaum clarifies his essentially pro-psychoanalytic stance; he makes clear that he fully credits the clinical situation of psychoanalysis with unique heuristic advantages for generating fruitful hypotheses about human psychology. He reiterates, however, that the detection of various connections among the thematic meanings of mental contents does not amount to the demonstration of the *causal* significance of such contents that is postulated in psychoanalytic theory. Consequently, Grünbaum concludes that the construction of convincing narratives (as hermeneuticists recommend in their version of the clinical aims of psychoanalytic treatment) cannot satisfy the requirements of developing valid analytic propositions. This is the principal reason for Grünbaum's judgment that the hermeneutic option can only trivialize psychoanalysis. (He calls it a kiss of death.)

Grünbaum devotes much effort to shoring up his thesis, against Edelson's arguments to the contrary, that clinical data can in principle never suffice to validate analytic hypotheses. However that may be, Grünbaum fails to acknowledge that the extra-clinical validation studies he deems essential should be focused on the unique observational data collected in a psychoanalytic setting; he overlooks the fact that combined research designs of that kind have already been devised (see, for example, P. Gedo 1988). To put this another way, the first priority in pursuing Grünbaum's probative research program should be to test the hypothesis that the process of free association yields data with unique characteristics. Regrettably, Grünbaum does not make the necessary distinction between simple introspection (the results of which he rightly regards as unreliable) and self-inquiry based on free association (see Gardner 1983).

Whatever its shortcomings, Grünbaum's challenge to psychoanalysis about its failure to validate its hypotheses has correctly gauged the intellectual tenor of our era of revisionism. In most ways, Grünbaum is more of a psychoanalytic traditionalist than most of the authors whose work will be reviewed in this book, for he very rarely claims that any of Freud's ideas has been refuted. From the viewpoint of an epistemologist, such caution is probably necessary; from that of psychoanalysis itself, it is clear that Polányi's account of the manner in which scientific paradigms succeed each other is the more cogent description of the recent metamorphosis of the discipline.

2
The Philosophy of Mind

- *The History of the Concept of Association of Ideas.* D. Rapaport.
- *Psychoanalysis and the Philosophy of Science.* B. Rubinstein.
- *The Psychoanalytic Mind.* M. Cavell.

Marcia Cavell begins her challenging monograph by stating that every version of psychoanalysis relies on a number of philosophical assumptions about "mind." This claim means that, in addition to empirical underpinnings, psychoanalytic theories also make use of a rationalist epistemology—and rival theories in the field are generally based on different philosophical assumptions. Well into the nineteenth century, psychology was an exclusively rationalist discipline and therefore constituted a branch of philosophy. David Rapaport's doctoral dissertation (for the University of Budapest), belatedly published in 1974, surveys the history of these philosophical developments through the seventeenth and eighteenth centuries, from Bacon, Descartes, and Hobbes, through Locke and Leibnitz, to Hume and Kant.

Rapaport focuses attention on the evolving concept of "association" because its clarification led to insight about the import of "psychic law," that is, of the relevance of scientific psychology to all of human behavior. Early in the seventeenth century, modern philosophy picked up the broken threads of Hellenistic thought about being and consciousness; at the time, associations were regarded merely as a source of errors in thinking. Descartes, who believed that innate ideas lead to knowledge, tried to specify the mechanism of associations in order to *limit* their supposedly undesirable influence. Hobbes was the first to view associations as vectors that often play the determining role in mental processes.

It was Locke who invented the term "association"; his views began to approximate recent concepts about mind. He believed that associations form the essence of reflection and intuition, and thus of all concept formation. In other words, he abandoned the mechanical concept of associations prevalent before his work. His conceptualization of "mental activity" gave birth to the genetic viewpoint in psychology. This viewpoint was extended by Leibnitz, who proposed that associations form an early stage of logical thought—a concept that decisively lifted associations out of the realm of pathology. Leibnitz was also the first philosopher not to exclude any part of the psychic domain from the realm of scientific laws, that is, not to exempt the "soul" from scientific scrutiny.

For Hume, the conception of the unity of mind as a system was no longer just a program to be pursued; he regarded such unity as a reality. This compelled him to initiate *dynamic* study of the associative process. Kant, in turn, systematized the work of his predecessors in philosophical psychology. In his system, associations gain validity by virtue of being a priori synthetic propositions; they constitute the mode of functioning of the imagination. For Kant, mind has three primary capacities: knowing, wishing, and experiencing pleasure and pain.

Rapaport concludes that the guiding thread within this history, from Descartes to Kant, is consensus on the conclusion that the emergence of associations is determined by desires. Cavell reminds us that Kant also realized that knowledge of the phenomenal world is inevitably organized in accordance with certain categories characteristic of human thought, so that human knowledge can never be absolute; it always remains a mere conceptual schema. In this regard, she believes that both Freud and Rapaport were Kantians, although Freud sometimes vacillated in this adherence to Kant's skeptical position.

In the twentieth century, Kant's skepticism has been extended by Wittgenstein's emphasis on the difficulties of precise communication, but in recent years many philosophers, including Cavell, have seen such "internalism" or "subjectivism" as exaggerated; she believes (*contra* Wittgenstein) that language constitutes a medium *linking* members of a community. In this view, language is always social; there can be no subjectivity without intersubjectivity. Contrary to her reading of Lacan (see the chapter on French Psychoanalysis), Cavell assumes that subjectivity does not exist prior to the acquisition of language (when there is as yet no "me"), so that the developmental step into the symbolic order does not constitute alienation from a prior state of being, as Lacan (1977) would have us believe. Cavell points out that language acquisition starts at birth, with the production of characteristic sounds to designate certain shared realities. These gradually overbalance a system of signaling by means of gestures (see also Muller 1996). At any rate, there is a human capacity for dialogue even before the acquisition of language: for instance, infants are able to create jokes without using speech.

Cavell's *philosophical* commitments about the "externalism" of language (and thought) entail the conclusion that psychoanalytic interpretations should correspond to something in reality and should, moreover, be congruent with all aspects of what is already known (see the chapter on the Narrative Option and Social Constructivism). Contrary to Spence (1982), she argues that psychoanalytic narratives can and should establish historical truth. (She rightly adds that, from a clinical viewpoint, it is often important to ascertain the actualities of past events.) In her view, deconstructionists illegitimately deny that the realities of human experience are socially shared, and this is the circumstance that enables people to have empathy for each other. In disagreement with Schafer (1976), she looks upon the reasons for human behavior as one category of causation. (This point is echoed in Rubinstein's treatise, as well as by Grünbaum in his books of 1984 and 1993.) Hence analytic interpretations should transcend the analyst's subjectivity; they should attain an objective standard. In other words, Cavell argues that psychoanalysis is rightly classified as a natural science, a judgment she also shares with Adolf Grünbaum (see the chapter on Epistemology). In her view, Schafer's disagreement with this classification is based on the fact that he conflates the concepts of action and activity, so that he can then disregard that certain organismic activities are not intentional; instead, he illegitimately regards them as if they constituted reasoned actions. (I believe she means that Schafer's error is to reduce human behaviors to the single category of the voli-tional, which can be encompassed within a mentalist framework. Un-like Kant, Schafer does not recognize that mankind often suffers against its will.)

Despite her commendable caution about the need for empirical validation, Cavell is more committed to a rationalist epistemology than are (most) natural scientists. Thus she *defines* thinking as a process dependent on language, a public activity wherein the unit of meaning is a sentence that can be communicated. In other words, according to her, chimpanzees and preverbal infants cannot "think." This view is directly contrary to that of cognitive psychology (see the account of Bucci 1997, in the chapter on the Input from Cognitive Science and its Uses). Of course, Cavell is entitled to define her terms in any way she chooses, but in this instance she has chosen the way least convenient for psychoanalytic purposes.

This point is best demonstrated by her claim that Freud's con-ception that thinking is possible without language refers to activi-ties that would better be described in somatic terms. She writes as if such prelinguistic neural processes were superseded (that is, stopped operating) when symbolic thinking becomes possible, an assumption both arbitrary and implausible. Although Cavell clearly states that "mentation" does not entirely coincide with intelligent behavior, and that infants acquire many skills before they have language, she insists that the control of such behaviors does not constitute thought. (By con-trast, most neurophysiologists classify even an act of perception as "thinking.") In accord with Cavell's rationalist definition of "thought," primary repression cannot exist, and unconsciousness is contingent on linguistic competence. But these are matters about which psychoana-lytic conceptualization should conform to the way that illuminates the broadest range of the empirical data collected in the analytic situation. It is probably unrealistic, however, to expect a professional philoso-pher like Cavell to be able to maintain the delicate balance psychoanaly-sis needs between its empiricist and its rationalist underpinnings.

On the other side of the interdisciplinary divide, among psycho-analytic clinicians, only Benjamin Rubinstein acquired sufficient ex-pertise in the philosophy of science to hold his own in discourse with epistemologists. In his lifetime, Rubinstein published about a dozen closely reasoned essays on the subject, but he died without assembling them into a monograph. The 1997 collection of his intellectual work was edited and meticulously annotated by Robert Holt. I should state, before commenting on this book, that my own conceptual work is heavily indebted to Rubinstein, probably to a greater extent than is that of most other contributors to these debates.

Rubinstein's very first publication tackled the mind/body problem, a subject avoided by most psychoanalytic theoreticians—as Rubinstein tactfully notes. Everyone concedes, of course, that mental functions are not disembodied, that is, they depend on a neural substrate; the "hard question" (as it has come to be called in scientific discourse) is whether to opt for a monist view, that psychology and neuroscience study identical processes from different perspectives, or a dualist one. Rubinstein notes that Freud wavered about this choice: in the 1895 *Project* and the 1940 *Outline of Psychoanalysis*, he was a pure empiricist who was ostensibly dealing with events in the central nervous system; at other times, he used a rationalist approach by introducing arbitrary postulates, notably that of a "principle of constancy." This unwarranted assumption necessitated, in turn, the concept of "psychic energy," then libido theory, and finally the 1923 structural theory. Because these hypotheses do not conform to our current understanding of brain function (see the chapter Toward a Biological Metatheory), Rubinstein holds that, in order to remain a scientific discipline, psychoanalysis must discard these a priori postulates and replace them with ones that conform to the current understanding of neurophysiology. In other words, psychoanalytic theories must simultaneously be psychologically tenable and fit into a valid physiological model. Wherever our understanding of brain functions is insufficient to do this, the model should specify the general nature of the neural processes that will have to be explicated in detail to validate the hypotheses in question. Rubinstein calls such models *protoneurophysiological*.

Ostensibly, Freud espoused the monist position, and his vitalist notions (such as that of psychic energy) constitute inadvertent solecisms in his theoretical work. Despite his disclaimers of the possibility that psychoanalytic psychology could rest on purely mentalist foundations, Freud resorted to constructs lacking referents in biology: it is not possible to translate many of his terms into components of any protoneurophysiological model. Rubinstein does not criticize the "lower level" constructs of psychoanalytic theory, only the "higher level" terms proposed to explain them. The lack of validity of these constructs is a matter of importance because the correlation statements used in the clinical situation are deductively derived from them.

Rubinstein points out that psychoanalysis describes all human behavior as motivated. Freud needed his metapsychology to specify how behavior is tied to motivation. In practice, these abstract propositions (e.g., the constancy principle) are translated into symbolic formulae that have remained noncommittal on the crucial question whether they correspond to brain processes. In Rubinstein's view, no mentalist theory is subject to confirmation or refutation, yet psychoanalysis can claim to provide *explanations* only if its theories can also be scientifically tested outside the psychoanalytic situation—at bottom, via neurophysiology. Thus psychic energy was a meaningful concept within a descriptive, mentalist framework; from a protoneurophysiological viewpoint, however, it is an unworkable explanation —for one thing, because it has no role in explaining either changes of function or ego autonomy. In Rubinstein's view, the concept that various structures in the central nervous system interact to process information provides the optimal explanatory framework for psychoanalysis. From that perspective, the experience of pleasure and pain is explained by the experimentally demonstrated operations of hypothalamic reward systems. Similarly, the activation of the central nervous system is understood as the function of a reticular arousal system in response to relevant information. Neither process entails any discharge of energy.

Another way to state Rubinstein's position is that psychoanalytic theory must simultaneously account for human reasons and organismic causes, and these alternatives are merely ways of describing the same events in two distinct languages. At the same time, he does not dismiss a dualistic view of mind and body as philosophically untenable; courteously, he merely calls it "unreasonable" to look upon psychological processes as nonbiological events. By providing a carefully reasoned, detailed protoneurophysiological model that can account for all phenomena relevant to psychoanalysis without resort to any of the unwarranted postulates of Freud's metapsychology, Rubinstein convincingly demonstrates that it is not necessary (or desirable) to pursue an exclusively hermeneutic option in our theorizing, thereby abandoning science and thus rendering it impossible to test the validity of our constructs (see also the chapter on the Narrative Option and Social Constructivism).

As I discuss in the chapter on the Challenge to Metapsychology, Rubinstein does not concur with scholars (such as G. Klein 1976 and Gill 1994) who believe that a purely clinical theory is feasible for psychoanalysis. In other words, for scientific purposes we have to conceive of human beings qua organisms, beyond understanding them as persons: "In clinical practice we see man unequivocally as a person. However, to justify our hypotheses about unconscious mental events, we must turn our attention to the organism this person is also" (p. 262). Rubinstein points out that "organism" is a theoretical concept within natural science. A person-as-agent engages in activities; an organism exists by means of physiological processes. The psychoanalytic abstraction "unconscious," a fortiori "unconscious wish," is a construct that stands for certain processes of this kind (let us recall that Freud thought these processes unknowable!). Consequently, psychoanalytic theory deals with more than a person-as-agent: "the unconscious" is precisely what transcends the human world of subjectivity. Those aspects of the theory that deal with organismic realities are of necessity beyond psychology: "metapsychological." If they do not, in fact, refer to such observable physiological processes, these terms become hollow, mere verbiage. Moreover, in the absence of potential scientific validation, our rules of interpretive inference must remain axiomatic, that is, arbitrary. (In those terms, even Jung's set of interpretations is as plausible as is any other.) Mentalist theories promote the illusion that the person is just as much an "agent" of unconscious processes as of conscious choices. Rubinstein does not spell this out, but this is his objection to Schafer's (1976) action language. At any rate, he specifies that a theory about organismic processes cannot legitimately be encoded in a language tailored to describe the actions of persons; a depersonified vocabulary is, in fact, more suitable for it.

Rubinstein's text is dense and difficult; its subtleties defy attempts to summarize his argument, although his thinking is always lucid. He takes for granted that psychoanalysis aspires to scientific status, and those aspects of his thesis aimed at clarifying that issue echo what I have summarized in the chapter on Epistemology in reviewing the work of Edelson and Grünbaum. In my judgment, Rubinstein's work is the most important contribution of our era to psychoanalysis as a science; anyone who would discuss its theory without considering his views is evading the difficult issues and cannot be taken seriously.

THE TURNING POINT

3
The Challenge to Therapeutics

- *A Developmental View of the Psychoanalytic Process.* N. Schlessinger and F. Robbins.
- *Forty Two Lives in Treatment.* R. Wallerstein.
- *The Psychology of the Self: A Casebook.* A. Goldberg, ed.
- *Termination in Psychoanalysis.* S. Firestein.

Perhaps the most original aspect of the analytic literature of the past generation has been the publication of a significant number of books and articles dealing with the therapeutic outcome of attempted psychoanalytic intervention. Studies of this kind began to appear around 1960 (Pfeffer, 1959, 1961), at first as demonstrations of the feasibility of reliable follow-up performed by someone other than the analyst who conducted the treatment. Essentially similar methods characterized subsequent reports by teams from San Francisco (Oremland, Blacker, and Norman 1975; Norman, Blacker, Oremland, and Barrett 1976), and Chicago (Schlessinger and Robbins 1983).

Among the books under consideration here, those of Firestein, Schlessinger and Robbins, and Wallerstein involve case studies prepared by authors who did not perform the completed analyses described. In the casebook edited by Goldberg, the reports were prepared by those who conducted the treatments, but they were discussed by an entire team of research collaborators. Only the Wallerstein volume was meant explicitly to focus on the issue of the clinical results of the treatments under consideration; as his title indicates, Firestein was most interested in the problem of termination, and the Goldberg casebook was intended to illustrate the clinical procedures of self psychology. Despite this limitation, both books contain sufficient detail about changes in functioning between the start of these analyses and their termination to permit readers to draw their own conclusions about the clinical outcomes.

Goldberg and Firestein report on six and eight analyses, respectively. In Wallerstein's sample of forty-two treatments, twenty-two were originally supposed to follow the psychoanalytic model. To these thirty-six analyses, we may add three described by Pfeffer, three by the San Francisco group, and seven by Schlessinger and Robbins, for a total sample of forty-nine available for evaluation. This patient population is reasonably representative of those who seek analysis in North America; because most of the treatments were conducted by candidates in various training programs, however, some of the less satisfactory results might be attributed to the relative inexperience of these beginners. In my judgment, however, this factor should not be given too much weight. Erle has studied the problem of analyzability in large samples treated by candidates (Erle 1979) and by respected senior analysts (Erle and Goldberg 1984); she found no significant difference in the outcomes reported. It should be recalled that analyses conducted by candidates are supervised by the best clinicians available at their institutes; these mentors are apparently able to bring the level of the students' clinical performance up to the standards of the profession as a whole.

On a purely quantitative basis, the overall population of forty-nine analysands may be somewhat skewed in the direction of problems of excessive gravity, for Wallerstein's group of twenty-two consists of persons who sought help by turning to the Menninger Clinic, renowned for its inpatient services. Ten of these twenty-two patients probably would not have received a recommendation to try psychoanalysis without the continuous availability of a psychiatric hospital as an emergency resource. One of Wallerstein's persuasive conclusions is that attempts to use classical psychoanalysis for remediation in these cases with "heroic indications" are misguided. Treatment plans of that kind either had to be changed or resulted in catastrophic outcomes. Three of these unfortunates actually died.

Wallerstein is also able to document that these errors in prognosis were based on misdiagnoses (on the part of those who performed the analyses) of the extent and depth of the psychopathology. The patients were simultaneously assessed by means of a battery of psychological tests; those results showed that analysis was contraindicated in at least five of these cases. Wallerstein concludes that the tendency to underestimate potential obstacles to analyzability applied to his entire sample: prospective analysts were ever ready to construct illusory "best case scenarios." In a similar study of analyzability from Boston, Kantrowitz (1987) found the same overoptimism about prospective patients among those who undertook their analyses and a more realistic assessment of prognosis on the part of psychological testers without therapeutic goals.

The remaining twelve patients in the Topeka study were not discernibly different from the analysands described in the other books and articles under consideration; they also happen closely to resemble the analytic population I have had the opportunity to treat over the past four decades (see Gedo 1979b; 1984, chapter 2; 1991, chapter 10). Except for the six cases in Goldberg's book, the analyses described by all these authors adhered to a model technique confined to interpretation; any departure from this classical procedure was considered to be a "parameter" (Eissler 1953), that is, an exceptional intervention the rationale for which had to be interpreted, in its turn, for the analysand.

Although the great majority of persons who enter psychoanalysis derive appreciable therapeutic benefits from treatment, such an improvement in adaptation cannot always be attributed to the specifically analytic aspects of the patient's overall experience. In his sample, Wallerstein singles out four cases of this kind; appropriately, he asks whether in these instances the great commitment of resources to an analytic effort was worthwhile. For example, he describes an economist followed for twenty-eight years who began this course with 1,364 hours in analysis and was still being seen in supportive therapy when the report was written. The patient was able to obtain a Ph. D. and a decent academic appointment, but he led a constricted life devoid of intimacy. The effort to treat him analytically was abandoned when a psychotic transference made its appearance; stability was achieved only after the overambitious treatment plan was altered. As I read them, there are similar cases of dubious "analytic" results in most of the other reports; for instance, one of the patients from San Francisco (case #2 in Oremland, Blacker, and Norman 1975) had a relapse after terminating a 5½-year analysis and then had to seek nonanalytic assistance.

Wallerstein's research team used a standard rating scale (of 0 to 100) to assess adaptation; prior to treatment, their sample scored an average of 48, after termination 62, at follow-up 65. (This was a disappointment; the team expected analysis to raise the average score to 74.) Altogether, some improvement was noted in sixteen of the twenty-two patients, but in only eight of these was it better than "slight." If the six cases that were explicitly changed from analysis to psychotherapy are left out of consideration, eleven of the sixteen who remain showed improvement, six significantly. Whichever set of these outcomes we accept as relevant, the analytic technique practiced in Topeka some twenty-five years ago appears to have paid dividends in only sixty percent of cases.

In my judgment, Wallerstein's criteria of analytic success were not stringent enough; the same can be said for those of Firestein or Goldberg (for details, see Gedo 1980). Let us, for illustrative purposes, consider one of the patients who, according to Wallerstein, derived the greatest benefit from the analytic experience. The patient was a medical scientist in analysis for 1,147 sessions; his oedipal transference neurosis was interpreted from every conceivable aspect. The analysand got out of a bad marriage and remarried, satisfactorily. The termination was, however, only accomplished through a process of "tapering off." At follow-up, a surprising identification with the analyst was evident; the patient's vocational activities had turned in the direction of (a simplistic form of) psychological medicine. In my judgment, this analysis achieved something useful, but it was incomplete—probably because it focused exclusively on derivatives of the oedipal phase of development. Psychoanalysts cannot afford to be self-indulgent in assessing their results.

It would be erroneous to attribute the neglect of preoedipal vectors in pathogenesis to some local tradition in Topeka: the eight analyses summarized by Firestein, conducted under the aegis of the New York Institute, used exactly the same focus, and so did most of the others I have included in this survey, except for those in the Goldberg casebook. The technical prescription prevalent a generation ago was based on an implicit theory of development: that the legacies of previous phases were recapitulated (and therefore transformed) by the oedipal crisis, so that analytic resolution of that crisis through a transference neurosis would suffice to remedy the maladaptive heritage of preoedipal vicissitudes. The research I am reviewing here has definitively refuted that contention.

Take, for example, case #4 reported by Schlessinger and Robbins (1983). The analysis of this young woman helped her to complete mourning for the loss of her father (and a brother) during latency; it then proceeded to the emergence of an oedipal transference neurosis. Despite some regression during the terminal phase, the analysis was concluded after some 850 sessions. At follow-up, the patient reported some vocational improvement, but she complained of frigidity, and the researchers noted that her characterological rebelliousness and manipulativeness remained unchanged. (They attributed the unresolved problems to the neglect of "separation-individuation" issues during the analysis.) The follow-up procedures confronted this person with the poor outcome of her treatment; she soon returned to the analyst for a renewed therapeutic attempt.

I single out this case for discussion because it so happens that, about twenty five years ago, the candidate-analyst presented it in a continuous case seminar I was then co-teaching at the Chicago Institute. As I heard the material of the first year or so of this treatment, it did not suggest an oedipal neurosis (complicated by parent-loss in latency). Over the heated objections of my senior co-teacher, I tried to point out that the analysand repeatedly engaged in rebellious enactments that did not become the focus of analytic scrutiny, indicating that major aspects of the personality were split-off and remained inaccessible to representation in words. For instance, early in treatment the patient, without warning or a by-your-leave, took a photograph of the analyst, who did not dare to limit this behavior or even to investigate its significance. I do not cite this detail to highlight the candidate's technical ineptitude but to point out that, according to a senior member of the faculty, it was sufficient to await the elucidation of this issue in the heat of the expectable transference neurosis. I argued in vain that his viewpoint was a prescription for analytic failure.

Of the seven cases discussed by Schlessinger and Robbins, five (including all four in which follow-ups were done) had to resume treatment after supposedly agreed-upon terminations; in each instance, the authors attributed the unsatisfactory outcome of analysis to the utter neglect of preoedipal issues, which had been uniformly interpreted as regressive evasions of oedipal anxieties. They draw the plausible conclusion that the crucial characterological attributes on which the resolution of oedipal conflicts depends are derivatives of the vicissitudes of the preoedipal phases of development.

Although Wallerstein does not consider his data from such a developmental viewpoint, his conclusions about the outcomes of the twenty-two analyses in his sample are congruent with it. He reminds us that more than half of these efforts made use of extensive parametric modifications of technique, that some of the better results were seemingly based on transference cures, that certain analysands had to remain in some kind of treatment indefinitely or were "weaned" only very gradually, that in a couple of cases improvements represented a defiant retreat from the transference relationship, in others the crucial transferences were enacted outside the analysis. Wallerstein prudently counsels settling for improvements, however they come about: through corrective emotional experience, reeducation, disengagement from a noxious milieu, or sheer good luck. It seems to me that this amounts to a repudiation of the theories of analytic technique and of change prevalent in North America when the Menninger project was conceived.

Despite the foregoing limitations of "classical" psychoanalysis, in one case alone does Wallerstein suggest that following a different analytic model might have produced a better result. (In several other instances, however, he points out that the analysis did not explore the "mother transference" sufficiently [e.g., the case on pp. 302–307]. In some of the cases, my own impression, based on Wallerstein's account, is that failure was more a matter of the incompetence of the analyst than one of applying the wrong theory [see esp. the case on pp. 279–283].) At any rate, Wallerstein labels one patient "Prince"; in that instance, the analytic relationship took the form that Kohut (1968, 1971) designated as "mirror transference." The analysis was broken off after 950 sessions; when the patient later returned, the analyst chose to treat him with psychotherapy. Wallerstein raises the possibility that, with this patient, using Kohut's technical prescriptions might have been more appropriate. I shall return to that issue when I consider the data presented in the Goldberg casebook.

It is noteworthy that, in 1978, Firestein's report still expressed no reservations about the efficacy of an interpretive analytic technique focused on oedipal guilts and anxieties. In a private communication (c. 1980), Firestein told me that, although the analyses he studied were performed by candidates, he had chosen only those of high reputation; in other words, the cases in his book were not damaged by inept handling—nor did he find evidence (as did Wallerstein in some instances) of troublesome problems of countertransference. Yet the follow-up interviews revealed a host of residual difficulties in every case. Several of these analysands had to seek further treatment relatively soon after terminating analysis, others sorely missed therapeutic assistance or led empty, isolated lives or felt subjectively ill. Those who managed to function somewhat better than before did so as a result of painful efforts. Insofar as the insights gained in analysis helped, in most cases it was sexual inhibitions that were relieved and there was less anxiety when a vocational success was achieved. Moreover, the nonspecific beneficial results of the relative peace that supervened while these persons were in analysis generally did not dissipate.

Although Firestein's summaries suggest that the Oedipus complex had been interpreted in a plausible and exhaustive manner in each of these analyses, it is striking that it remained unresolved in every instance. For example, the analysis of Charlotte E. was characterized by a sadomasochistic struggle in the transference. (The patient felt that the opportunity to vent venom in treatment was a safety valve that prevented the psychotic decompensation she dreaded.) Her sexual excitement during the sessions had been attributed to reliving oedipal experiences vis-à-vis the analyst. At the prospect of termination, she reacted to impending loss of the relationship with a feeling of emptiness. Her vituperativeness with the analyst persisted; after termination, she was barely able to suppress her masochistic inclinations. After six years of analysis, she remained claustrophobic and led an isolated life. In my judgment, behind the overt oedipal manifestations, there had to be profound archaic problems. Little wonder that the patient was overtly dissatisfied with the outcome of her analysis and consoled herself with how prestigious it was to have been analyzed.

A year after termination, another patient (Shirley T.) was drinking to excess and her sadomasochistic battles with her husband were worse than ever. At follow-up, she described the nature of her therapeutic needs with clarity: she needed analysis to repair her deficient self-esteem; the seven years of treatment had "invigorated" her. In still another case (Frank B.), the temporary emergence of a delusional (mother) transference was ignored, in favor of interpreting passivity vis-à-vis father figures; when behavioral improvement was noted, termination was suggested, precisely because the analysand seemed "addicted" to treatment. At follow-up, Firestein found a man full of grief and rage, one who felt castrated by the loss of his relationship to the idealized analyst. (This follow-up resulted in the patient's return to his former analyst for renewed assistance.) Firestein's contact with patient Joseph V. was even less encouraging: V. was overtly paranoid about his former analyst. He also had colitis and was resorting to nonanalytic treatment.

Two of the analysands in Firestein's sample took the initiative to break off their treatment. Thomas F.'s analysis was focused on primal scene material. He became more and more silent; after four years of work, he decided to terminate. He had had mystical experiences in the past; now he revealed that entering analysis had satisfied his lifelong search for a transcendental power. At follow-up, he disclosed that his silences had concealed that he was experiencing the worst time of his life; he felt that a "demon had been trying to break out" of him. The other patient who fled, Martha R., had for four years refused to adhere to the basic rule of free association, apparently in the conviction that the analyst was omnipotent. She broke away when his *discovery* of her covert lack of cooperation revealed his lack of omniscience. One of the two remaining analyses in Firestein's series was interrupted by a move to another city; he classifies this as an "adventitious" event. I have my doubts: in my career, I undertook the analysis of 62 individuals, and none of them left town "adventitiously" while we were collaborating. To put this differently, in my experience, analysands do not run away if we are ready to accept their transferences, no matter how archaic these may prove to be.

It is striking how the analytic work at the clinic of the New York Psychoanalytic Institute remained unaffected by object relations theory or the influence of Kleinians; moreover, at the time these analyses took place, self psychology was not yet part of the analytic scene. By 1978 Firestein could have made reference to any of these alternative schools, but heterodoxy of that kind was not as yet possible in a New York context. In contrast, a dozen years later Pine (1990) published a book advocating the selective use of a variety of models of treatment, and his proposal did not provoke outrage. I can only assume that, in the interval, the "voice of the intellect" did gain a hearing, as Freud always desired: the cumulative published evidence has rendered the position some regarded as classical untenable. In the real world of clinical practice, in the vast majority of cases, the procedure of the psychoanalytic mainstream proved to be inadequate, and the mainstream responded by shifting course.

That history speaks well for the scientific status of American psychoanalysis—nowhere else in the analytic world have outcome studies of this kind been performed. Nor have the adherents of any of the schools of psychoanalysis outside of the American mainstream validated their claims of superior results. It should be noted that Goldberg's casebook presents a highly select sample of precisely those analysands whom Kohut believed to be most suitable for the therapeutic method he had developed; this work does not address the question of how such a prescription would work out with the gamut of persons who seek psychoanalysis. Nor are follow-ups available for any of the patients described; in that sense, these reports of analytic results are less reliable than those of the other research groups I am reviewing.

Another way to approach this issue is to recall that what is looked upon as the successful termination of an analysis is determined by the observer's theoretical preconceptions. (Contrast this indeterminacy with the rating scale for adaptation agreed upon in advance of collecting the data that permitted quantification of the results in Wallerstein's study.) Goldberg's book was prepared at the very time when Kohut (1977) decided that the appropriate end point for analysis (of "narcissistic disorders" in particular) is the acquisition of "compensatory structures" that make better adaptation possible. This viewpoint is more or less in accord with the modest therapeutic ambitions recommended by Wallerstein at the conclusion of his study. For my part, I have never accepted such a purely pragmatic goal for analysis, albeit it may be satisfactory as a psychotherapeutic outcome (see Gedo 1980). By my criteria, three of the six analyses described in *The Psychology of the Self* (Mr. B., Mr. M., and Mrs. A.) remained incomplete. In his later work, Kohut (1984) explicitly stated that unending reliance on selfobjects is the normal state of humankind; I understand that claim to mean that it is not even desirable to attempt to resolve analysands' archaic transferences. Another patient in Goldberg's sample, Mr. I., cut his analysis short, allegedly for external reasons.

However complete or incomplete these analyses might have been (and in none of the six were oedipal issues dealt with at all), at termination there were appreciable adaptive improvements in every case. Mr. B. seemed to have overcome a tendency to become disorganized; Mr. E. had become able better to manage issues of tension regulation; similar gains on the part of Mr. I. were only put in doubt by the premature termination of his treatment. The case summaries are not sufficiently explicit to judge whether the resort to perversions previously present in every patient had disappeared at termination. It is certainly clear that several continued to idealize their analyst—Mr. I. actually attributed God-like powers to his.

Because of the frequency of relapse following incomplete analyses in the patients included in the various follow-up studies, it is impossible to compare the clinical results of the self-psychology casebook with those of the analyses conducted along traditional lines. The only series of terminated analyses that is more or less comparable to that of the casebook is my own (Gedo 1991, chapter 10). I attempted to conduct a psychoanalysis for 62 individuals; with 50, we reached mutually agreed upon termination, with satisfactory improvements in adaptation. In four cases, I abandoned the analytic effort in favor of psychotherapy; one patient had to be hospitalized (and therefore had to seek a therapist in another city), and one was transferred to another analyst (for good reasons intrinsic to the analysis). One person who stopped prematurely subsequently did relatively well; about the other five I have no information, but most of them left treatment because we had reached an impasse.

Although the way I conducted analyses kept changing over the years, at no time did I confine myself to the kind of narrow focus (either on oedipal issues or narcissistic ones) pursued by the analysts represented in all the studies considered here. (One might say that, for the first decade of my analytic activities, I adhered to the viewpoint Pine espouses in his 1990 book; since around 1968, I have used a hierarchical model of mental life and a complex theory of technique based upon it.) I do not cite my results as evidence for the validity of my theories of technique; rather, I wish to underscore why I judge the analytic work reported in all the follow-up studies so harshly.

In terms of process criteria, my methods led to a higher proportion of terminations by mutual agreement than are reported in any of the books under review. In terms of outcome at the time they terminated treatment, my analysands did much better than any of those described by Firestein or Wallerstein—if the analysands they describe had been my patients, I would have looked upon my work with them as analytic failures. I suspect that my analysands did at least as well as the patients in the Goldberg casebook, but I do not wish to put this in competitive terms. All I am trying to say is that good results are contingent on paying proper attention to archaic issues (as Schlessinger and Robbins rightly concluded) but that Heinz Kohut's specific prescription for doing that is not necessarily the best.

4
The Challenge
to Metapsychology

- *Freud Reappraised: A Fresh Look at Psychoanalytic Theory.* R. Holt.
- *Modern Psychoanalytic Concepts in a General Psychology.* A. Rosenblatt and J. Thickstun.
- *Psychoanalytic Theory: An Exploration of Essentials.* G. Klein.

Without a doubt, the greatest agent of change within recent psychoanalysis has been accelerating disenchantment with the metapsychology Freud proposed a century earlier to form the biological anchor for his conceptual system. Many authors have contributed to the successful challenge of Freud's assumptions, but only a few in the form of monographs. Perhaps the most concise statement of the objections to Freud's metatheory was that of the eminent, psychoanalytically trained physicist Don Swanson (1977), who concluded that, as a set of biological propositions, Freudian metapsychology has been refuted by the results of neuroscientific studies; as a philosophical enterprise, it is epistemically unsound (among other things, because it violates certain physical laws); and as a guide for the clinician, it is based on circular reasoning, so that it is actually redundant and therefore trivial. (The philosophical issues relevant here have been discussed in Essay One of this volume.)

In terms of intellectual history, the metapsychological revolution was led by those students of David Rapaport who founded the *Psycho-*

logical Issues monograph series, notably George Klein and Robert Holt, and by Benjamin Rubinstein, whose indispensable contributions to this debate were collected only very recently (see the chapter on the Philosophy of Mind). It is noteworthy that Rubinstein's papers of 1965 and 1967 (in Rubinstein 1997) are frequently cited by the other contributors to the discussion, and Holt reports that as early as 1962 Rubinstein alerted him to the fact that the notion of psychic energy covertly introduces vitalism (that is, the postulation of a non-material spirit or soul) into Freud's ostensibly mechanistic theory.

Holt's own book of 1989 contains papers he wrote on this subject from 1962 to 1988. The earliest (chapter 4) was an examination of the meanings of the "bound" and "free" cathexis of psychic energy postulated by Freud; in a 1989 introduction, Holt notes that in this study he was not yet skeptical about the existence of psychic energy in nature, and he adds that he now considers Freud's classification of cathexes to be a mere metaphor, based on analogies to certain chemical concepts. Perhaps the core of this volume is chapter 5 (originally published in 1965), where Holt discusses Freud's biological assumptions and their influence on his psychoanalytic theories; this fundamental contribution spells out the reasons for Swanson's later conclusion that, as biological science, Freud's metapsychology proved to be incorrect.

As Holt acknowledges, the 1965 version of this chapter overlooked Freud's adherence to Darwinism, an omission rectified by Frank Sulloway in an important (albeit overly polemical) monograph of 1979. Holt had concentrated, instead, on Freud's commitment to the "school of Helmholtz," to which the future founder of psychoanalysis came to adhere by way of the instruction of his professor of physiology, Brücke, and his professor of neuropsychiatry, Meynert. These scientific predecessors taught him to conceive of the central nervous system as passive, a "reflex arc" through which stimuli pass as excitations from afferent (sensory) to efferent (motor) termini. It was also from these neuroscientists that Freud got the notion that the goal of this biological apparatus is to conserve energy. Freud enunciated this "conservation principle" as a paramount need to accomplish the reduction of tension within the nervous system. Because endogenous stimuli (in contrast to exogenous ones) cannot be escaped, in this view "drives" constitute the primal source of human motives. These biological hypotheses have subsequently been tested, and every one of them has been refuted.

Holt points out that, in its thoroughgoing materialism, Freud's 1895 *Project for a Scientific Psychology* tried to carry out the program of Helmholtz to banish vitalism from biology. Contrary to prevailing opinion, Holt demonstrates that Freud did not abandon such a neurological platform in *The Interpretation of Dreams* (1900) or his later works, although this continuing reliance on biology becomes covert as of 1900. In his theoretical chapter VII of *The Interpretation of Dreams*, Freud explicitly retained the reflex arc model; he added that pleasure is to be equated with tension reduction. (After 1920, this notion of nirvana is elaborated as the "death instinct.") In parallel, the constancy principle was renamed the "pleasure principle." Holt concludes that Freud's "psychic apparatus" (putatively fueled by "psychic energy") actually constitutes a plausible power engineering model of the brain, albeit an incorrect one.

Holt goes on to demonstrate that, contrary to Freud's assumptions, the central nervous system is ever active; stimulation merely lends this activity its patterning. Nervous tissue conducts not energy but impulses that serve as signals; similarly, the sense organs merely *traduce* stimuli into a transmissible code; the organism does not seek nirvana but needs moderate levels of stimulation—an actual deprivation of stimuli causes unpleasure. (To be sure, trauma consists of persistently excessive stimulation that produces an information load the brain is unable to integrate, so that disorganization follows.) Freud's purely quantitative explanations for pleasure and unpleasure (as changing levels of tension) have been overthrown by the discovery of neurochemical causes for these sensations, produced in discrete cerebral centers. In summary, Freud's power-engineering understanding of brain function has to be replaced by one based on information science.

Holt points out that numerous subsidiary concepts of psychoanalytic theory stem from the foregoing biological assumptions, all of which have been refuted. For instance, the notions of cathexis, stimulus barrier, aim inhibition, even that of "ego," are directly derived from the hypotheses falsified by biological research. Because it has been thought, incorrectly, that Freud had abandoned the neurophysiological basis of his theories, later disproof of his biological assumptions has had no immediate effect on psychoanalytic thinking: metapsychology had been illegitimately severed from its roots in natural science. Perceptively, Holt observes that psychoanalysts have, by denying their biological assumptions in this way, permitted themselves freely and irrationally to shift between "psychological" and "physiological" frames of reference as it suited their immediate rhetorical convenience, an epistemic critique more fully explored by Rubinstein (1997). As an example of such an illegitimate shift, Holt cites Freud's postulation (already present in the *Project*) of an "observing ego" without specification of any physiological basis for it. Because Freud was pursuing a materialist program, such a conceptualization without a basis in physiology was an illegitimate resort to covert vitalism.

In a 1967 paper (now chapter 6), Holt went on to spell out Rubinstein's insight that the very concept of psychic energy constitutes a resort to vitalism, for the idea nowhere fits into the only alternative to it, the mechanistic viewpoint. By conceiving of a psyche (an "ego homunculus") operating within a soma that is in turn conceived as a mechanism, Freud implicitly turned from his epistemic commitment to psychophysical parallelism to unwitting adherence to the dualism of psyche (spirit) and soma enunciated by Descartes. Any postulation of a "soul" is, of course, untestable; Holt believes such a lapse into vitalism was congruent with Freud's repeated flirtations with overt spiritualism. Further, he points out that the development of information science has rendered *both* vitalism and mechanism obsolete as biological frameworks; Rubinstein's epistemological papers spell out a way to transcend this sterile dichotomy (see the chapter on the Philosophy of Mind).

The foregoing considerations call into question the Freudian attempt to explain motivation through the concept of "drives." Holt looks upon this idea as a reification and concretization of the very concept of a motive. He offers alternative explanations: because it is aroused by specific stimuli, sexuality is best considered an *appetite*; in exact analogy with flight reactions, aggression is a *reaction* to threat; hunger and thirst are *signals*—in other words, better explanations are available for them all than is the dubious concept of drive (which, in its turn, is dependent on the fictive construct of psychic energy).

The same issue is discussed in chapter 3 of George Klein's 1976 book (a paper previously published and thus immune from the bias of the editors of this posthumous volume who, in my judgment, in some ways tried misleadingly to reframe Klein's viewpoint in line with their own). Keenly aware that sexuality has been of central importance in the evolution of psychoanalysis, Klein concentrated on differentiating the meta-psychological theory of libido (based on the model of obligatory drive discharge to reduce tension) from clinical theories about the role of conflicted sexual wishes in neurosogenesis. He stressed that, as an explanatory theory, the concept of drive does nothing to enhance understanding of the data of clinical observation (as Rubinstein put it in 1967, the concept of psychic energy is a tautology: this is why Swanson was to judge metapsychological explanations to be clinically trivial). The drive concept belongs in the mechanistic realm, that of a "psychic apparatus" irredeemably divorced from the world of wishes and object relations. To replace the libido theory as an attempted explanation for the occurrence of sexual wishes, Klein proposed that children formulate wishes in accord with cognitive schemata they construct on the basis of memories of past experiences of pleasure (see also Dorpat and Miller 1992).

In parallel with this demonstration that abandoning Freud's metapsychology need not alter the psychoanalytic understanding of the role of sexuality in human existence, Klein published an analysis of the concept of ego (in his book, reprinted as chapter 4). He pointed out that the term can be defined narrowly (to denote only defensive operations) or quite broadly (as an "organ of adaptation"), as the representative of reality, as a regulator that makes choices and signals dangers, or as the initiator of various psychic processes. In Klein's view, all these conceptions are unsatisfactory because they do not account for what Hartmann (1939) named a "synthetic function." In this Hartmannian sense, psychoanalytic theory needs to encompass the *correlation* of the activity of all psychic systems—to posit a supraordinate integrator that acts in a manner that transcends "the mind in conflict" (Brenner 1982). In other words, as a theory, "ego psychology" has remained vague on the crucial question whether "ego" refers to an organized system or to a list of functions. It has also been insufficiently clear about the "conflict-free sphere" (Hartmann 1939), having failed to specify whether such a postulated set of functions implies the existence of motivations in which no drives are implicated. Klein ends up by suggesting that ego psychology merely turned out to be an empty conceptual stratagem that tried to patch over the insufficiencies of the drive-discharge model of mentation as a comprehensive explanatory framework. (For a similarly devastating critique of the concept of "id," see the excellent paper of Anne Hayman [1969].)

At his death, Klein's own proposals for an adequate psychoanalytic theory were left in draft form and incomplete. He did specify (see chapter 5) that such a theory must be epigenetic and must encompass the legacies of all development phases, a viewpoint I had previously endorsed in a collaborative monograph (Gedo and Goldberg 1973). Our views also coincided in supporting Hartmann's concept that theory must be able to account for mental organization (that is, issues beyond the intersystemic conflicts highlighted in Freud's 1923 structural theory). Both Klein and I believed that this is best accomplished by postulating some kind of self-structure or schema (see Gedo 1979a, 1993a, and Lichtenstein 1965). Self-organization, in this view, is a cardinal biological necessity and constitutes the core of psychological development: it is essential for integrity, coherence, and a sense of continuity. In these terms, conflict is produced by incompatibilities between a new adaptive challenge and the organized schema of self. Hence development occurs by way of a series of crises that compel changes in self-organization. From such a perspective, conflict cannot be equated with pathology, and psychoanalytic "cure" must consist of a change in the self-schema. These were the radical aspects of Klein's manuscript that its editors tried to downplay in their Introduction and certain interpolated footnotes.

In the manuscript he left at his death (then published without his imprimatur), Klein seemed incongruously to propose that it is not necessary to specify the biological assumptions that are implicit in such a theory; as he put it, the natural-science causes of mental organization are clinically irrelevant. Hence he apparently regarded metapsychology as "expendable," a viewpoint enthusiastically promoted by one of the editors of Klein's book, Merton Gill. Of course, such a view can be maintained legitimately only if one's clinical theories are truly free of natural-science assumptions, and this is by no means the case with regard to Klein's theoretical attempts. How he would have dealt with this inconsistency if he had lived is, of course, an unanswerable question.

In a multi-author volume published to honor George Klein (Gill and Holzman 1976), Gill (1976) reviewed most of the critiques of Freud's metapsychology hitherto published by Holt and Klein (as well as by Basch 1975a, 1976c) and not only contended that it is unnecessary to specify our biological assumptions, but went further by claiming that psychoanalysis need not adhere to natural science in any way. In other words, Gill asserted that psychology can remain a science without being a branch of biology. From an epistemological perspective, this is the most overt endorsement of mind/body dualism in the history of psychoanalysis. Later, Gill (1994) made explicit his view that psychoanalysis should concern itself only with "human meanings," a contention from which it follows that its subject matter is confined to the mental contents conveyed in free association (possibly supplemented by observations of the analysand's overt behaviors in the clinical situation).

In the same volume, Rubinstein (1976) published a rebuttal of the Klein/Gill position on the possibility of a strictly "clinical" psychoanalytic theory (chapter 7 in Rubinstein 1997). He emphasized that divorcing this theory from natural science would emasculate psychoanalysis by making it impossible to study *how* mental functions operate. He also pointed out that many of the constructs, such as "thought" or "wish," used by those in the anti-natural science camp are, in fact, meaningful only in a biological framework. Although such unobservable activities are often subjectively experienced, basically they always operate on a non-experiential level that transcends the boundaries of what Gill defined as "psychology." We might add that in the intervening years neuroscientists have developed PET-scan techniques that permit us actually to visualize these non-experiential thought operations. Thus Freud's inference that mental activities are largely unconscious is a hypothesis that belongs within natural science. Rubinstein rightly asserted that it is impossible to choose among competing interpretive schemata on clinical grounds alone; any particular clinical hypothesis can be invalidated only if it is shown that the brain cannot function in the manner implicit in that hypothesis. In my judgment, it is the developmental theory of psychoanalysis that is especially dependent on the findings of natural science, for clinical data yield little information about functioning in the presymbolic era of childhood.

Rubinstein agreed with Holt and Klein that Freud's metapsychological proposals have turned out to be invalid, that they have been refuted by the evidence of neurophysiology. He disagreed with Gill about the legitimacy of dispensing altogether with biological assumptions; in fact, he thought that, despite the author's seeming disclaimers, Klein's manuscript contained a proposal for a new metapsychology. However that may be, Rubinstein himself had made a cogent effort to develop one in a 1974 paper in which he outlined a model for the kind of neurobiological data needed to permit the development of valid clinical theories in psychoanalysis. (This and other contributions by Rubinstein have been discussed in more detail in the chapter on the Philosophy of Mind.) Moreover, within a year, Allan Rosenblatt and James Thickstun (1977) added another new metapsychological proposal to this growing list, with explicit acknowledgment that their work was an extension of that of both Holt and Rubinstein.

On the mind/body question, Rosenblatt and Thickstun endorse a position of philosophical monism; they dismiss the notion of psychic energy because, epistemically, it implies a position of dualism. In their view, psychology is one possible language used to articulate the nature of certain central nervous processes; they demand that its hypotheses be stated in a manner that makes refutation possible—in other words, they proscribe the use of metaphors in psychoanalytic theory. They devote a chapter to a survey of the main components of standard psychoanalytic theory, wherein they specify which of these they see as invalid (concepts of forces and energies, instinctual drives), useless (topography), or faulty (the structural theory). They also decry the illegitimate tendency of many theoreticians to reify psychic processes.

In lieu of the paradigm of psychic energy, Rosenblatt and Thickstun propose that of the communication of information, a process that does not, as a matter of biological fact, require transfers of energy. They note that there have always been some concepts in psychoanalysis that belong to information theory, such as that of signal anxiety. This idea has explained how the input of information may activate some subsystem of the mind/brain, generally without the attainment of consciousness. In their view, the actual significance of reflex arcs in the nervous system is that of delivering information. The activity of the brain is animated by way of cybernetic mechanisms of feedback; taking part in these is the true function of affects. (On the same point, Holt [1989] describes the "tonic support" to the reticular system in the midbrain provided by cortical stimuli; this system is the principal activator of the entire neural apparatus.) Such cybernetic processes are hierarchically organized into sets and integrated programs, so that the person has a stable hierarchy of goals that guarantees autonomous functioning but constitutes, at the same time, what we have called psychic determinism. When the usual priorities lead to adaptive failure, the hierarchic system is capable of alternative choices at a lower level of integration.

In the twenty years since the publication of the last of the books under review, no voice within psychoanalysis has been raised to argue in favor of Freud's outdated biological assumptions. At most, some *retardataire* adherents of the status quo might contend that the old metapsychology was meant only metaphorically, a last-ditch defense soon abandoned in face of objections to a pseudoscience of mere rhetorical devices. In contrast to this honorable admission of defeat in the face of fresh scientific evidence, the psychoanalytic community has largely disregarded the epistemological issues involved in this controversy. I have discussed the relevant literature on the philosophy of science in Essay One; suffice it to repeat here that a considerable faction of the profession has followed Gill, as well as Schafer (1976), in their denial that we need viable roots in natural science. Most of these authors therefore feel free to dispense with a metapsychology and the epistemic requirements of biological science; they rely instead on a variety of speculative philosophical systems (Hegel, Heidegger, Gadamer, existentialism, and so on). Only Opatow (1989) has, to my knowledge, made an attempt to justify Freud's metapsychology as a respectable *philosophical* proposition (putatively derived from Hegel); in my judgment, this *tour de force* overlooks the fact that, as an adherent of Brücke and Meynert, Freud always intended to remain within the fold of natural science, even when his hypotheses were subsequently falsified by its findings. In a fundamental sense, his psychoanalysis has been a science of motivations that he conceived in biological terms as innate, preprogrammed dispositions for action. (For motivational theories proposed as substitutes for Freud's drive psychology, see the next chapter, the Theory of Motivation.)

5
The Theory of Motivation

- *Psychoanalysis and Motivation.* J. Lichtenberg.

Sigmund Freud devised psychoanalysis as a psychology of motivation built around the concept of drives. His basic model of mind was that of a mechanical apparatus driven by forces fueled by psychic energy. When, in the 1970s, these metapsychological postulates were successfully challenged (see the chapter on the Challenge to Metapsychology), it was incumbent on Freud's critics to propose some novel theory of motivation that would be epistemically and biologically tenable. To his great credit, George Klein (1976) was not only among the first to discard Freudian metapsychology; in the very same work, he also addressed the need to articulate valid motivations for human behavior.

In order to meet the requirements of science, Klein was determined to make only testable statements. He tried to do so by inferring a valid theory of motivation from a "map" of subjective intentions, one best drawn on the basis of clinical observations. Klein postulated that such a schema of motives becomes hierarchically structured into a system he called "self." In other words, Klein conceived of the "inner world" of humankind as an assembly of cognitive schemata (see Bucci 1997; Dorpat and Miller 1992). He also assumed that behavior is motivated by the premium of pleasure, and he supplied a list of "vital pleasures" as a proposed classification of human motives. Klein did not consider the possibility that some motivations may not be experienced subjectively.

Klein's list includes six types of pleasure, albeit he had some doubt about one of these, that of the reduction of tension (which, in Freud's now discredited view, actually defined "pleasure" as such). His categories of sensual pleasure and functional pleasure are probably self-explanatory: from Robert White (1963) he took the concept of competence (which White renamed "effectance"), and he proposed two additional categories, the pleasure of pleasing and that of synthesis (or creating order). One consequence of the posthumous publication of Klein's incomplete manuscript is a failure to resolve the inconsistency of confining this classification of pleasures to the foregoing categories but, elsewhere in the book, using further motivational concepts to explicate behaviors. For instance, he discussed the propensity to repeat passive experiences in an active mode (highlighted by Freud in 1920) as a need for mastery. Klein brought this up as an example to demonstrate that Freud himself sometimes dealt with motivations that could not be accounted for on the basis of any drives. Another source of motivation Klein mentioned is the need to maintain continuity. In other words, he did not live to develop an internally consistent and inclusive theory of motivation, although he did succeed in showing that cogent substitutes for drive theory are readily available.

The need to devise a tenable motivational theory for psychoanalysis was reconfirmed in 1977, when Rosenblatt and Thickstun devoted much of their monograph (also reviewed in major part in the chapter on the Challenge to Metapsychology) to this issue. They provided a detailed recapitulation of the history of psychoanalytic hypotheses about motivation, starting with the notion that the early attribution of motive power to "instincts" was a way to acknowledge that certain motivational systems are determined by genetic endowment. For instance, the organismic tendency to seek pleasure surely denotes the operation of a neural process that has evolutionary advantages because it facilitates the appraisal of environmental conditions.

Rosenblatt and Thickstun followed both Rubinstein and Holt in discarding the concepts of instinct and drive because these depended on the postulate of some non-physical energy, that is, of a non-material spirit. Moreover, in their view, biological evidence does not support any concept of homeostatic *drives*: specific human behaviors are initiated and terminated by means of physiological *signals*. They emphasized that even sexual and aggressive actions cannot be completely understood on the basis of any drive theory, because their occurrence is absolutely dependent on the context of meanings attributed to the milieu. In addition, they pointed out that drive theories are unable to account for the human propensity for exploratory behaviors. In fact, numerous kinds of human activity are so divorced from sexual or aggressive motives that drive theorists were forced to postulate some unobservable process that tames drives, such as "sublimation," to account for them, a purely speculative solution lacking any referent in biology and therefore unsatisfactory from the scientific viewpoint.

Even those features of behavior most suggestive of drive motivation, its occasional attributes of peremptoriness or cyclicity, are satisfactorily explicable in alternative ways: the patterning of central nervous system functions is a sufficient source for all human activity. Within the brain, it is the affects that have the role of activating signals; Rosenblatt and Thickstun viewed affects as the felt phase of the organism's appraisal of its circumstances. They credited Bowlby (1969) for the earliest psychoanalytic statement of the function of affects for monitoring and communication. At any rate, the existence of such neural correlates for "feeling" renders the concept of drives superfluous. As for the activation of the entire nervous system, sensory input satisfactorily accounts for the necessary levels of arousal (via the reticular activating system).

The foregoing view of the central nervous system as a processor of information aligned the conception of Rosenblatt and Thickstun with George Klein's cognitive model for motivation; in their estimation, it also supports Holt's contemporaneous contention (1989, chapter 7) that psychoanalysis must replace drive theory with one focused on wishes and fears, conscious and unconscious. The neural processes that correspond to the qualities of such mental contents make possible both positive and negative feedback to adjust behavior. This is accomplished by activating and inhibiting further neural processes. In other words, these authors espoused a cybernetic model or "systems" conception of motivation. Although the neural activities they highlighted are, of course, functions performed by the constitutionally ordained structure of the soma, the specific systems that control behavior are gradually built up in the course of a process of development. Rosenblatt and

Thickstun pointed out that, in fact, various psychoanalytic theories had for some time used cognitive concepts congruent with their proposals (and not with drive theory) to explain certain motivations—for instance, a need to ward off certain affects, the need to adapt to the milieu, or the operation of an "organizing function."

To recapitulate: Rosenblatt and Thickstun proposed a neurophysiologically based motivational theory in which human action is controlled by a "behavioral system." This system is activated by sensory information processes by means of feedback loops, especially those known as affects. The entire system appraises the match between inborn organismic goals and current opportunities; by establishing a hierarchy of priorities, the child develops a supraordinate control system for behavior the authors propose to call the "self" (cf. Gedo and Goldberg 1973; G. Klein 1976). Note, however, that Rosenblatt and Thickstun did not commit themselves about the nature of the organismic goals subserved by this control system.

The first psychoanalytic attempt to specify the inborn goals of the human organism was Joseph Lichtenberg's 1989 monograph, *Psychoanalysis and Motivation*. Lichtenberg starts out by stating that human behavior is guided by a combination of innate programs (note the vocabulary of information science) and learned patterns. Like Rosenblatt and Thickstun, he postulates a center for the organization and integration of the gamut of motives that he also proposes to call "self." (This is a departure from the viewpoint of self psychology, to which Lichtenberg generally adheres. In contrast to the phenomenological commitment of self psychology—its exclusive focus on subjectivity—this definition of "self" assumes the structural viewpoint I have long insisted is essential [Gedo 1979a, 1981b; Gedo and Goldberg 1973]. Unfortunately, Lichtenberg fails consistently to follow this nonphenomenological definition of "self" throughout the 1989 book.)

Lichtenberg carefully defines "motivation" as a system that promotes, fulfills, and regulates some basic need. This concept is congruent with the assumption that *all* human behavior must be motivated. *Psychoanalysis and Motivation* classifies inborn motivations on the basis of the evidence provided through systematic observations of (normal) children from birth through the consolidation of symbolic capacities; although Lichtenberg aims to integrate this information with psychoanalytic knowledge, clinical evidence from the psychoanalytic setting is not cited in the book. In contrast, Lichtenberg reviews a number of psychoanalytic proposals concerning motivation (all of which he deems to have been unacceptably reductionistic) that were unconnected to the concept of "drive": Bowlby's (1969) theory of attachment, White's (1963) of effectance, or Kohut's (1984) of self-cohesion, among others.

Explicitly, Lichtenberg aims to extend George Klein's work of classifying motives by reviewing the implications of observational data about the presymbolic phases of development, and he makes clear his agreement with Stern (1985) that infants possess a number of diverse motivational systems that are eventually ordered hierarchically. These systems call forth functions relevant for the fulfillment of organismic needs; with the addition of the affective repertory, feedback cycles are established that may, in turn, give priority to various alternative motivational systems. Such a theory, involving a complex hierarchical system, makes clear that a number of reductionistic proposals from the past may have made valid suggestions with regard to one of the subsystems of this hierarchy.

It should be noted that evidence from the observation of infants does not lend itself to direct translation into a classification of organismic needs; Lichtenberg's theory of independent motivational subsystems is based on his interpretation of the significance of that evidence. Although these inferences are generally plausible, on occasion they are decidedly speculative. For instance, Lichtenberg asserts that a child's capacity for solitary play denotes that he or she has a sense about the prior establishment of a "holding environment," à la Winnicott (see chapter on the Rise of the Relational Option). There is simply no way of ascertaining whether this is really so. At any rate, Lichtenberg's interpretation of the data has led him to postulate the existence in human infants of five independent motivational systems; the effects of each on observable behavior are continuously waxing or waning. Evidence from neurophysiology cited by Hadley (1989) in a chapter appended to *Psychoanalysis and Motivation* lends corroboration to these conclusions.

The first of the subsystems discussed regulates the child's physiological requirements; this more or less corresponds to the "self-preservative instincts" Freud postulated in 1915b. According to Lichtenberg, the availability of sucking competence in the neonate shows that this subsystem is active before the child forms any attachment; in other words, physiological regulation is a motive independent of object relationships. It is true, as noted by Spitz (1962), that such regulation is greatly influenced by the infant's "reciprocity" with its caretakers, so that dysregulation is often brought about by unsatisfactory nurture. These transactions are at first mediated, for the most part, by way of tactile and proprioceptive experiences. It is the caretaker's ability to respond in ways well correlated with the infant's various physiological states (such as sleep/wakefulness) that establishes the rhythms of the mother–infant dyad and thus leads to the child's early affective experiences. The latter are then organized into memories (in Stern's [1985] view, ultimately into "generalized" internal representations or RIGs). When the infant becomes aware of its affective memories, that information can be used as feedback to correct and refine the regulation of physiological needs.

The second preprogrammed, innate subsystem considered is that of "attachment–affiliation," previously singled out as a motivation by Bowlby. The reciprocity stressed by Spitz is seen, in this context, as mutual interregulation mediated through various communicative channels; the mother's voice and smell are among the earliest and most important of these. Relatively quickly, infants are enabled to integrate the information gained via discrete sensory modalities, and this capacity for cross-modal integration facilitates the differentiation of "mother" (and of the mother–infant dyad) from other people. The formation of RIGs constitutes the initial emergence of a "core self"; Lichtenberg believes that subjectivity is attained around the age of nine months. One of the most significant conclusions he draws on the basis of this view of the onset of object relations (and of the self-system) is that the normal infant never functions in a manner homologous with the (regressive) pathological states observable in adults.

By the age of one year, infants show unmistakable signs of attachment to their primary caretaker; their characteristic responses to the latter's departures give evidence of a capacity for intentionality in behavior. Attachment offers great evolutionary advantages, because human toddlers, lacking in the capacity to adapt to the environment when left to their own devices, must accept guidance from an adult. This is accomplished by way of reciprocal affective signals; the establishment of such a communicative exchange is called "affective attunement" (Stern 1985). On the way to autonomous competence in self-regulation, many infants learn to soothe themselves by using a Winnicottian "transitional object" in some manner that echoes their experiences with their caretakers. The capacity to call upon memories (RIGs) in this manner shows that the child has acquired the ability to re-imagine the past, that is, to form "images."

Lichtenberg goes on to consider the motivational system he names "exploratory–assertive," his version of the White/Klein concept of competence. He believes that this is already in operation during fetal life, because some capacity to "learn" (to recognize the mother's voice) has been shown to be present before birth. One of the most important observations Lichtenberg cites, one first reported by Sander (1983), is that infants are most likely in various respects to achieve competence not in a dyadic context, but when they are comfortably alone, in "open space." As they learn to organize their experiences, babies gradually acquire the skill (based on procedural memories) to change their own physiological state (see also Sander 1986). The caretakers may promote such competence through appropriate intervention and nonintervention. At first, infants experience joy about the very fact that they are able to take initiative in action; such initiatives expand into "play" and lead to learning. These observations demonstrate that human beings actively seek stimulation.

The fourth motivational system considered is the "aversive" one, which combines the programs formerly attributed to aggression ("fight reactions") and propensities for withdrawal ("flight reactions"). Parens (1979), in an elaborate observational study, found evidence of aversive behaviors (rage) by the age of twelve weeks, but he never encountered spontaneous sadism: sadistic behavior always followed the infliction of pain on the child. Lichtenberg therefore concludes that aggression is a reaction to actual or threatened unpleasure, and it turns to destructiveness (by mobilizing the assertive subsystem) only as a result of very dire experiences. As for withdrawal, even neonates are capable of some such actions in response to environmental noxae, albeit these attempts tend to be ineffective except insofar as they function as signals to the caretakers. Later in development, it is the caretakers who transmit signals of "danger" to toddlers. Thus manageable experiences of controversy actually promote development by teaching the child to tolerate and manage both anger and fear or shame.

In his fifth subsystem of motivation, Lichtenberg combines both sexual and sensual propensities, because he considers these to be alternative responses to the same stimuli. Wrily, he notes that we scarcely have more direct observations concerning infants' sexual behaviors than were available to Freud in 1905; the outstanding exception is the detection of erections in babies during REM sleep. In her chapter on physiology, Hadley (1989) took no issue with Lichtenberg's decision to combine sensuality and sexuality in one system; however, in a subsequent paper (1992), she reported that neuroscientific data have shown that these experiences are mediated through separate neural structures, so that they constitute two motivational subsystems rather than one. Moreover, she stated that the sexual system becomes functional considerably later in development than does the sensual one.

Because Lichtenberg nowhere claimed that his listing of motivational systems was complete or definitive, Hadley's expansion of his schema does not constitute a major problem for his conception: Lichtenberg has been successful in presenting a theory of motivation based not on the concept of drives pressing for discharge but on a system of preprogrammed biological (neural) patterns evoked by varied adaptive requirements throughout the life cycle. What Lichtenberg left out of consideration is the fact that, in accord with his own definition, motivation extends beyond the realm of the preprogrammed patterns essential for adaptation during the presymbolic phases of development (see Gedo, 1996a, Epilogue). This omission has led to the paradox that, despite his adherence to self psychology, Lichtenberg's schema does not deal with Kohut's (1977, 1984) conception that self-cohesion is a vital organismic need. Hadley (in press) now believes that there exist neural structures that function to maintain an autonomous self-organization, so that "autonomy" constitutes a seventh subsystem of preprogrammed motivation, albeit one that comes "on line" later than the ones Lichtenberg considered.

In my view (Gedo 1988, Epilogue), the hierarchy of motivations is even more complex: the acquisition of ideals and acceptance of imperatives that follow the maturation of symbolic capacities add another class of motivations—what Thomas French (1952) called "counter-motives"—to the system, and so does the attainment of competence in learning the requirements of adequate adaptation within some communities. (One tries to gain expertise in financial matters not merely to enjoy the pleasure of effectance, but also to take pleasure in pleasing one's family through the provision of decent living standards. That is not to say that George Klein's unsystematic list of vital pleasures is a schema preferable to the one proposed by Lichtenberg—I am merely using one of its components to show the incompleteness of the latter as a consequence of its exclusive focus on the first two years of life.) Be it noted that it is the addition of countermotives that first necessitates the organization of the dynamic unconscious.

Once again, we must await the findings of brain science that will specify the physiology and biochemistry underlying the motivational systems that operate on the basis of symbolic transformations. We must never lose sight of the fact that symbolic functions are just as completely products of preprogrammed neural capacities as are the organismic adaptations considered in Lichtenberg's schema. In that sense, the countermotives highlighted by French have conceptual parity with the motivations wired into the brain at birth or shortly thereafter.[1]

---

1. Greenberg (1991) has proposed a theory of motivation imbedded in a mentalist view, that is, one based on entirely different epistemic premises from those of the authors discussed in this chapter. Greenberg's work will be discussed in the chapter entitled Toward a Paradigm of Self-Organization.

6
The Narrative Option and Social Constructivism

- *Between Hermeneutics and Science.* C. Strenger.
- *Beyond the Psychoanalytic Dyad.* J. Muller.
- *Historiography and Causation in Psychoanalysis.* E. Wallace.
- *Narrative Truth and Historical Truth.* D. Spence.
- *Retelling a Life.* R. Schafer.

In *Between Hermeneutics and Science*, the psychoanalyst and philosopher Carlo Strenger traces the rise of "hermeneutics" (as a branch of scholarship) within continental philosophy and its influence on psychoanalysis by way of the works of Habermas (1968) and Ricoeur (1970, 1981). He sees the positive contribution of this development as an insistence on the need for a shared culture to make possible the communication of meaning through an intelligible text. For psychoanalysis, this insight has necessitated the modification of the claim that the analyst is an objective observer, in favor of the realization that intersubjectivity plays a role in collecting our data (see Mitchell 1997).

According to Strenger, acceptance of hermeneutics as the sole organizing framework for psychoanalysis would entail five consequences: 1) analytic theory would have to discard metapsychology; 2) in its discourse, it could use only personal terms; 3) it could offer no causal explanations; 4) it would focus on meanings via narratives; and 5) it would have to sanction interpretive pluralism. Strenger concludes that, if it were construed in that manner, psychoanalysis would fail to qualify as natural science. (For a work that precisely fits these criteria, see D. B. Stern [1997].)

Strenger agrees with Grünbaum's (1984) judgment that the hermeneuticists' interpretive criterion of narrative coherence is insufficient for psychoanalytic purposes, for it is too easy to meet. In his view, interpretations must *at a minimum* also meet the criterion of congruence with secure knowledge in cognate fields. He means that one must not resort to explanations based on science fiction or supernatural interventions, for example. In this sense, Strenger deems many standard Kleinian interpretations to be illegitimate. Another way Strenger puts this is that even narratives that are complete, intelligible, and "adequate" may be absurd.

It was in the context of widespread loss of confidence in Freud's metatheoretical assumptions—and a lack of consensus about replacing them (see the chapter on the Challenge to Metapsychology)—that certain theoreticians proposed to abandon the effort to integrate psychoanalysis within biological science. Instead, they advocated that it accept the status of an exclusively hermeneutic discipline. The earliest overt advocate of this position within psychoanalysis proper was Roy Schafer (1976) who put forward a linguistically based conceptual schema he called "action language," a viewpoint he intended to divorce from biological considerations. Perhaps the most detailed exposition of a putative rationale for such a choice was provided by Donald Spence in *Narrative Truth and Historical Truth* (1982).

Spence based his argument on the premise that the observational data of psychoanalysis constitute a text. (It will be recalled that "hermeneutics" is basically the science of textual exegesis. This has recently been broadened to a view that persons can be read as "texts.") He was certainly justified in stating that psychoanalytic discoveries are generally introduced in the form of coherent narratives about specific analytic transactions. He was also right to caution that the need for narrative coherence may inadvertently lead to falsifications, so that the degree of polish possessed by a case history says nothing about the historicity of its claims. In explicit disagreement with Lacan (1977), Spence asserted that experiences registered unconsciously are not organized in a code that is linguistic; consequently, he pointed out, these matters are exceedingly difficult to articulate in words. He stressed that they are likely to emerge in the form of visual imagery (as in dreams or fantasies), and that verbal descriptions of the latter are likely to be highly inexact. Moreover, despite the analyst's best efforts, even the *semantic* meaning of the analysand's associations is difficult to establish. According to Spence, the obstacles are particularly severe when we deal with dreams or memories, because the analysand's report has inevitably altered such mental contents in the process of encoding them in words. Finally, Spence warns us that our interpretations tend to focus the understanding of material in particular ways, so that premature and/ or inexact interpretations may seriously skew the subsequent dialogue.

Spence's argument is particularly cogent about the cumulative distortions introduced into the analytic transaction through the analyst's undetected emotional bias, the technical use of unwarranted rules of thumb, and the tendency to reach premature closures. He pointed out how often the tendentiousness of some of the analysand's communications is overlooked and how easy it is for the analyst to bypass their ambiguities. He caps his summary of the difficulties of psychoanalytic hermeneutics by focusing on the ease of mismatching primary data with familiar narrative patterns. According to Spence, these difficulties make it all but impossible to arrive at historical truth by way of psychoanalytic reconstruction.

Spence's detailed deconstruction of numerous published interpretations of psychoanalytic data (such as Freud's reconstruction of the primal scene allegedly witnessed in childhood by the Wolf Man) is everywhere persuasive. In fact, it might well be used as a set of model cautionary tales about the *abuses* of psychoanalytic interpretation. It is therefore rather surprising that Spence is relatively tolerant of such practices, as if such a worst-case scenario were both routine and unavoidable: fundamentally, he proves to be unconcerned for historical accuracy. According to him, the task of the analyst is not to find enduring psychological patterns but to bring about new ones. In this sense, Spence appears to condone the use of any interpretive schema whatsoever (no matter how arbitrary), provided it is applied skillfully from an aesthetic and a rhetorical viewpoint.

The foregoing espousal of "narrative truth" as the proper criterion of psychoanalytic adequacy is, in my judgment, a counsel of despair. Narrative fit is a necessary but not a sufficient condition for competent analytic work; I do not believe that adaptive changes based on plausible illusions shared by analyst and patient are likely to endure. Moreover, Spence lost hope about establishing historical truth largely because the "facts" he was interested in were those of the actual transactions between the child and its objects; the historicity of such putative events is indeed impossible to establish on the basis of psychoanalytic data alone (although decisive, independent documentary evidence sometimes does become available). Facts of that kind are, however, seldom of crucial importance; the historical truths that always matter for analysis concern the internal psychic changes that succeeded each other in the course of development, and these are, at least *in principle*, detectable on the basis of the successive vicissitudes of the analytic transference. (Spence recognizes our therapeutic concern with these vicissitudes but fails to give weight to their value as historical evidence, as repetitions of the past in the analysand's inner world. It is of some relevance that this is not the only instance in the book where Spence seems to have been unmindful of clinical priorities.)

In contrast to that of Spence, the work of Roy Schafer has always borne witness to its author's clinical mastery. Nevertheless, starting with his 1976 book, *A New Language for Psychoanalysis*, Schafer has reconceptualized psychoanalysis as a process wherein the participants reformulate the narrative of the analysand's life (see also Schafer 1978). *Retelling a Life* is the latest version of this new concept. One crucial respect in which it transcends Spence's book is that Schafer does not look upon the observational data of psychoanalysis as a mere spoken text: he gives equal weight to the nonverbal enactments within the psychoanalytic situation—in his words, the "showings" that supplement the "telling." Disillusioned with a biologically based metapsychology, because Freud's nineteenth-century version has not endured, Schafer has sought a philosophically sound metatheory, devoid of biological considerations, with but rare lapses into Freudian terminology based on biological assumptions, such as "repression," "introject," or "working through." Although Schafer asserts that a successful analysis deconstructs the analysand's initial narrative of his or her life, he nowhere claims that the new version then constructed by the participants may disregard historicity.

Schafer provides several examples of typical life narratives that have to be altered in analysis, such as phallocentric sexual beliefs, myths of destructiveness for which one has to make reparation, narratives of entrenched suffering that cover over the active pursuit of failure and idealization of unhappiness, and so on.[1] Schafer looks upon the competing clinical theories espoused by various psychoanalytic schools as "master narratives" that codify such typical biographies. He insists, however, that the reformulated life story must define the analysand as the sole agent responsible for his or her fate: he makes no allowance for "happenings" wherein one is merely passive. One may respond to threats via (active) defensiveness; if this involves becoming unaware of something, in Schafer's system that amounts to self-deception, the creation of a fiction. Such a hard-line commitment to an a priori postulate about psychological life (one that at bottom makes covert assumptions about the operations of the central nervous system) is not entirely consistent with Schafer's claim that the reformulated narrative has to be constructed collaboratively by analyst and analysand. For instance, Schafer asserts that reports of subjective deadness or emptiness always mean that the analysand is "playing dead" (or playing empty)—as if human beings could never be overwhelmed. (So much for eschewing biological assumptions!) In this sense, some of Schafer's interpretations may fail to reach the standard of historical truth, however persuasive his proposed narratives may be.

Despite their differing premises, both Spence and Schafer explicitly take psychoanalysis out of the realm of natural science. (In *Between Hermeneutics and Science*, Strenger names George Klein, Merton Gill, and Arnold Goldberg as further significant contributors who advocate such a view. In my opinion, he is right about Gill [see Gill 1994] and Goldberg [see Goldberg 1995]. I do not believe that Klein ever made his position on this matter explicit). It is worth noting that Ricoeur (1981, chapter 10 and editor's Introduction), although he also states that psychoanalysis is not a natural science, recognizes that Freud's effort— in Ricoeur's view, largely an unsuccessful one—to integrate the hermeneutics of clinical discourse with the biological "forces" of the drives was indispensable. In other words, Ricoeur acknowledged that, however necessary the hermeneutic aspects of psychoanalysis are, they do

---

1. Schafer may be the most persuasive voice within psychoanalysis consistently to espouse a feminist point of view.

not constitute the whole story of the enterprise; he stressed that a view of psychoanalysis exclusively based on its linguistic aspects overlooks the essential task of explaining the psychic processes of symbolization and desymbolization (that is, the problems Freud tried to address by means of his economic viewpoint). *Between Hermeneutics and Science* addresses not only the arguments of the hermeneuticists but also those of the epistemologist Adolf Grünbaum, as he articulated these in his 1984 monograph. (For further discussion of Grünbaum's work, see the chapter on Epistemology.)

Strenger (like Grünbaum before him) disagrees with Schafer's contention that there is a significant distinction to be made between reasons for behavior and its causes. He argues that if the reason for one's choice of behavior is a particular understanding of reality, that understanding is the cause of the behavior. Causality of that nature must, however, be attributed to processes in the brain—witness the impairment of judgment that accompanies intoxication. Hence for our purposes a hermeneutics of coherent narratives is insufficient: to effect changes in behavior, the analysand has to be convinced that the analyst's interpretations are *true*.

Strenger is fully aware of the difficulties in the way of making accurate reconstructions of the past, obstacles shared by all historical disciplines (chapter 5; see also Wallace 1985). Yet such conclusions may be rationally assessed, even if they are seldom amenable to scientific proof. As for the objection that the differing interpretive schemata of rival schools of psychoanalysis all appear to be effective, Strenger suggests that these therapeutic results, which are not quantifiable, are probably incommensurate. In this regard, he might have done better to postulate that it is the accepted explanation of therapeutic change, as primarily dependent on interpretation alone, that is faulty. (For more complex—and adequate—explanations, see Gedo 1979a, 1988, 1995a, b; Levenson 1983).

In *Historiography and Causation in Psychoanalysis*, Edwin Wallace (1985) also subjects the historicist viewpoint of Spence and Schafer to philosophical scrutiny. Wallace regards the reconstruction of the meaning of past experiences as the heart of psychoanalytic treatment, on the assumption that current adaptation crucially depends on those meanings (cf. Weiss and Sampson 1986). In this sense, the analysand is a historian who provides a narrative of his or her biography; the analyst, who reinterprets these matters in the light of the evidence provided by diachronic transference vicissitudes, plays the role of historiographer. Wallace acknowledges that neither participant deals in "facts" and that, as the hermeneuticists claim, analytic interpretations are subject to the distorting effects of the subjectivity of both members of the dyad. Nonetheless, multiple observers are able to obtain reliable data through the analytic method.

A historian of medicine and psychiatry, Wallace is persuasive about the status of psychoanalysis as a historical discipline: like all of history, it deals with symbolically mediated behaviors through the exercise of empathy. In neither discipline is pure empiricism (that is, the sole use of inductive methods) possible. In the view of Wallace, however, Spence and Schafer exaggerate the difficulties in the way of reconstructing "historical truth," and they overlook the fact that the narratives they construct are also necessarily organized on the basis of preexisting theories. Despite the risks of reductionism and circularity (that is, belief in the validation of hypotheses by data selected in accord with their preconceptions), Wallace believes that both history in general and psychoanalysis in particular can organize meaningful data without inventing them (see also Friedman 1988).

Wallace rightly points out that psychoanalysis is simultaneously an ideographic and a nomothetic discipline: it focuses on individual instances but aims to develop general laws. It is essential to keep in mind that no psychoanalytic proposition should be regarded as an absolute one; it is always merely probabilistic. In order to arrive at universals, it is necessary to supplement clinical data with evidence from nonanalytic sources (see also the chapter on Epistemology). Wallace is also aware that psychoanalysis differs from history in one crucial respect: the analytic effort is intended to *alter* the analysand's (future) history. For this purpose, engendering belief in a narrative (*à la* Spence or Schafer) may not be sufficient, for it is often necessary to determine what the actualities were in the past. In other words, in particular instances, only certain interpretations will ultimately prove to be adequate to change the analysand's personality. To put this in another way, according to Wallace psychoanalytic propositions should both be coherent and as nearly as possible correspond to the historical truth of past experience. Although certainty in historical matters is unattainable, psychoanalysis does possess reasonable rules of inference for its reconstructions, such as the requirement for analyst–patient consensus.

Wallace points out that, in proposing his "action language," Schafer (1976) actually denied the cogency of a genetic viewpoint for psychoanalysis, as if personality structure did not exercise a determining influence on behavior and thus constitute part of "reality." As a result, Schafer cannot regard (his version of) psychoanalysis as a natural science, while Wallace properly classifies his (historical) version of the discipline as a science akin to paleontology: a non-experimental natural science. But he also points out that the difference between his view and those of the hermeneuticists goes even deeper, to the very conception of causality—one of the unresolved problems within epistemology.

Freud's commitment to exceptionless psychological determinism regarding human behavior makes him the philosophical successor of Hobbes, Locke, Hume, Kant, Schopenhauer, Darwin, and Mill (some of whose works he translated into German; see also Rapaport 1974). Wallace defends psychoanalysis against Schafer's accusation that the commitment to determinism entails mind/body dualism[2] by asserting (rightly, in my judgment) that, *as a therapeutic modality*, psychoanalysis is a somatic procedure; only as an explanatory system has it been focused on "non-physiologic" matters. (It is regrettable that Wallace fails to express more discomfort about this problematic disjunction; Schafer's thesis does present a formidable objection to the claims of Freud's psychoanalysis to constitute a natural science.) At any rate, in his view (contrary to that of Schafer) human purposes can be causative, personality development is historically determined, and the past makes its meaningfulness manifest in the present by means of affectivity. Wallace effectively refutes Schafer's contention that there is a significant difference between "causes" and "reasons"; he demonstrates that Schafer has merely invented synonyms for causation that sound less mechanistic.

In my judgment, Strenger and Grünbaum have demonstrated that the hermeneutic option would precipitate psychoanalysis from its meta-

---

2. Schafer's point is cogent because unconscious vectors necessarily operate on a biological level (Rubinstein 1997), but Freud's insistence on the operative role of mental contents (in all circumstances) lacks any connection to the somatic realm.

psychological frying pan into the fire of unrestrained fantasy. At the same time, we cannot afford to disregard the arguments of Spence and Schafer concerning the difficulties of understanding the communications of analysands. Psychoanalysis as a discipline, with the exception of Lacan and his followers (see the chapter on French Psychoanalysis), has paid insufficient attention to semiotics. (For the clinical relevance of semiotic issues, see Gedo 1996a.) In *Beyond the Psychoanalytic Dyad*, John Muller (1996) has made an attempt to remedy that neglect. The book is divided into two parts: the first proposes a "developmental semiotics"; in the second, Muller surveys a series of Lacanian propositions about archaic mentation. It is the first section that merits inclusion here, because a semiotic perspective should resolve the unproductive dichotomization of natural science versus hermeneutics.

Muller starts with the insight of Charles Peirce, the originator of semiotics, that culture, in the form of language, constitutes a "third" that supplements the mother–infant dyad. In Muller's view, it becomes a constituent of a holding environment, and it helps to structure relevant portions of the brain. Communication begins in the context of the mutual gazing of mother and infant that makes possible the earliest exchange of signals. In this manner, by the age of four weeks the newborn learns to recognize familiar percepts; in other words, expectancies are established through social interaction. These early signals are "protolinguistic," but they suffice to initiate the recognition of differences and the correction of erroneous perceptions. Around the age of three months, the exchange of signals becomes sequential and makes possible the communication of information about affectivity. At first, it is the mother who tends to take the initiative in these matters, and the infant mirrors her signals in what amounts to the occurrence of "coerced empathy"; only between the ages of four and six months is the infant released from this kind of stimulus-boundedness and enabled to take the initiative in communication.

In my judgment, it is crucial to note that infants periodically turn away from these social transactions, presumably in order better to process the information they have collected; this means that even in early infancy mental functions take place in a private space (see Modell 1993). In the course of development, children then learn the rules of their culture for semiosis. These rules constitute a syntax for human action that evolves into a hierarchy of codes. Muller points out that the developmental theories of psychoanalysis (even the 1985 proposals of Stern) have generally neglected the significance of such a semiotic framework. Yet, from the viewpoint of a depth psychology, one of the crucial issues is the manner in which the individual develops from a zoösemiotic organism into one capable of "anthroposemiosis." Peirce divided this progression into three stages; he named these "icon," "index," and "symbol." (Lacan renamed these the "real," the "imaginary," and the "symbolic.") It is important to note that zoösemiosis implies communication without subjective experience. It has been shown that already during fetal life it is possible to register repetitive percepts. Muller therefore concludes that the unconscious is *semiotically* structured. In the course of development, early memories are then retranscribed in newly learned semiotic codes. Although Muller could be more explicit on this score, I believe that he has shown that Lacan's (1977) claim that the unconscious is structured *linguistically* is too adultomorphic and therefore unwarranted.

The infant's early capacities for semiosis rapidly establish a condition of intersubjectivity with caretakers. Muller therefore concludes that psychoanalytic hypotheses about developmentally universal phases of autism and/or symbiosis are manifestly incorrect. By around nine months, the foregoing primary intersubjectivity is succeeded by a secondary form that is uniquely human. The Anlagen of this capacity are the "protoconversations," starting in the second month of life, in which the mother's voice is a carrier of affect. Around the age of three months, these signals begin to function as indices that point to significant matters (for instance, dangers); by around six months, the physical properties of the caretakers' particular spoken language alter the infant's auditory perception in specific ways. Thereafter, the child is able to engage in playfully mirroring the vocalizations of others, although disruptions of semiosis, with confusion about agency, frequently occur. Muller conjectures that conditions of that kind are the Anlagen of projective identification. The next developmental step is the active use of vocal signs to produce desired effects; the infant is alert for the mother's signals of feedback to these initiatives. By the age of nine months, the infant is able to make use of such signals as instructions about future conduct; in other words, a shared reality has been established.

The symbolic world, that of Peirce's "thirdness," gains predominance around the age of three; contrary to the views of Piaget, it develops on the basis of presymbolic semiosis. The acquisition of symbolic capacities gives the child the ability to experience self-continuity; at the same time, such adherence to shared cultural modes safeguards the individual against the pull of symbiotic possibilities. This idea has been current in German philosophy in the form of the aphorism, "*Kein du, kein ich*": If you are not differentiated, neither am I; in other words, it is essential to achieve mutual recognition, instead of mistaking others for alter egos. It is this achievement of differentiation that underlies the secondary intersubjectivity that is characteristically human. In a clinical aside, Muller cogently observes that in the psychoanalytic situation intersubjectivity does not call for mirroring the analysand's affects; it requires clarification of the importance of recognizing the latter's needs and desires. In conclusion, he reiterates that a dyadic universe always constitutes a pathological retreat from existence in the cultural matrix, so that the currently popular "intersubjective" paradigms within psychoanalysis wrongly privilege undesirable developments. I would agree: neither a one-person nor a two-person psychology is sufficient for psychoanalytic purposes.

Muller's book does not explicitly touch upon the work of the psychoanalytic hermeneuticists, but in my judgment it does demonstrate that as soon as the need for a semiotic viewpoint in psychoanalysis is taken seriously, that communicative framework is clearly revealed as a branch of natural science. Moreover, the claims of social constructivism as an adequate approach within psychoanalysis ring hollow; in unguarded moments, its proponents have to admit as much: "Analysts in these postmodern days remain just as passionate as analysts have always been in searching for what is most true and useful, and they maintain the strongest kind of feelings that one thing is more true and useful than another" (D. B. Stern 1997, p. 168). Reality, including psychic reality, is no mere social construction.

7
The Rise of
the Relational Option

- *Object Relations in Psychoanalytic Theory.* J. Greenberg and S. Mitchell.
- *Object Relations Theories and Psychopathology.* F. Summers.
- *Theories of Object Relations: Bridges to Self Psychology.* H. Bacal and K. Newman.

The past generation has seen repeated efforts to review the intellectual history of the growing movement to focus psychoanalytic theory on the vicissitudes of object relations. (For the theoretical necessities that set this development into motion, see Gedo & Goldberg 1973. I shall return to these issues later in this chapter.) By and large, these attempts surveyed most of the same contributions; they differed, however, because of the varied conceptual agendas of their authors. The earliest of the surveys considered here was that of Greenberg and Mitchell (1983). These writers emerged from the Sullivanian "interpersonal" school of psychoanalysis. Understandably, they were intent on showing the kinship of their own point of view with the broadest range possible of respected alternatives; consequently, they reduce the multiplicity of psychoanalytic theories into two varieties: the drive theories of Freudian tradition and a more recent "relational perspective" that, according to them, includes the interpersonal viewpoint. Bacal and Newman

(1990), equally committed to the concepts of Kohut and Winnicott, consciously rewrite the history of object relations as a record of steady progress crowned by the development of self psychology. Summers (1994), a member of a more recent cohort of psychoanalysts, appears to be neutral about the intellectual disputes of previous generations; his (unstated) agenda involves the promotion of a concept of the therapeutic action of psychoanalysis based on the "internalization" of a benign new relationship. Despite these tendentious aims, all three surveys are lucid, informative, and generally accurate. It is important to note that, among these authors, only Summers undertakes systematically and critically to assess the various contributions discussed; the other books generally do not go beyond their exposition.

There is agreement among these authors that, because of her conceptualization of "internal" (that is, intrapsychic) object relations, Melanie Klein deserves credit as a crucial pioneer of this school of thought. Nor do they differ about the fact that Klein herself refused to abandon drive psychology, so that her theoretical position remained ambiguous. All see the British object relations theorists, particularly Winnicott, Fairbairn, and Guntrip (Bacal and Newman add Balint and Bowlby), as unequivocal adherents of the new viewpoint, and they all make an attempt to correlate the position of the interpersonalists with that of the Britons. In line with their postulation of a relational perspective, Greenberg and Mitchell include Hartmann, Mahler, Jacobson, and Kernberg among theorists who tried to come to grips with the significance of object relations; of these, Bacal and Newman consider only Mahler and Kernberg, and Summers deals with Kernberg alone. More surprising is the authors' unanimous verdict that "self psychology" constitutes an object relations theory. (Bacal and Newman specify that this judgment applies to Kohut's work only after 1977. For details, see the chapter on the Kohutian Legacy.)

Greenberg and Mitchell start with the acknowledgment that every theoretician within psychoanalysis recognizes the significance of object relations. Every theorist postulates that mental representations of objects are formed, and that these become discernible in treatment by way of transferences. "Objects" may be conceived as entities invested by drives, or they can be defined without reference to a drive concept; this choice leads to alternative models of mind: those of drive/structure and of object relations/structure. Freudian drive psychology did not allow for non-libidinal attachments to objects; in response to the challenges of Adler and Jung, however, Freud developed the concept of narcissism, that is, of the investment of the "ego" (in this context, this meant self-representation) with libido. Freud's most prominent use of the concept of object relations occurred with regard to the potentiality for identifications, particularly those that lead to superego formation. In contrast to Freud's purely intrapsychic focus, the interpersonalists have concentrated on observable relations in the social realm. Greenberg and Mitchell point out that throughout his work Sullivan emphasized that human relatedness is the prerequisite of satisfactions and a safeguard against anxiety. In treatment he urged concentration on the here and now of the analyst–patient transaction.

Bacal and Newman make the valid historical point that the relational perspective in psychoanalysis was actually introduced by Ferenczi. They fail to note, however, that Ferenczi's thinking was transmitted to Sullivan by way of the former's analysand, Clara Thompson. The Ferenczi tradition was carried on mainly by Balint (1985), whose postulation of the neonate's capacity for "primary love" asserted that object relations are already crucial at birth. Balint believed that unsatisfactory early relationships create a "basic fault" in the personality that is not an outcome of preexisting conflict. In London, Balint's ideas probably influenced the analysts who formed the "middle group" (between Freudians and Kleinians), notably Winnicott. Moreover, we should in this connection recall that Melanie Klein was an analysand of Ferenczi's, and that it was his encouragement that led her to pioneer the psychoanalysis of young children, the field where her clinical conclusions culminated in her theoretical notions about internal objects.

In his overview of the object relations paradigm, Summers (chapter 8) concludes that it constitutes resort to "pure psychology." Were this judgment valid, it would mean that object relations theories are divorced from all biological assumptions—in other words, that they should be classified as instances of "mentalism" (see the chapter on the Philosophy of Mind). Although this conclusion about the theories of Winnicott, Fairbairn, Guntrip, and Kohut concerning those of Klein (and, by extension, Kernberg's version of the latter) is probably valid, its cogency is more difficult to determine. All commentators agree that Klein's theoretical schema has a constitutional basis, one that postulates crucial individual variability in terms of inborn drive propensities. Greenberg and Mitchell correctly stress that Klein's system is, in fact, focused on the ontogeny of a "death instinct." They point out that, in describing this process, Klein implicitly changed the very definition of drive; in their view, she understood the concept in terms of love or hate, thus cutting it off from somatic roots. This interpretation is in accord with Summers' characterization of object relations theories as pure psychology. We should note, however, that both Greenberg and Mitchell and Summers erroneously equate "death instinct" and aggression (or hate); they thereby evade the conundrum that Klein actually based her system on the alleged self-destructiveness of the human organism. She was therefore obliged to posit some forces that could counteract such a drive, and she came up with the hypothesis of the neonate's capacity for projection (turning the destructiveness outward) as well as one for internalizing good nurture (that is, the consequences of actual human relations). In my view, these are biological assumptions; hence, I prefer to classify the Kleinian system as an id psychology, albeit one covertly infused with vitalism (Gedo 1986, chapter 6), because these biological assumptions are fictive. (For a similar assessment of Klein's position, see Ogden 1986.)

Although at bottom Klein may be misclassified as an object relations theorist, her concept of internalized object relations clearly did become the central tenet in the theories of certain others in the relational camp, so much so that Summers sees the drive concepts Klein (and Kernberg) employed as superfluous features in her system, and Greenberg and Mitchell assert that the basic mental processes she deals with are solely the vicissitudes of internalized objects. It would seem that the commitment of these authors to object relations theory has rendered them unresponsive to Klein's (very appropriate) concern with issues that transcend it.

Bacal and Newman point out that internalized object relations do not merely record the infant's actual experiences with the caretakers: these memories, according to Klein, are formed via the prism of unconscious "phantasies." Summers correctly notes that, in this regard, Klein was committed to the postulate of innate ideas. Greenberg and Mitchell concur by stating that Klein postulated phylogenetically transmitted unconscious knowledge. It is remarkable that none of these surveys raises any objection to an epistemological view so contrary to that of all natural sciences. Nor does any of them take issue with Klein's failure to specify how various internalized transactions might have a bearing on each other and thereby influence behavior. Formulations such as "persecution by a bad object" assign a motivational role to a memory, as if it were an actual person. Such reification of a concept substitutes mere verbiage for the explanation that is actually required. (It is true that Greenberg and Mitchell concede that Klein altogether neglected to spell out how the personality is organized.)

Although he is critical of Klein's schema because of its adultomorphism and its assumption that expectable development is a result of negotiating a sequence of pathologies, Summers credits her theory with the virtue of constituting a systematic framework. I shall shortly return to this issue as it concerns object relations theories in general. Here I wish to note that Summers claims that Winnicott's contributions (which, according to Greenberg and Mitchell, do not add up to a coherent system) may also be systematized, and that is what he attempts to accomplish in his review of Winnicott's work (chapter 4). He organizes Winnicott's ideas along a developmental axis subdivided in accordance with the characteristics of infant–caretaker transactions, that is, "object relations" in the interpersonal realm. According to this schema, the internalization of object relations can begin only in the second half of the first year of life, following various maturational steps that promote self–other differentiation. Winnicott's concept of development envisages the child's eventual attainment of independence, so that in his schema the vital import of internal objects is largely limited to an intermediate phase of "relative dependence" (cf. Gedo and Goldberg 1973, chapter 5); even then, this influence is mitigated by the infant's capacity to create "transitional objects." In other words, it is not entirely appropriate to pigeon-hole Winnicott's contributions as object relations theories—his conceptual work had broader implications.

If one makes a list of these contributions, as reported in these three books, the contention of Bacal and Newman that Winnicott's work as a whole is a stepping stone in the direction of a theory centered on the "self" concept does not seem to be entirely unreasonable. They point out that even in the (initial) phase of "absolute dependence," Winnicott postulates the gradual development of a sense of self; in that of "relative dependence," after the integration of temporality, he hypothesizes the acquisition of a concept of "me-ness"; if circumstances inflict unmanageable experiences on the child, he conceived that a "false self" may develop. It is entirely possible that Winnicott shied away from systematizing his ideas because he suspected that they were more radical than his contemporaries realized. (Bacal and Newman correctly point out that the next stepping stone in the direction of a psychology of self was provided by Guntrip, who looked upon object relations as building blocks for a sense of self.)

If neither Klein, nor Winnicott, nor Guntrip unequivocally qualifies as an object relations theorist, the attempt of Greenberg and Mitchell to dichotomize psychoanalytic theories into those based on drive and those they call relational is severely compromised. Evidently, their thesis commits the fallacy of the undistributed middle: as Bacal and Newman rightly imply, it is now feasible to base analytic theory on the organization of "self." Of course, this is precisely what, since 1977, Kohut and his followers have claimed to have accomplished. It is of the highest interest, therefore, that Bacal and Newman explicitly contradict this claim; they also quote Kohut's disciple Michael Basch in support of their conclusion that Kohut's theory is centered *not* on a concept of self but on that of "selfobject." Be it noted that in self psychology "selfobject" is now used to designate any object that affects the sense of self—a definition broad enough to encompass any conceivable object. I am therefore in complete agreement with their conclusion that, in view of these facts, Kohut was an object relations theorist. (In the entire literature of "self psychology," Bacal and Newman found only one statement [that of Wolf 1984] that deals with "self" as mental structure.)

By contrast, Summers views the proper aim of the object relations paradigm as the development of theories outlining the structuralization of a self that is eventually subjectively experienced as well. Such hypotheses view psychopathology in terms of some defect in self-structure. But I should add that the most explicit theory centered on self-organization has been the one I have tried to outline (Gedo 1979a, 1981b, 1988, 1993b). If one accepts that object relations concepts can serve the subsidiary function Bacal and Newman assign them, Greenberg and Mitchell's ecumenical efforts in this area are even further undermined; the theories they tried to collect under one umbrella are simply too heterogeneous. Fairbairn's (1954) theory probably best approximates Greenberg and Mitchell's criteria for the relational paradigm.

Viewed as competing conceptual schemata, none of the theories surveyed in these books is sufficiently comprehensive. For instance, even Greenberg and Mitchell concede that Sullivan failed to consider how structuralization takes place, particularly in a manner that yields good adaptation. They also acknowledge that the other major interpersonalist, Fromm, ignored developmental considerations altogether. In my judgment, it is the insistence of all these theorists on reducing mental life to dyadic experiences that is unacceptably reductionistic. (To illustrate this by a common example: no object relations theory can account for the devastating effects of chronic illness or perceptual defects on personality development [see Freedman 1997].)

Because the authors of all three books are adherents of one or another object relations viewpoint, none of them considers the consequences of the acceptance of mentalism by most of the theoreticians they discuss, and, in the instance of Klein and her followers, they misread her ambiguous theories to conform with mentalist (that is, nonbiological) presuppositions. If psychoanalytic theories do not have to be constrained by valid biological information, every hypothesis about early mentation, however scientifically implausible, is as legitimate as any other. Hence none of the authors of these books is bothered by the fact that the specific hypotheses of the various theorists they survey are mutually incompatible: without biological referents, the only criterion on which one can base one's theoretical preference is that of putative therapeutic utility, and (alas!) clinical interventions all too often seem to succeed irrespective of their validity (cf. Grünbaum 1993).

Another way to approach the impossibility of refuting (or affirming) the validity of these competing hypotheses is to note that none of the theorists surveyed has articulated a general proposition about the manner in which "mind"—the realm they are allegedly mapping—functions.[1] This indeterminacy allows them freely to propound ad hoc developmental hypotheses without a shred of empirical evidence and without fear of contradicting any presuppositions of their own. It is a conceptual world worthy of Pirandello's "Right you are—if you think

---

1. The failure to address this vital issue has continued to characterize the works of relational theorists to the present day (see Greenberg 1991; Mitchell 1997; D. B. Stern 1997).

you are!" Conceptual anarchy of this kind is what allows Winnicott to deal with all psychopathology as the result of a simple arrest of development caused by environmental failure and, as Summers concedes, to disregard the fact that analysands have grown in many ways since they suffered pathogenic experiences. The same judgment is applicable to Guntrip's reduction of all psychopathology to schizoid developments in infancy. And so on.

Despite these glaring weaknesses, object relations theories have become popular because they offer a number of guideposts for clinicians responsible for the care of patients whose psychopathology is more archaic than the oedipal problems psychoanalysis was initially concerned with. To put this differently, most of the contributors included in these volumes have put forward specific clinical propositions that have proved to be cogent. All commentators agree on the value of Klein's observations about mental operations such as splitting and projective identification, Winnicott's transitional experiences or his true-versus false-self dichotomy, Fairbairn's "need–fear dilemma," and many other discrete clinical notions of this kind. Moreover, the consensus within the "relational perspective" that object relations are sought not to satisfy libidinal wishes but because of attachment needs (independent of other motivational considerations) has been borne out by extrapsychoanalytic evidence (see the chapter on the Theory of Motivation).

Summers has pointed out that, Klein and Kernberg excepted, object relations theorists advocate the expansion of psychoanalytic technique "beyond interpretation" (to use terminology I introduced in 1979a). Recently, even Klein's followers have begun to view the therapeutic action of psychoanalysis as the consequence of new internalizations. In the judgment of Summers, these ideas have moved the discipline, in a desirable development, to look upon treatment from an interactional perspective. From that viewpoint, even the provision of interpretations serves to form a new (and generally unprecedented) object relationship.

The idea that a novel relationship in treatment will lead to new and more adaptive identifications and thereby constitute a "new beginning" for analysands was first articulated by Balint (1932). In cases of uncomplicated developmental arrest, such fortunate developments may indeed occur; as I have discussed in some detail elsewhere (Gedo 1993b), in disorders of character we cannot expect such a smooth therapeutic course, for negative transference attitudes almost always preclude using the analyst as a new object. Consequently, I believe that Summers has adopted an oversimplified view, one that has encouraged him to be more indulgent of the reductionism and incoherence of various object relations theories than is warranted. (The reading of Greenberg and Mitchell is even more partisan, especially in view of their unsparing critique of traditional psychoanalysis.) Perhaps because of their a priori assumption that self psychology forms the apex of psychoanalytic progress, it is Bacal and Newman who best preserve a proper distance from other aspects of their subject matter and thus permit readers to form their own conclusions. Later developments in this psychoanalytic school of thought are discussed in chapter 13 (The Relational Perspective: New Departures).

INPUT FROM COGNATE DISCIPLINES

8

The Theory of Development and the Yield of Infant Observation

- *The Interpersonal World of the Infant.* D. Stern.
- *On Infancy and Toddlerhood.* D. Freedman.
- *Psychoanalysis and Infant Research.* J. Lichtenberg.
- *The Psychological Birth of the Human Infant.* M. S. Mahler and A. Bergman.

Psychoanalysis began to report on studies of the behavior of preverbal infants, observed in naturalistic settings, over 50 years ago (Spitz 1946; Spitz and Cobliner 1965). Margaret Mahler was among the first investigators to adopt this research strategy (see Mahler and Furer 1968); her enormously influential collaborative report of 1975 summarized the results of an elaborate, well funded study conducted over a period of fifteen years. Mahler approached this research with convictions about the early development of the human infant formed through previous observations of psychotic children. On that basis, she postulated that mental life begins with a phase of autism, that this is normally followed by a phase of symbiosis, and that around the age of eighteen months a process of individuation culminates in the successful separation of child from mother that she called "the psychological birth" of the infant.

Mahler designed her research to determine whether these hypotheses are valid for children from intact families who suffer from no gross pathology. Her subjects volunteered to allow longitudinal observations of the infants (and their interaction with their mothers) through the first three years of life, in exchange for the opportunity of twice weekly attendance at Mahler's well-reputed nursery school. These observations were supplemented with monthly home visits.

Although Mahler proposed a novel focus for the attempt to understand early development, she unquestioningly accepted the traditional drive theories of psychoanalysis and the postulate that infants pass from a stage of primary to one of secondary narcissism. Mahler's team gathered a massive data base of behavioral observations (on a total of thirty-eight infants—seventeen in a pilot project and twenty-one in the standard setting they ultimately devised), but the open-ended research design permitted them to ascertain only whether the raw data could be fitted into the theoretical framework they had postulated. Neither did they compare this fit with that of alternative schemata, nor did they look for data that could have disproved any of their hypotheses. Although the authors acknowledge that their population sample was not representative, they do not seem aware of the principle that no amount of "evidence" congruent with a hypothesis suffices to substantiate it.

What the research did accomplish was to suggest that the process of "separation-individuation" (starting at four or five months and ending at thirty to thirty-six) can be reliably subdivided into a number of phases. The authors rashly assume that, before the process starts, there is a phase of normal autism in which self and others cannot be differentiated, aggressive energy is deflected via projection, but the infant can distinguish between good and bad experiences. These purely speculative notions are difficult to correlate with the available observational data, which are concerned with overt mother–infant behaviors, mostly in connection with feeding. The first subphase described begins with a process of "hatching," which the authors attribute to increased alertness as a result of maturation of the central nervous system. The second is the "practicing subphase," propelled by the infant's increasing skills in locomotion that permit moving away from the mother. The toddler's pleasure in mastering these skills produces a "love affair with the world," like an intoxication with the joy of effectance. The authors arbitrarily assert that this joy also expresses the toddler's pleasure at escaping from symbiotic fusion. The third subphase they postulate is one of "rapprochement," which begins around fourteen months or a bit later, when the toddler's joy subsides and increased separation anxiety becomes observable, an indication that the child has become aware of its own limits. In this subphase, joy accrues mostly from socialization; these transactions show that the child now recognizes that the caretaker's volition differs from its own. The last subphase, roughly coincident with the third year of life, is that of the achievement of libidinal-object constancy and the consolidation of individuality.

A substantial section of the book is devoted to five detailed reports of the manner in which specific infants went through the foregoing phases. (In terms of Mahler's aim to focus on "normal" development, it is noteworthy and disturbing that four of the children featured had a rocky course during the period of observation, two of them to the extent of causing serious concern.) The authors conclude that variations in the precise timing and pattern of this sequence of subphases have no clear import for subsequent adaptation, but that follow-up observations show that individuals largely retain the characteristics they have assumed by the age of three. As for the process of individuation as a whole, they believe that it is innate (cf. Hadley, in press), so that it exerts a "maturational pressure." They make clear, however, that the process is also determined by the specifics of nurture: a "parasitic mother," who unconsciously does not wish her child to be independent, can provoke vehement efforts, even on the part of young infants, to create physical distance from her; other kinds of poor nurture may produce what the authors regard as a prolongation of symbiosis.

Aside from Mahler's own developmental hypotheses, the research team was able to confirm many of the conclusions of previous observers, such as the emergence of a "social" smiling response around three months of age, that of "stranger anxiety" around eight months, an increased tendency to explore at sixteen months, to say "no" at eighteen, and so on. In other words, at the level of overt behaviors, the project yielded many valuable generalizations. When the investigators tried to correlate these observations with putative intrapsychic processes in the infant, they frequently produced speculations that can never be tested, so that neither confirmation nor refutation is possible. For instance, they describe the tendency of toddlers to return to their mothers as "refueling," on the assumption that some kind of libidinal exchange must be taking place. It is more plausible (and parsimonious) to postulate that toddlers return for guidance when the "brave new world" has bewildered them.

Despite this unfortunate overlay of useless speculation, *The Psychological Birth of the Human Infant* rendered psychoanalysis enormous service by calling attention to numerous significant phenomena during infancy and toddlerhood that its developmental hypotheses had previously simply left out of consideration. In the book, Mahler and her co-workers lean over backward to put the square peg of their behavioral data into the round hole of traditional metapsychology; their only concession to the need for theoretical revision is occasional resort to the vocabulary of Kohut (in the version he used *before* the formulation of "self psychology"). This circumstance probably accounts for the fact that Mahler's work has gradually lost its influence. Nonetheless, Mahler's efforts proved to be the thin end of a wedge that would pry open the doors to the revision of developmental psychology.

Joseph Lichtenberg's book of 1983 for the first time brought to the attention of the psychoanalytic community the extensive observational data collected by researchers uncommitted to the analytic viewpoint. (Such data have greater weight for testing psychoanalytic hypotheses than observations made with psychoanalytic assumptions taken for granted.) Lichtenberg began with the assertion that the complexity of the neonate's organization demonstrated by these studies has undermined the psychoanalytic theories of drives and psychic energy. Infants seek stimulation and continue active even during REM sleep; they are object oriented, and not only when they are in need. They have intrinsic potentials for regulation, organization, self-righting, and adapting to the caretakers' patterns of nurture. Their "adaptedness" is based on the availability of numerous functions that are, in Hartmann's (1939) terms, "autonomous," such as the ability to classify the input of information. By the age of four to six months, infants gain the ability to be guided by cues from the mother; this interactional system permits the milieu to have its effects on the child's genetic ground-plan. In other words, infants possess built-in patterns (such as crying) that have the power to evoke the responses they need from caretakers. One of the cardinal tools of this information exchange is the child's affectivity, which becomes functional in an ordered maturational sequence; at the same time, it serves as a system of internal signals within the organism.

Lichtenberg rightly stresses that psychoanalysis and infant research use distinct concepts and languages that can be correlated only in the domain of neurophysiology. The organization of the neonate depends entirely on biological processes (in the central nervous system) that produce states of alertness, crying, quiescence, REM and non-REM sleep. The organization of stimuli leads to a system of reciprocal feedback between child and mother; these communications are impregnated with affect. This system of attachment should be sufficiently under the infant's control to permit the latter to experience being "alone in the presence of another," as Sander (1980) put this, using a phrase coined by Winnicott. The evidence suggests that learning by way of self-initiated activity best takes place in the absence of the caretakers.

According to Lichtenberg, the infant can call on mental representations only in the second year of life yet is capable of many complex behaviors without this ability. For instance, late in the first year there is already evidence of a capacity to engage in planned behavior. Depending on the fit or mismatch between percept and memories, infants at this age will engage in exploration or avoidance; facial cues are particularly important in this regard. Infants engage in various activities despite the absence of conceptual capacities—on a reflexive basis, so to speak. In Lichtenberg's judgment, these data about the organization of infants on the biological level refute the developmental hypotheses of Melanie Klein as well as those of Margaret Mahler: contrary to the assumptions of these theorists, only affect/action patterns are available prior to the acquisition of symbolic functions; fantasies become possible only sometime during the second year. Even at the stage when cues are taken from the mother's facial expressions, the infant remains incapable of conceptual thought; neither is anticipation possible until well into the second year. Defensive operations can begin only after the establishment of long-term memory makes representation possible.

In summary, Lichtenberg concludes that in the first year of life the most important experiences are actual "exchanges" with the mother. In the second year, evocative memory begins operating, so that the toddler transcends the limit of acting solely on the basis of immediate exchanges (that is, by way of action sequences); rather, it is now able to learn from *signs*. This means that deductive thinking begins before the acquisition of symbolic capacities! When the child becomes capable of "imaging," this makes possible the discrete representation of oneself and others. Thenceforth the toddler can recognize its image in a mirror. This is the first indication of a capacity for conceptual thinking that makes it possible for the child to assume "executive functions" independently—in other words, to make a choice among alternatives and to monitor autonomous activities. In relation to other people, the child can now conceive of intersubjectivity; at the same time, the need for "open space" (Sander 1983) becomes even more important than it was during the first year.

In agreement with Mahler, Lichtenberg views the toddler's ability to say "no" as the earliest sign of an independent sense of self. Thereafter children tend to show more assertiveness, and this is likely for the first time to generate internal conflicts; these, in turn, may lead to regressive developments, such as splitting.

Finally, Lichtenberg concludes that the evidence from infant observational studies has shown all existing developmental theories within psychoanalysis to have been grossly faulty. In explicit agreement with my position in *Beyond Interpretation* (Gedo 1979a), he stresses the need in psychoanalysis to deal with such derivatives of the presymbolic phases of development as basic regulatory deficits, cognitive deficits, and bodily symptoms (see also Krystal 1988). The implications of his work for psychoanalytic theory as a whole are much more radical than were those of the Mahler volume, for not only does he show the need to rethink our developmental hypotheses, but his work challenges the relevance of Freud's (1900, 1923) models of the mind for much of human behavior.

Lichtenberg's work in the field of infant observation was strictly conceptual, the integration of the results of a wide array of research in a manner meaningful for the psychoanalytic community. In contrast, Daniel Stern wrote *The Interpersonal World of the Infant* (1985) after lengthy first-hand immersion in infant observation. Nonetheless, his book is an attempt to use such "ethological" observational data to construct an epigenetic, hierarchical schema for the development of the "sense of self": that is, he hopes to trace the genesis of human subjectivity. Stern starts his exposition with the judgment that all the developmental theories extant in psychoanalysis are untenable because they deal exclusively with conditions possible only after the acquisition of consensual language. The subjectivity of a verbal child is characterized by a sense of organization, continuity, cohesion, personal agency, affectivity, and meaning; it is an invariant pattern of awareness that encompasses the capacity for intersubjectivity. To reach such a state, children must traverse a process of development that goes through several organizational increments, prominently at the ages of two to three months, nine to twelve months, and fifteen to eighteen months, less obviously so at five to six months.

Self-awareness begins as awareness of the body, soon that of the body in action. Awareness of an inner life—one's own and that of others—appears around nine months of age. Stern stresses that at no time are (normal) babies autistic or symbiotic in the sense claimed by Mahler: interpersonal experiences can already be organized by the neonate's central nervous system, and sometime between two and six months of age the infant shows signs of experiencing continuity, agency, affectivity, and cohesiveness. The infant's attachment to the mother is a developmental achievement that does not compromise the child's autonomy. In other words, the sense of self is organized in parallel with the organization of social experience. Stern proposes the following epigenetic sequence for the sense of self: phase of emergence, core self, subjective self, verbal self, these phases being separated by the organizational nodal points listed above.

Stern reiterates that preverbal infants are incapable of having wish-fulfilling fantasies or of forming delusions, abilities all previous developmental theories in psychoanalysis have wrongly assumed to be present. He attributes these errors to the incorrect belief that the clinical issues relevant to the conflicts of the verbal child must be central for normal development in the preverbal era. Contrary to these speculations, observation has revealed that what is crucial for development is the manner in which the mother–child dyad deals with various adaptive tasks.

In the first two months of extrauterine life, the neonate is "organizing": very quickly, it learns to recognize its mother by her smell, and a sense of agency is experienced as a result of sucking and of hearing human voices. Soon the neonate has periods of alert inactivity and begins to seek stimuli; among these, there is innate preference for the human face. By two months, the infant makes eye contact, coos, smiles. Sleep patterns stabilize. These changes are paralleled by changes in EEG patterns. The child begins to be able to evaluate percepts, and affectivity comes on line; physiological regulation is effected through social interactions with caretakers. As changes in internal states are experienced, the infant learns to apprehend sensory percepts cross-modally. In other words, there is a supramodal integrating capacity that registers the world without consideration for the sensory organs and pathways activated. Soon the infant will imitate the perceived actions of others; both motoric and perceptual schemata are being organized. This leads to the ability to recognize individuals (and to distinguish the human face from a mask). Early in the postnatal second trimester, some consciousness emerges and with it a characteristic hedonic tone. Stern cautions, however, that, in this phase of emergence, the infant registers experience in a global way, without differentiating details.

In the second and third trimesters of extrauterine life, the sense of core self develops further. Contrary to the views of Mahler and Winnicott, Stern puts emphasis on the rich social interactions prevalent at this age. Infants need an optimal range of stimulation, that is, both novelty and order; gradually, they acquire the ability to regulate their level of excitement on their own. When their intentions are frustrated, it is easy to note that they are aware of the circumstances, because appropriate motor patterns are activated to effect their "plans." At the age of four months, Siamese twins are already cognizant of which set of fingers belongs to whom—just one piece of evidence of how infants define their core self on the basis of the felt consequences of proprioceptive experience. In this manner, they acquire a coherent sense of the body that is cross-modally integrated. Concurrently, more and more episodic memories accumulate, consisting of combinations of percepts, affects, and motor events; these contribute to a sense of existential continuity. Memories of similar events are then combined into more generalized categories, invariant "expectations" that Stern calls "RIGs (representations of actions that have been generalized)." These are the main constituents of a core self.

From an observer's perspective, the infant's physiology is regulated through the ministrations of caretakers. From that of the infant, however, this does not amount to "fusion," for the infant is able to distinguish who is the agent responsible for specific actions. The RIGs formed as the core self develops eventually make possible the "evocation" of companionship, a conclusion that differs from Freud's (1900) postulate of hallucinatory wish-fulfillment only in terms of the later timing of onset and an emphasis on the affective component over (visual) imaging.

The third subphase begins as the infant acquires the ability to apprehend that the mother's subjectivity does not always coincide with its own. This capacity does not depend on symbolic thinking; Stern points out that it is present even in dogs. From around seven to nine months on, children are able to communicate feelings by way of bodily signals, leading to experiences that Stern calls "intersubjective." This ability to evaluate the dyadic situation (for instance, to experience the mother's empathy) provides such advantages for adaptation that it is essential to acquire it . The experiences various psychoanalytic authors have called "mergers" become possible only after the child has learned to distinguish the emotional position of another person. Through such nonverbal communication, the infant may by "contagion" be swept up by the affectivity of an adult. Stern calls events of that kind "mis-attunements." Proper attunement involves consensus about affective intensities, timing, and "shape"—that is, directional gradients.

The acquisition of language ushers in the "verbal self," the sense of individuality produced by the capacity for reflection. Stern notes, however, that words are not generally available to describe the experiences of the preverbal era, so that the verbal self may not include all the relevant experiences of the child. Although he does not comment on this, I believe Stern's cautionary statement refers to the process Freud (1915a) called "primary repression" (see also Frank 1969). This is the only hint in *The Interpersonal World of the Infant* about the significance of differentiating conscious from unconscious mentation. At any rate, the attainment of a verbal self is indicated by the beginning use of pronouns and the child's recognition of its image in a mirror; this is paralleled by the child's ability to show empathy with someone else. Stern also notes that it is only through words that it is possible to *falsify*; hence in the era of the verbal self it becomes possible to construct a "false self" as well. Because such a development comes about only on the basis of interpersonal vicissitudes, Stern would prefer to designate it as the erection of a "social self." In parallel, he calls Winnicott's "true self" the "disavowed self" or the "private self" (cf. Modell 1993).

In conclusion, Stern asserts that infant observation has found untenable the concepts of "normal autism" and of needing to reduce stimulation to a minimum; it has shown those of libido, ego, and id to be useless; and it has demonstrated the need for a general theory cognizant of multiple systems of motivation. He deems all the psychoanalytic theories of development to have gone wrong because they relied on the assumption that infants engage in fantasy and failed to understand that it is real experiences that are crucial for development.

David Freedman's *On Infancy and Toddlerhood* correlates the yield of infant observations, recent neurobiological research, and psychoanalytic clinical studies. Freedman's observational work followed the strategy of physiological research that uses the ablation of specific structures to infer their functions from the disabilities that follow. Obviously, in humans, this can be done only on the basis of "natural experiments" such as longitudinal studies on handicapped infants. For instance, Freedman explains the greatly increased incidence of autism in blind infants (but not in the deaf) as the consequence of the vital role of visual stimuli during the first year of life; this, in turn, is the result of the innate timetable for the myelinization of those structures in the central nervous system that subserve the various sensory modalities: those for vision come on line earlier than those for hearing.

Much of infantile behavior is preprogrammed, that is, it does not have to be learned. In contrast, Freedman points out that the neonate has no "object relations"; both parents and psychoanalytic theories that attribute such abilities to infants are engaged in adultomorphizing. The infant does have *experiences* that produce dendritic connections the function of which constitutes "unconscious mentation." By the age of six or seven months, memories of experience are so organized that familiar percepts produce a smiling response and unfamiliar ones cause distress. Such an ability for recognition is the prerequisite for initiating relationships. The psychoanalytic notions of primary narcissism and infantile omnipotence are also adultomorphic; in fact, the only Freudian idea about early development that has found support in biology is that of bisexuality: embryonically, the brain is at first always female and becomes more or less masculinized under the influence of fetal sex hormones. As a consequence, there is an innate distinction between the behaviors of males and females.

The intervening variable between the effects of heredity and of environment is that of patterns of concrete experience in early life; the effects of these are so profound that they are generally taken for constitutional givens. This explains the fact that monozygotic twins who have different early experiences may later seem constitutionally different. Freedman illustrates the specific effects of unusual early experiences in several unique instances, such as cases of congenital esophageal atresia (a condition that prevents feeding by mouth) or that of a child raised in a sterile bubble because of an immune-deficiency syndrome (who could be touched but could not have closer human contact).

Freedman's review of the evidence from all sources leads to conclusions congruent with those of Lichtenberg and Stern. He stresses, in addition, that the infant's learning is mostly procedural (*how*, not what); this has been recognized in psychoanalysis through its stress on unconscious identification. The notion of "introjection" was an attempt to conceptualize changes in functioning (that is, structural changes in the brain!) by means of a metaphor of interiority. This idea becomes concretized by authors who write about a gamut of introjects as if they were quarreling homunculi. I strongly agree with Freedman's view of the development of a "self-system"—this conception is structural rather than phenomenological/subjective. Because both sensorimotor schemata and identifications may be unconscious, the self-system in Freedman's work transcends the "sense of self" Stern (and Lichtenberg in most of his discussions of this matter) chose as the focus of theirs. Freedman is therefore able to conceive of self-organization either as cohesive or as "split" into parallel, walled-off subsystems that can produce seemingly inexplicable, repetitive behaviors (cf. Freud 1920).

9
Toward a Biological Metatheory

- *Affect Regulation and the Origin of the Self.* A. Schore.
- *Mapping the Mind.* F. Levin.
- *Mind, Brain, Body.* M. Reiser.

A generation ago, at the time analytic theoreticians abandoned Freud's metapsychology as a valid biological substrate for psychoanalysis (for details, see the chapter on the Challenge to Metapsychology), only one respected contributor persisted in calling for its replacement by a tenable metatheory based on biology. In a series of meticulously argued papers, originally published between 1965 and 1976, Benjamin Rubinstein (1997) restated that the central postulate of psychoanalysis, that of the import of unconscious mental processes, necessarily requires consideration of psychological events beyond subjectivity and introspection. Rubinstein agreed that Freud's metapsychology was epistemically flawed, because a concept of psychic energies could be maintained only within a dualistic system (one that splits a mental realm from the soma). This insight revealed an internal inconsistency within Freudian thought, for Freud (1891, p. 55) was also explicit in postulating that mind is merely a dependent concomitant of the activity of the brain. (See also Swanson 1977.)

Through the mid-1970s, Rubinstein had no access to sufficient valid information about brain function to propose a neurophysiological alternative for Freud's metatheory. In order to demonstrate that, once we learn enough about the central nervous system, we shall be able to explicate the regulation of behavior on a biological basis, he proposed a purely hypothetical "proto-neurophysiology" that could illuminate psychology without resort to speculative bridging concepts, like that of psychic energy. In the decade that followed, among clinicians, I was almost alone in supporting Rubinstein's position (see Gedo 1979a, 1981b, 1984; see also Rosenblatt and Thickstun 1977); most psychoanalytic authors continued to use Freud's metapsychology, albeit in a nonbiological (i.e., metaphoric) sense, or they explicitly endorsed a hermeneutic/linguistic view of psychoanalysis (see the chapter on the Narrative Option and Social Constructivism).

The agenda of devising a biological metatheory for psychoanalysis was substantially advanced by Morton Reiser in his 1984 monograph, subtitled "Toward a convergence of psychoanalysis and neurobiology." In a cogent methodological introduction, Reiser confronted the unsolved problem posed by the fact that the respective domains of the disciplines that study the regulation of behavior from the "psychological" and the "biological" vantage points use distinct methods and terminologies. According to Reiser, the former have focused on the question of meanings, while the latter deal with issues concerning energy and matter. Reiser concluded that the resulting conceptual gap does have to be bridged, not by inventing new metaphors, but through the discovery of "translation rules" capable of correlating the data of these separate fields of investigation. (For one recent suggestion along these lines, see Bucci 1997.) Reiser accepted Freud's position that the central nervous system subserves the functions we call "mind," but he did not claim that neurophysiological data can be turned into psychological concepts without some intermediate template that can serve as a "traducer." Nor did Reiser propose such a Rosetta Stone in this book; modestly, he aimed to explore whether tracking parallel data from psychoanalysis and brain science could generate hypotheses about the requisite template.

In *Mind, Brain, Body*, Reiser pursued but two paths toward that goal, the issue of memory storage and that of stress. I shall return to his substantive contentions shortly; here, I want to mention that in *Mapping the Mind* (chapter 10) Fred Levin (1991) soon made a plausible proposal about one focus of study that may serve as an intermediate domain where psychoanalysis and brain science intersect: he saw the development of the human communicative repertory and of information processing as such an intervening variable. Levin pointed out that the acquisition of language (in ontogeny as well as in phylogeny) has an organizing role for the brain and that brain function may even be influenced by the specific language spoken. In this connection, it is well to recall once again that brain scientists now look upon the central nervous system primarily as a processor of information (Hadley 1992).

From a developmental viewpoint, Reiser's contention that psychology is a science of meanings is not entirely valid: before entering the symbolic realm, humans (like other species) are organized on prelinguistic or protolinguistic levels (see Levin, p. 117n.), and derivatives of these modes of organization continue in functional use throughout the life-span. Hence psychology should, in addition to "meanings," encompass certain biological matters, as I have always argued. The relevant functions operate automatically and unconsciously; they are therefore explicable on the basis of physiological criteria. To illustrate: Hadley (1989) has explained that the earliest developmental achievement is the capacity to maintain the familiarity of neural firing patterns; these are measured by comparator mechanisms in the limbic system. In her view, this neurophysiological requirement is the basis of the repetition compulsion. The next development is the addition of affect to the operation of the comparator mechanisms, giving rise to the experience of pleasure or pain. (Pleasure reward takes place through dopamine circuits, anatomically distinct from the pain centers.) The matching system and the pleasure/pain system are hierarchically related, and hence the more fundamental mechanism of the repetition compulsion is able to override the pleasure principle.

As this example demonstrates, the earliest phases of development in behavior regulation and their subsequent derivatives may be directly illuminated by relevant neurophysiological data. Both the papers of June Hadley (1983, 1985, 1989, 1992, in press) and Alan Schore's book of 1994 approach the convergence of psychoanalysis and neurobiology on the basis of such developmental information (see also Freedman 1984). To illustrate, let me list a few additional psychological conclusions Hadley (1992) draws from neurobiological data. She states that the basic motive force for behavior originates in internal generators, cell groups in the brain stem that are modulated by stimuli from the external and the internal milieu. She finds evidence that "motives" are a series of subsystems of hierarchically organized complex behaviors, orchestrated in the hypothalamus and coordinated/prioritized by higher cortical centers. The foregoing data argue against the Freudian concept of *Trieb* (drive) and for the cybernetic theory of motivational systems proposed by Lichtenberg (1989; for details, see the chapter on the Theory of Motivation). Hadley stresses that the central nervous system is inherently active, so that it is redundant to postulate forces that would give it power; it is "wired" to explore the environment and, depending on circumstances, to respond to it with assertiveness or aversion. And so on.

Thus the neurobiological evidence has made it possible to invalidate certain psychoanalytic hypotheses, while it supports certain others. For instance, Hadley (1989) reports that there is no evidence for (nonreactive) aggression that requires discharge. Elsewhere (1992), she finds that the evidence contradicts Lichtenberg's (1989) conjecture that sexuality and sensuality form a single motivational system, a conclusion that also calls into question Freud's (1905) concept about polymorphous infantile sexuality. At the same time, she reports (1992) that cortical processing that eventuates in conscious experience takes place only when perceptual mismatch with expectation, or novelty, or overstimulation occurs: conclusive evidence for the Freudian concept of the Unconscious.

In *Mapping the Mind*, Levin (1991) also makes correlations between certain theoretical propositions in psychoanalysis and neurobiological data, and in some instances he does so where such postulated homologies are rather speculative. Levin believes that, if we learn *how* various functions are carried out in the central nervous system, we shall better be able to define what actually occurs psychologically—in other words, he is committed to the notion that neurobiology and psychoanalysis should operate on isomorphic principles. From this perspective, the concepts of "neural control" and "adaptation," each used by one of the disciplines concerned, are actually equivalent.

Perhaps the most intriguing of his applications of this idea is Levin's discussion (chapter 2) of recent data about the development and functional interrelationship of the two cerebral hemispheres. Levin infers that the defenses of repression and disavowal constitute, respectively, the elimination of input from the left and the right hemisphere (in right-handed persons), a suggestion independently made by Basch (1983). Levin reports that direct connections between the hemispheres via the corpus callosum become well established around the age of $3\frac{1}{2}$. He concludes that the fact of hemispheric differentiation inevitably produces internal conflict (cf. Brenner 1982), especially after the left hemisphere begins to gain a dominant role as a result of the importance of language for adaptation.

Suffice it to say that Levin tries to document that psychological variables are always manifestations of such known (or at least potentially knowable) brain processes. He is at pains to point out (chapter 5) that the findings of neuroscience about the hierarchical arrangement of the developing brain dovetail with certain hierarchical models of psychic function and development, particularly those I have proposed (Gedo and Goldberg 1973; Gedo 1979a, 1988, 1996a). What in theoretical works I have called "self organization," Levin terms a "hierarchy of self-in-the-world potentials." He postulates that a core sense of self is established in the cerebellum (which is active at birth); this "map" of one's body in space is ultimately retranscribed in the basal ganglia and the central parietal cortex. Levin assumes that when this representation becomes a long-term memory, the person has achieved what psychoanalyts call "self-cohesion." As cross-modal sensory integration supervenes, the self-schema becomes more abstract. Thus a series of maps of self-in-the-world become hierarchically integrated in the course of neural development.

Alan Schore's (1994) massive monograph is focused on the neurobiology of *emotional* development. The recent insight that carries his work beyond earlier contributions is greater appreciation of the role of early experience (with the primary caretaker) in influencing the structuralization of the immature nervous system. This neurobiological finding forms a bridge between incompatible psychoanalytic theories, those that deal with attachment and those postulating autonomous self-regulation. It is particularly noteworthy in this regard that the prefrontal cortex takes about two years to become structured, and these developments are especially sensitive to the nature of the infant's human ties (chapter 3). Schore reviews in detail the structuralization of the ventro-medial surface of the prefrontal cortex (particularly in the right hemisphere), with its connections to the limbic system. These structures and circuits are essential for the development of emotions and, consequently, of motivations; through hypothalamic connections, they regulate the autonomic nervous system and thus play a decisive role in psychobiology. This subsystem of the brain, through neuroendocrine mechanisms, activates the centers for pleasure and pain (reward and punishment), and it forms the apex of the hierarchy of psychosomatic control.

Adequate environmental input facilitates the foregoing development of affectivity and, somewhat later, of its control; in this sense, Schore claims that the mother regulates the biochemistry of her child. Moreover, he persuasively demonstrates that even later in life neurochemistry continues to underlie psychology: human attachments are mediated by exactly the same neuroendocrine events that take place in chemical addictions! Like the other authors whose interdisciplinary work is cited here, Schore accepts Hughlings Jackson's concept of the hierarchic organization of the central nervous system, and he adopts the term *self-organization* to designate its psychological correlates. He understands that this view implies a sequence of developmental phases and a sequence of phase transitions that constitute periods of instability, principles that inform the hierarchical models I have proposed (see Gedo 1979a, 1988).

Schore outlines the following phases: 1) recognition of the mother's face imprints the expressions of her emotional repertoire by about eight months of age; this produces a symbiotic system that tends to elicit the same emotion in the infant, thus playing an organizing role.

2) By around twelve months, a reorganization takes place, as inhibitory structures gradually begin to overtake those promoting excitement and joy. This change is facilitated by the mother's expressions of disapproval, which give rise to shame, transactions that enhance the functions of the inhibitory (vagal, norepinephrine-mediated) subsystem. Mother–infant attunement produces a vitalizing reciprocity that sets body rhythms, establishes affective parameters, and leads to learning through the conditioning effects of the mother's reaction. Shame is induced by a lack of attunement, wherein the mother's changed facial expression appears unfamiliar.

3) In the middle of the second year, a crisis of socialization takes place that by around eighteen months leads to a new phase in which affects begin to operate as signals. This development coincides with

the acquisition of significant symbolic capacities and the beginning predominance of the left cerebral hemisphere; this corresponds to the establishment of a "dynamic unconscious."

Schore's description of the earliest phases of development of the mind/brain certainly justifies—and amplifies—Levin's contention that the line of development of neural control dovetails with my hierarchical model. Because Levin was less than explicit about the details of such a line of development, let me repeat how Schore subdivides it. According to him, Phase I is characterized by a lack of cortical input; Levin adds that in its course the infant forms a cerebellar map of self-in-the-world. Phase II is that of right hemispheric prefrontal control and affective input that is added to the core self-organization. Phase III is characterized by predominance of the left cerebral hemisphere; self-cohesion is stabilized through replication of the self-schema as a map in the parietal cortex. Levin has postulated a Phase IV that begins when the corpus callosum vastly increases interhemispheric integration.

Perhaps I have now given a sufficient number of examples, culled from the books under review, of the successful correlation of the simultaneous growth (and reciprocal influence) of neural structure and psychic function. Compared to this fruitful harvest, the yield from the strategy chosen by Reiser, to attempt such correlations for adult conditions, is relatively meager. His best effort at integration happens also to deal with early development: he points out that the capacity for signal anxiety must depend on a cortical function, the anticipation of noxae, albeit the affect of anxiety is produced in the brain stem (locus ceruleus). This explanation is congruent with Schore's conclusion that anticipatory anxiety becomes possible in the second half of the second year of life. Reiser's discussion and classification of stress disorders is cogent, but (apart from explaining the major psychoses as stress disorders *of the brain*, caused by dysfunction of neurotransmitter systems) it does not advance the agenda for finding a template to bridge the gap between psychoanalysis and brain science. Nonetheless, Reiser concluded his book with statements that were to be echoed by Levin and Schore: both the central nervous system and what he calls the "mental apparatus" are capable of functioning in multiple modes and consequently are prone to undergoing abrupt changes of state.

In addition to the crucial attempt to formulate a biological metatheory, these interdisciplinary works deal with a number of issues of importance for clinical theory and the theory of technique in psychoanalysis. For instance, all the books under review touch upon the question of learning, about which there seems to be a fair degree of consensus. Thus Levin (in chapter 3, co-authored by the neurologist M. Vuckovich) asserts that learning at all levels of the nervous system takes place not by changes in "hardware," but by way of chemical changes that reshuffle the synaptic deck, establishing new circuits. He describes the process as the establishment of a short-term memory; when and if this receives reinforcement, it is retranscribed as a long-term one (see also Palombo 1978, and Reiser, chapter 10). Hadley (in press) believes that it is the maturation of the limbic system at about three months that enables the brain to initiate representations, and that maturation of the frontal cortex, by around ten months, produces "immediate" memory storage. (This, in turn, enables the infant to form simple plans.) Memories are then modified by new experiences. A process of multimodal scanning, largely unconscious, leads to *recognition* through the activation of lattices of cells and to *recall* through the interaction of assemblies of such systems. Long-term memory storage takes place by way of chemical changes.

Because procedural memories may not involve such cortical participation, Levin stresses that they may be recoverable only through pump-priming that activates the vestibulo-cerebellar system—for instance, by repeating certain postures or gestures. Whatever the pathways utilized, priming will activate various modules of the central nervous system adapted for learning. Hence Levin conceives of psychoanalysis as a procedure that permits people to learn new methods of information processing, such as more appropriate use of each cerebral hemisphere (see also Gedo 1988, Epilogue; Schore reviews the same issues in his chapters 13 and 14). Levin's prescription for promoting the participation of both hemispheres is that the analyst must communicate in a manner that will reach every relevant module in the brain (see his chapter 1). He particularly recommends the use of metaphors that, by virtue of their evocation of concrete imagery in the various sensory modalities, may integrate hitherto disconnected representations. To the same ends, the analyst may use musical or gestural communications as well as his or her own affectivity. (I have reached similar conclusions on the basis of my clinical experience; see Gedo & Gehrie 1993; Gedo 1996a.)

Although I consider the three monographs highlighted in this chapter to be important stepping stones on the road to a valid biological metatheory for psychoanalysis, I should also mention that they are best used as works of reference rather than read from beginning to end. (In this regard, Schore's massive bibliography of 105 pages will remain a valuable resource for years to come.) Because they attempt to cover a vast field that has yet to achieve integration, these books inevitably lack total coherence; to some extent, they show that they have been put together somewhat disjointedly from previously prepared independent drafts. Although I detected no internal inconsistencies in any of them, Schore's volume is often repetitive and Levin's occasionally ventures far afield from its ostensible subject matter (the intersection of psychoanalysis and neuroscience), with chapters that deal primarily with language. Reiser's book was intended not only for psychoanalysts, but for brain scientists as well; as a result, much of it outlines certain premises and findings of psychoanalysis in a manner too elementary to offer very much to our profession. Yet, in each case, a discerning reader can easily choose to read the sections of these books that will provide the most new knowledge.

10
The Input from Cognitive Science and Its Uses

- *Psychoanalysis and Cognitive Science.* W. Bucci.
- *The Shadow of the Object.* C. Bollas.

Wilma Bucci contends that the realms of psychology and neurophysiology (that is, conceptions of mind and of brain) can now be integrated, because cognitive science provides a middle ground through which the concepts of these disciplines may be translated into each other's discourse. Bucci thereby hopes to change the status of "mind" from a *philosophic* abstraction to one within natural science, to make it a concept defined as a network of behavioral control through information processing. The subsidiary concepts of such a science of mind must be well enough defined to permit laboratory studies that can test the validity of its hypotheses. Bucci's viewpoint is in explicit opposition to that of authors who would confine psychoanalysis to clinical theory; she points out that all such proposals have covertly retained aspects of the metapsychology they purportedly rejected, so that, like that axiomatic system, they have necessarily remained unverified. At the same time, Bucci holds Freud's energy postulates to be untenable, and she agrees with Holt (1989) that the analytic conception of thinking (that of primary and secondary processes) constitutes an oversimplification. (See also the chapters on the Challenge to Metapsychology and Toward a Biological Metatheory.)

The cognitive hypothesis Bucci proposes for psychoanalytic use is a "multiple code theory" that encompasses both symbolic and subsymbolic processing and the integration of these realms through "referential activity." In other words, in disagreement with philosophers such as Cavell (1993), Bucci is committed to the existence of "prelinguistic thought"—what Bollas, in *The Shadow of the Object* (1987), calls "the unthought known." In agreement with Noy (1969), Bucci postulates that symbolic and subsymbolic thinking are both present and continue to mature through the life span. (This conclusion makes superfluous the notion that nonverbal processing constitutes a "regression in the service of the ego.")[1]

Symbolic codes may utilize either words or images, but these two varieties of encoding have to be processed in different ways. In addition, certain ideas *cannot* be verbally encoded; they can only undergo "subsymbolic" processing. This takes place separately for each perceptual modality, by way of "parallel channels." Yet the continuing operation of subsymbolic components within long-term memory may lead to increasingly skilled performance, as in that of trained dancers or wine tasters, for example. Evidence from neurophysiology demonstrates that the perceptual apparatus and the process of imaging make use of the very same channels. The various channels of this subsymbolic system form a network so organized that any stimulus will produce arousal in the entire system. Bucci's multiple-code theory of cognition constitutes the kind of model Rubinstein (1997) calls "protoneurophysiological," for (as she makes explicitly clear) it is not a model of brain function per se, but it conforms with all available evidence from brain science.

The cognitive model implicit in most psychoanalytic theories and most explicit in that of Lacan (see the chapter on French Psychoanalysis) is that of a single basic common code comparable to language. Not only is empirical evidence for such a single symbolic code lacking, that hypothesis is, in fact, in disagreement with the neurophysiological data cited by Bucci. For instance, there are separate systems of memory, declarative and procedural, for the cognitive operations Bucci designates as symbolic and subsymbolic processing, respectively. This is a matter

---

1. D. B. Stern (1997) argues against the possibility of prelinguistic thought but offers no evidence for his conviction. His notion of "unformulated experience" remains murky because he fails to spell out its putative biology.

of crucial therapeutic significance, for behavioral change is contingent on altering matters encoded in the procedural system. In other words, in order to be effective, treatment must go beyond processing verbalizable mental contents to enhance procedural skills (see also Gedo, 1995a, b, 1997a). Moreover, the distinction within the declarative subsystem between episodic memory and semantic memory (the subjective encoding of specific events versus that necessary for linguistic processing) suggests that Freud's classification of cognitive functioning into primary and secondary processes constitutes an oversimplification.

Bucci describes the mode of operation of the various subsymbolic systems for each perceptual modality, some of which are relatively simple, while others (like vision and audition) are relatively more complex. In any case, after these are integrated into a network, they become more or less linked to language. For instance, olfactory data are notoriously poorly connected to the verbal code. By contrast, the cross-modal scheme as a whole is intimately linked to emotions. Bucci understands emotion as a response to meaningful stimuli, mediated within the limbic system, that serves as a guide for action, a regulatory capacity that takes the place of the instincts of simpler organisms. Although emotional processing may become conscious, it may also bypass the cerebral cortex (through direct hippocampal-amygdalar connections), so that it may occur largely out of awareness.

As for the cognitive operations of infancy, Bucci points out that the views of Piaget, Winnicott, and Mahler have all been invalidated; it is Vygotsky's concept of prelinguistic thought processes that has been borne out. The subsequent linkage of subsymbolic processing with language (by way of the intermediate stage of "inner speech") does not alter the fact that man's affective core is linked to nonverbal perceptual schemata (what Daniel Stern [1985] designates as RIGs—see the chapter on the Theory of Development and the Yield of Infant Observation). These early memories constitute the basis of the human sense of animacy and agency, of containment, support, and coherence—in other words, a self-system. The organization of cognition depends on that of the central nervous system: the lateralization of verbal processing in a dominant (left) hemisphere; the modularity of the brain that makes possible operations parallel to conscious thinking that occur outside of awareness, including processes that may remain nonverbal; and the capacity to bar emotions from the cortical operations that involve symbolic processing.

Bucci calls the integration of the multiple codes available to process information *referential activity*. She postulates that various codes expectably become available in a regular sequence: first the subsymbolic codes of the gamut of perceptual modalities, then the nonverbal symbolic code of imagery, later the verbal code. When these become integrated via referential activity, a fourth phase of cognition has supervened. (Note that this line of development might well be continued by postulating a fifth phase of cognition characterized by achievement of the ability to construct a narrative.) Bucci points out that each of these various codes may operate consciously or unconsciously; she also notes that the nonlexical aspects of speech express subsymbolic aspects of the speaker's thinking. In her view, psychoanalysis as treatment must be an attempt to enhance referential activity; in other words, a failure to integrate the various codes of information processing may come about albeit each code is available in isolation. Because Freud assumed that a single common code had to be assisted so that it could mature, psychoanalytic technique has overlooked the necessity to devise different modalities of intervention at each phase of the referential cycle. Bucci clearly means interventions "beyond interpretation."

The interpersonal world and the sense of self are constructed on the basis of emotion schemata (RIGs) to which, at later stages of development, verbal symbols may be attached. Such schemata may turn out to be more or less adaptive; in accord with Gerald Edelman's (1987) views about memory, they may be recategorized in the light of subsequent experiences. Bucci believes that it may be most difficult to alter cognition if it is encoded subsymbolically, although, to be sure, in psychoanalysis one attempts to bring the influence of symbolic thinking to bear upon such matters. In other words, for good or for ill, these archaic memories form the basic fabric of the personality (see also Gedo 1981b). These microstructures constitute the core of psychopathologies. Hence they have to be altered through disorganization and resymbolization, made possible if they have been reactivated by way of transference—provided the "fabric" is not excessively rigid. If maladaptation is caused by unfortunate experiences in earliest infancy, transference may not occur; the therapeutic task in such cases (such as instances of alexithymia) is to assist analysands to learn a symbolic code for the first time. (This is the kind of psychological deficit I have named "apraxia" [see Gedo 1988].) In disagreement with the views of Kernberg and McDougall, Bucci understands both enactments and the formation of symptoms as partial advances toward symbolic thinking.

Any failure to link subsymbolic processing with language makes it impossible to change established patterns. In psychoanalytic treatment, referential activity is promoted by means of free association, which permits the correlation of feelings with words (see also Muller 1996). These correlations are facilitated by the emotional attunement of the analyst with the analysand, a process through which feelings may be assigned new meanings. Bucci points out that such referential activities, like creative activities in general, are not regressive; on the contrary, they involve optimally developed psychological skills in subsymbolic processing, imagery, narration, and reflection.

Dreams, akin to symptoms and enactments, constitute efforts to process the meaning of experiences on a nonverbal level. In other words, Bucci denies that any verbally encoded information is being censored by the dream work; she proposes that activation of the brain stem arouses subsymbolic emotional schemata, that these are represented via the dream imagery and (in treatment) subsequently narrated. The dream work merely constitutes the standard ways of subsymbolic processing (see also Palombo 1978). Any attempt to put the dream into words inevitably constitutes a secondary revision, a reordering in the mode of the dominant cortical hemisphere, that subsequently makes reflection about the mental contents possible. As Bucci also puts this, there are no preexisting latent thoughts that have been transmuted into the imagery of the dream, or, for that matter, into such waking experiences as the Isakower phenomenon. Her hypothesis satisfactorily accounts for dreaming without the necessity of postulating "psychic energy," as Freud was obliged to do.

Bucci presents her integration of psychoanalysis and cognitive science as if her conclusions were at variance with all previous psychoanalytic hypotheses. From the viewpoint of intellectual history, I think in this she is mistaken, for those conclusions are entirely congruent with proposals I have put forward (in part with Arnold Goldberg) ever since 1973. Moreover, some other analytic authors have also explored these matters, notably Dorpat and Miller (1992, see the chapter on Toward a Paradigm of Self-Organization, this volume), as well as Christopher Bollas in his 1987 monograph. (Bollas is a member of the British school of object relations theorists, and regrettably his book also neglects adequately to review the previous contributions of American colleagues.)

Bollas writes about "the unthought known," about analysis as a wordless dialogue, about "somatic knowing." In the tradition of Winnicott, he stresses that psychoanalysis should constitute a novel experience wherein the true self is enhanced. The new experience must be discovered and shared, often in silence; this is made possible not by interpretations but through the provision of a holding environment wherein the unthought known can be reprocessed. The analyst's contribution to such transactions is largely self-analytic, for it is the monitoring of countertransference reactions that can complete the semiotic exchange that communicates the unthought known. In other words, Bollas sees the heart of psychoanalysis as the clarification of affectivity by means of a proxy illness of the analyst—a process Bollas beautifully illustrates by means of clinical examples.

Insofar as the analyst collaborates to provide patients with the experiences needed to affirm their true self, Bollas calls the role that of a transformational object who helps to recreate the past and to apprehend the unthought known. (This concept coincides with that of the "selfobject" in the work of Kohut [1977, 1984].) Bollas views dreams as repetitions of remembered experiences, unconscious, unthinkable, but not repressed, which have been given form through the dreaming process. Archaic experiences may be remembered only in this form, for children may avoid putting them into words if language comes to be seen either as useless or as dangerous. Alternatively, these unthought memories may be represented by way of certain character traits. This archaic language of character may have to be decoded by the analyst; to accomplish this, enactments must be regarded not as manifestations of resistance but as a form of semiosis. Bollas adds that, in certain contingencies, it is a narrow focus on what is verbalizable that constitutes resistance.

About the matters I have summarized, I believe Bollas, Bucci, and I are in essential agreement, although Bollas and I have reached these conclusions on clinical grounds, while Bucci has done so through the application of cognitive science. In The Shadow of the Object, Bollas deals with a number of other issues that pertain to topics covered in other chapters of this guide. In my judgment, however, the principal contribution of his monograph is his concept of the unthought known.

INDIVIDUAL SCHOOLS

II

The Evolution
of Ego Psychology

- *The Ego and the Analysis of Defense.* P. Gray.
- *The Mind in Conflict.* C. Brenner.
- *The Psychoanalytic Process.* J. Weiss, H. Sampson, and the Mt. Zion Psychotherapy Research Group.

Ego psychology, as one of the schools within psychoanalysis has been known, was long designated by its adherents as the American "mainstream." Those who abandoned it in favor of alternative viewpoints have tended to deprecate its traditionalism, and it is probably true that for some time the energies of its intellectual leaders were overinvested in fending off the challenge of alien traditions. Hence it is easy to overlook far-reaching evolutionary changes within ego psychology (see Rothstein 1983), best exemplified by the three volumes to be considered in this chapter.

The earliest of these influential books is Charles Brenner's *The Mind in Conflict*, a well written, authoritative, and lucid position statement that does not make any effort to rebut the contentions of other schools of thought; Brenner simply makes clear his own scientific commitments. These include the explicitly biological postulate of a mental "apparatus" that is given impetus by somatic processes. Consequently, Brenner endorses the use of extraclinical data in theory construction and validation. He correctly designates Freud's notion that the concept of "drive" is at the frontier between psyche and soma as an epistemic error: mind and body are not contiguous domains with a common frontier but separate categories. Mind is a designation for certain functions of the central nervous system. Nonetheless, Brenner retains the concept of drives qua motivational forces that can be postulated on the basis of the wishes to which they give rise (cf. Greenberg 1991).

Such wishes are therefore understood as "drive derivatives," that is, mental representations of constitutional needs that fluctuate in intensity. Although Brenner thus gives weight to quantitative considerations, he rejects Freud's assumption that these can, in analogy to physical systems, be conceptualized in terms of "energies." On clinical grounds, Brenner classifies all drive derivatives as either sexual or aggressive wishes; he does not consider whether this classification of what he considers clinically relevant about human motives is fully inclusive (see the chapter on the Theory of Motivation). He argues that Freud's concept of a "repetition compulsion" is superfluous because the satisfaction of aggressive wishes does not lie "beyond the pleasure principle." This contention overlooks the fact that Freud (1920) attributed compulsive repetitions not to the operation of aggression but to that of entropy. Although Freud's causal explanation for the repetition compulsion was biologically untenable, Brenner's argument still attacks a straw man.

As the title of the book indicates, Brenner's ego psychology is focused on the assumption that both drives inevitably produce conflicts that, in turn, lead to symptom formation. In his view, however, it is not various drive derivatives that conflict with each other; these wishes come into conflict with the unpleasure generated by the dangers they threaten to bring about. The ego's defensive functions are designed to forestall such unpleasure. Brenner rightly stresses that the functional capacities Freud called ego and id can be differentiated only when there is intrapsychic conflict (see also Gedo & Goldberg 1973). He does not postulate that the defensive functions consist of an array of specific "mechanisms"; to the contrary, he holds that all mental functions, even drive derivatives, can be made to serve any adaptive goal, including that of defense. The failure of defense brings about increasing unpleasure that may culminate in disorganization. Brenner therefore sees even this calamity as a consequence of conflict.

According to Brenner, defenses may be aimed either against unconscious wishes or against the affects generated by a conflict. When a wish creates a threat of future calamity, the organism responds with anxiety; when a calamity has already occurred, the response is depression. Brenner believes that guilt responses basically consist of combinations of anxiety and depression. Despite his acknowledgment that unpleasure can be disorganizing, Brenner dismisses the concept of overstimulation, essentially because Freud's version of the idea (that of "actual neurosis") was based on an erroneous etiological hypothesis. He argues that trauma cannot occur without *psychological* causation. It must be noted that, in forming such controversial opinions, Brenner is always decisively influenced by evidence from psychoanalytic experience—largely his own. This is a methodological issue about which I shall have more to say below.

Although he cautiously reminds the reader that it is never safe to assume that any particular configuration has either an oedipal or a preoedipal genesis, nowhere in *The Mind in Conflict* does Brenner deal with preoedipal material. His account of childhood calamities begins with those of the oedipal period, which he places between the ages of $2\frac{1}{2}$ and $5\frac{1}{2}$. The issues of self-esteem prominent in that era are skillfully explicated in terms of his notion of "castration depression" (see the chapter on the Kohutian Legacy). In other words, Brenner does not attribute depressive reactions exclusively to the consequences of object loss. Nor does he reduce the dangers of the oedipal era to the sole issue of castration: in his view, every conceivable danger is present throughout the life span.

Freud's concept of "compromise formation" is central for Brenner's discussion of the consequences of conflict. Not only does he view symptoms as consequences of compromise; for Brenner, jokes, fantasies, and dreams also represent such adaptive solutions. Compromises may lead to good adaptation as well as to psychopathology, and the result of successful treatment is the adoption of compromises less disadvantageous than were those of childhood. Transferences represent compromise among the agencies of the tripartite model, but Brenner looks upon the superego itself as the legacy of the moral compromises of the oedipal period.

The foregoing account of mental functioning is generally coherent, and it represents a considerable departure from Freud's ultimate theoretical schema. Brenner clearly recognizes many of the flaws of Freud's metapsychology that had been challenged in the previous decade (see the chapter on the Challenge to Metapsychology), and he tries to avoid those pitfalls by articulating a psychological theory the biological basis for which he fails to specify. Hence, despite his declared willingness to seek extraclinical validation, Brenner's theory is actually a mentalist one. This raises the question of what the concept of "drive" means in a purely psychological framework: if it does not refer to physico-chemical processes, is it not a covert allusion to soul or spirit? Rubinstein (1997, chapter 9) has demonstrated that the concept of "unconscious wish" can refer only to neurophysiological processes; hence Brenner's synonym for that concept, "drive derivative," cannot fit into a mentalist framework. In my judgment, in other words, Brenner's effort to solve the epistemic problems of metapsychology is not successful.

At the same time, Brenner realizes that abandonment of the postulate of psychic energy entails having to stop differentiating ego from id, as Freud did, on the basis of distinct bioenergetic properties. He does assign some supraordinate adaptive functions to the ego—to maximize satisfaction and minimize unpleasure—but he does not look upon it as an organized system, à la Freud (1923). In my judgment, Brenner's version of ego psychology is no longer a theory of (more or less) stable structures; it merely delineates the adaptive resources of the individual vis-à-vis the postulated tendency of sexuality and aggression for *unchecked* gratification: the ego maximizes satisfaction by means of compromise. In my judgment, Brenner's proposal conforms to the limits implicit in Schafer's (1992) contention that psychoanalytic theories merely provide a mode of discourse for the construction of specific narratives (see the chapter on the Narrative Option and Social Constructivism).

The Mind in Conflict is addressed to the analyst already committed to ego psychology; even in that context, it is extraordinary in its complete disregard for the organization of behavior in the first thirty months of life. Brenner is explicit in privileging data obtained in the psychoanalytic situation; he does not comment on the rationale of excluding the discordant observations of analysts of other theoretical persuasions. Because of his technical prescriptions (the unrelenting focus on conflicts about sexuality and aggression), the presymbolic era is for him a blank. Consequently, he constructs a theory that presupposes the availability of symbolic functions. Such a framework, in turn, allows him to confine himself to the analytic database he trusts. That reasoning is irredeemably circular. If every person reached the age of 2½ without any disturbance in development, Brenner's description of mental life would (more or less) hold water, but (as Eissler already noted in 1953) the notion of undisturbed development is a theoretical fiction. Brenner's psychoanalytic views are *axiomatic*: they are put forward as if they were self-evident truths.

All of that is not to say that Brenner's clinical observations are faulty; what he utterly fails to demonstrate is the causal connection between the mental contents he reports and maladaptation. (In the process, Brenner goes a long way toward justifying Grünbaum's [1984, 1993] contention that clinical evidence cannot validate the causal hypotheses of psychoanalysis.) Brenner ignores everything but the compromises that result from intrapsychic conflicts; he never considers the possibility that unresolved oedipal conflicts might be based on unfavorable developments at proedipal stages (see Gedo 1988, 1995a). His attempt to show that putatively archaic syndromes, such as depersonalization, are also compromises (between drive derivatives and the threat of unpleasure) by citing a single case where he contends this might have been so is unconvincing. Brenner even believes that the psychoses are manifestations of such compromises, although his evidence for this is confined to the putative clarification of a few specific symptoms.

The Mind in Conflict is an effort to salvage the ego psychological paradigm by deleting its indefensible features. It is a highly significant work precisely because it constitutes the acknowledgment of those problems on the part of one of the leaders of the "mainstream." To retain as much of the old paradigm as possible, Brenner constructed a tight theory (albeit one not immune to challenge either on epistemological or biological grounds) that leaves out of account a host of clinical phenomena, including those of Freud's observations that necessitated the use of economic and structural concepts. This particular evolution of ego psychology is a disastrous retreat that barely avoids admitting defeat.

In contrast to Brenner's predominant focus on clinical theory, Paul Gray's *The Ego and the Analysis of Defense* concentrates on the practice of psychoanalysis. Gray's aim appears to be to eliminate the last vestiges of "id psychology" from analytic technique, a goal he attains with distinction. The clinical theory implicit in his presentation in many ways echoes that of Brenner (who is frequently cited with approval), except for one crucial difference: Gray makes it clear that his discussion is applicable only to "neuroses" (narrowly defined), and he leaves open the question of how other conditions are structured and how they might be approached therapeutically.

In other words, *The Ego and the Analysis of Defense* is an excellent primer that outlines an optimal prescription for the management of (oedipal) transferences. Gray's principal contention is that analysands whose difficulties are confined to that sphere can be assisted to focus the work in the analytic here and now on the crucial issue of the manner in which their own mind operates (see also Edelson 1988). Such a focus implies less attention to extra-analytic behavior; the analyst should be able to stay out of the patient's actual life. Gray agrees with Gardner's (1983) recommendation that the analyst should concentrate on helping analysands to improve their self-observation, an aim that entails an explicit effort never to preempt functions patients could perform on their own.

Assisted self-inquiry, as Gardner (1993) called this (see the chapter on the Principles of Therapeutics), can take place only if the analyst gains the cooperation of the analysand—in Gray's terms, of the latter's ego. Self-understanding implies that resistances should not be overridden (through transference manipulations) but closely observed in the service of voluntary mastery. Gray's technique is notably anti-authoritarian. He strongly endorses the precept that analytic work should proceed from the surface down, as well as its correlate, that it should focus on defensive activities and not on the id. Such a procedure can be carried out only if priority is given to current dynamics rather than to the role of the past—despite all countertransference-based temptations to displace attention to externals, whether past or present.

Gray is particularly good at outlining how the analyst can promote analysands' self-observing abilities, and he is entirely explicit in regarding these activities as educative endeavors. Obviously, the first step is to convey that the analysand's primary responsibility is to associate freely. Gray then proceeds to form an observing alliance by demonstrating the fruits of reviewing associative sequences in terms of defensive fluctuations. He recommends that the rationale of all analytic procedures be clearly explained to patients, for instance, that reliving conflictual matters provides an opportunity for mastery, or that any obstacle to free association is a manifestation of the pathology properly designated as neurosis. The analyst's principal technique of instruction is to perform the observational task in the very manner the analysand needs to learn. If the focus on mental operations demonstrates that certain functions are impaired, it is essential to focus the patient's attention on that difficulty. With certain analysands, a failure to attend to the analyst's communications is the crucial impairment to be corrected; with others, it is merely the need to cooperate in the task of reassessing the sequence of associations.

I am in complete agreement with Gray's technology of analytic instruction, as well as with his claim that it should lead to understanding the sources of patients' anxieties and thus improve access to their inner world. I particularly applaud his stress on the therapeutic responsibility to make certain that the analysand has grasped the analyst's intended meaning and to employ rhetorical devices of the kind that promote optimal communication (see also Gedo 1984, chapters 8 and 9; 1996a).

The technique Gray recommends amounts to focused attention on intrapsychic conflicts. This helps to highlight transference developments and their affective components, and reliving these vicissitudes will lead to experiential insight. It is interesting to note that Gray's theory of technique echoes that of Ferenczi and Rank (1924), although he is at pains to disavow any adherence to Ferenczi's tradition. In agreement with Brenner, Gray regards the influence of the superego as the equivalent of defensive operations, but he points out that, as transference develops, superego functions are externalized onto the analyst. Such vicissitudes are easily overlooked, particularly with regard to so-called benign aspects of the superego. Although Gray is cognizant of superego pathology (for instance, lacunae), his recommendation to deal with superego standards as if they constituted symptoms strikes me as one-sided: in my experience, if the analyst does not preserve neutrality in these matters, he or she is likely to be regarded as the proponent of forbidden impulses, a veritable serpent.

At the same time, Gray concedes that, with certain primitive ("infantile") personalities, the analyst may have to shoulder the burden of acting as an "auxiliary superego." Again, in my experience, such an approach has not been fruitful; I have had greater success in demonstrating to such patients the pragmatic disadvantages of dissocial behavior. This is only one example of Gray's ambivalence about the appropriate technical approach to pathologies beyond neurosis. He would prefer to call all such modifications of technique something other than "psychoanalysis," but (unlike Brenner) he acknowledges that they are sometimes necessary. Admittedly, unfortunate technical choices are occasionally made by everyone. In my judgment, however, it is more dangerous to underestimate the archaic nature of an analysand's difficulties than it is to misdiagnose oedipal problems (see the chapter on the Challenge to Therapeutics), so that I am uneasy about Gray's clear preference for using an "unmodified" approach.

My gravest criticism of *The Ego and the Analysis of Defense*, however, is for its failure to consider the high probability that any particular analysand will have difficulties referable to the legacies of more than one developmental stage. A technique narrowly focused on neurotic problems, such as that advocated by Gray, will prove to be of limited efficacy in mixed cases of that kind. If we accept this boundary to its applicability, however, Gray's treatise constitutes a major evolutionary advance for the theory of technique within ego psychology.

The Psychoanalytic Process is an unusual book: its Theoretical Section was written by one author (Weiss), the one on Research by another (Sampson), and the entire volume is also credited to the numerous participants in a psychotherapy research group. I shall make no comment on the research project, which the authors deem to have been successful in buttressing their hypothesis. This holds, arbitrarily, that the primary aim of behavior regulation is safety, which is promoted through unconscious control based on thoughts and beliefs. It follows from this postulate that psychopathology is the consequence of having "pathogenic beliefs." The psychoanalytic situation provides a safe milieu, encourages the relaxation of defenses, and permits the analysand to test the validity of such beliefs. Weiss correctly classifies this control/mastery theory as a variant of ego psychology; I am by no means convinced, however, that the evolution it betokens has been welcomed by a majority of the "mainstream." Weiss is aware of disagreement among ego psychologists about the extent of an organizing function of the ego (see his chapter 2); his position, that the unconscious ego produces behavioral *plans*, is at one extreme of the spectrum of opinions.

Weiss attributes many pathogenic thoughts to the influence of the unconscious superego: he points out that irrational guilt about separation or survival must be based on erroneous beliefs. He does not consider, however, what might cause the persistence of such false beliefs. In the clinical illustrations he provides, for example, guilt is perpetuated by a need to idealize parents who fell far short of idealizable behavior; as I read this material, the persistent cognitive error was the secondary result of the patient's continuing inability to bear the affective consequences of facing certain realities. None of Weiss's discussions of pathogenic beliefs questions why patients have to hold on to such absurdities. Weiss does not use the concept of splitting (or disavowal), which might at least clarify *how* childhood cognitive errors could be perpetuated, nor does he explain why these inconvenient mistakes had to be repressed. In his view, the most common pathogenic beliefs are those of self-blame and of threatened object loss.

Perhaps most controversial is Weiss's teleological assertion that patients enter analysis with the unconscious wish and plan to disconfirm pathogenic beliefs and therefore master their problems. In other words, he affirms that analysands repeat the past in order to disconfirm it. Note that this hypothesis is exactly the opposite of most views about repetition, generally understood as the perpetuation of patterned behavior without regard for its adaptive value. Weiss does not explain how anyone can develop a rational but unconscious plan to get well (and precisely by means of the control/mastery pathway). Such putative potentialities go beyond all previous powers attributed to ego qua organized system—I see the hypothesis put forward by Weiss as a vitalist degradation of ego psychology. (For a more rational and restricted view of the role of cognitive schemata in pathogenesis, see Dorpat and Miller 1992). It is also worth pointing out that, like Brenner or Gray, Weiss and Sampson make no reference whatsoever to the era before the acquisition of language and conceptual thinking or to the legacies of that era in adult life.

12
The Kohutian Legacy

- *Borderline Psychopathology and Its Treatment.* G. Adler.
- *Contexts of Being: The Intersubjective Foundations of Psychological Life.* R. Stolorow and G. Atwood.
- *How Does Analysis Cure?* H. Kohut.
- *The Restoration of the Self.* H. Kohut.

Twenty-five years ago, Heinz Kohut was widely seen as the preeminent innovator within Freudian psychoanalysis. In his 1971 monograph, *The Analysis of the Self*, Kohut summed up his pioneering extension of classical clinical theory to the field of the narcissistic disturbances, thereby stretching the purview of psychoanalysis beyond the transference neuroses, without abandoning traditional premises. The clinical data he reported dealt with psychological issues prevalent prior to the onset of the infantile neuroses on which analytic practice had been focused; he recounted, persuasively, that certain archaic problems can be dealt with in analyses conducted in the usual manner if the transferences he designated as "narcissistic" are given weight as independent vectors in pathogenesis. Because these mental dispositions are crucial in the regulation of self-esteem (as well as for the sense of self), Kohut began to call his contribution "the analysis of the self."

One way to summarize Kohut's lasting contributions is that he discovered that excessive ambitions develop in early childhood as a result of emotional vicissitudes unconnected with fantasies of incest and/or parricide, that failure to establish stable ideals is related to early disappointments in the caretakers, and that difficulties in self-esteem regulation are generally based on a propensity to become either apathetic or disorganized under stress. In my detailed assessments of Kohut's work (Gedo 1975, 1986, chapters 7 and 8; 1991, chapter 11), I concluded that these were valid clinical observations that required reconsideration of the entire clinical theory of psychoanalysis.

For a number of years, Kohut was hesitant to launch such a radical program. In his 1977 book, *The Restoration of the Self*, he was content to use two "complementary" clinical theories, based on incompatible premises: for the transference neuroses (which he called the problems of "Guilty Man"), he continued to use traditional theory; for the problems of "Tragic Man" (as he named the set of issues to which his work had called attention), he proposed a series of novel explanatory concepts. Kohut postulated that, to reach the structural dispositions characteristic of Guilty Man, a "cohesive self" must already have been formed; without this development, Tragic Man's more ominous fate cannot be averted. Consequently, in this middle period of his work he asserted that mixed cases (those combining neurotic and narcissistic features) are unusual.

Elsewhere, however, Kohut suggested that the foregoing dichotomy was not a nosological distinction but merely the application of competing hypotheses to the same set of phenomena. Hence it came as no surprise that, in his posthumous *How Does Analysis Cure?* (1984), Kohut asserted that oedipal problems are caused by "self-pathology"; by this he meant that anxiety about threats to self-cohesion undergirds oedipal problems. In other words, by the time he died, Kohut was wholly committed to the novel clinical theory that came to be known as "self psychology." It should be noted that Kohut's new theory explicitly abandons the metapsychology under severe attack from many quarters in the last decade of his life (see the chapter on the Challenge to Metapsychology), albeit his work through 1972 had been cast in the mold of Hartmann's (1964) psychoeconomic postulates.

In this regard, Kohut probably yielded to the persuasion of some of his followers, notably Michael Basch (1975a,b,c, 1976a,b,c, 1977). It is also likely that Kohut came to realize that some of the ways in which he had forced his clinical generalizations to fit into Hartmann's theory were implausible. For instance, his notion that mature assets of the personality such as wisdom, humor, and empathy constitute transformations of narcissism (that is, sublimations of narcissistic libido) had put forward a purely verbal formula as if it constituted a scientific explanation. Nonetheless, Kohut obviously found it difficult to abandon the conceptual framework he had used for decades; *The Restoration of the Self* at times falls back on explanations in terms of vicissitudes of narcissistic libido. Perhaps this inconsistency was forced upon Kohut by his failure to indicate the biological assumptions with which he replaced those of Freud and Hartmann. His silence on this score gives the appearance of an adherence to a mentalist position (see the chapter on the Philosophy of Mind).

Kohut was also reluctant to commit himself (perhaps prematurely) to a precise definition of what he meant in speaking of a "self." In his 1971 book, the word is never used as a psychoanalytic construct; through the mid-1970s, Kohut continued to use it only to refer to certain mental contents. In *The Restoration of the Self* (p. 207n.), Kohut acknowledged that such narrow usage of the term was out of keeping with the clinical phenomena he was trying to illuminate, but his discussion of self-as-structure in that work remained quite sketchy. He was particularly vague about the formation of such a structure; he simply asserted the truism that a "nuclear self" comes into being through internalizations. As for later conditions, he characterized them by means of the metaphor that the self functions as an "energic tension arc" that links a pole consisting of ambitions and one of idealized goals by way of the skills at the person's command. I, for one, have never grasped what this metaphor could mean; it is easier to follow Kohut when he describes "self" in anthropomorphic terms as weak or strong, deadened or vitalized, coherent or fragmented. Kohut's concept is particularly difficult to follow because he attributes ambitions and idealized goals to the nuclear self but acknowledges that the former crystallize between the ages of two and four and the latter even later. Nor did Kohut clarify his definition of "self" in his posthumous book; he merely reiterated that it refers to the individual's "nuclear program" of ambitions and ideals. If Kohut really meant that such a program is entirely learned from the caretakers (as his writings lead one to conclude), that view would constitute a position of unparalleled extremism in denying the role of "nature" in human development.

Alone among those using "self" as an analytic construct, Kohut conceived it purely phenomenologically (that is, as a summation of the person's subjectivity). He was certainly not alone in advocating that we center psychoanalytic theory on such a structure (for other such proposals, see Lichtenstein 1965; Gedo and Goldberg 1973; G. Klein 1976); by contrast, his hypothesis that objects who meet the infant's needs are experienced as executors of the latter's volition (and are therefore best designated as "selfobjects") was entirely original (see Kohut 1971, p. xiv). This empathic conjecture is entirely plausible, but it fails to specify what kind of transactions (if any) in early childhood might be experienced in a manner different from this. To put this in another way, once Kohut abandoned drive theory, it no longer made sense for him to look upon *any* object relationship as other than need-satisfying. Indeed, in recent years, a number of self psychologists have expanded the explicit functions to be classed as characteristic of a selfobject. Thus Wolf (1980) conceived of adversarial relationships in these terms, and Lichtenberg, Lachmann, and Fosshage (1997) include even sensual/ sexual experiences among those provided by selfobjects.

The murkiness of the selfobject construct was compounded by the fact that in Kohutian discourse "self–selfobject relations" may refer to an interpersonal relationship (in childhood or in the analytic transference) or to intrapsychic events involving *representations* of the person and of need-satisfying objects. (For confirmation of this inconsistent usage, see Goldberg 1988, p. xvi). At any rate, Kohut's novel clinical theory focuses exclusively on self–selfobject transactions (in treatment, on selfobject transferences), "selfobject needs," and "selfobject functions." Implicitly, Kohut came to view bonding with the selfobject as the sole norm of human existence, the only source of significant motives, and therefore the only potential cause of maladaptation.

Kohut initially defined selfobject needs quite narrowly; he confined them to the "narcissistic" issues implicated in self-esteem regulation in analytic patients, the need to idealize a selfobject and to have one's subject-centered grandiosity affirmed (1977, p. 33; see also 1978, p. 557). Before the birth of "self psychology," he had discerned these configurations through the emergence of "idealizing" and "mirror" transferences. At the end of his life, he began to realize that this classification was incomplete; as a first remedy, he proposed elevating "alter ego" transferences (also called "twinship" transferences)—conditions wherein analysands require the analyst to be their exact psychological double—into a third category on this list. Because he left *How Does Analysis Cure?* in an unfinished state at his death, it is likely that, had Kohut lived, he might have reconsidered this issue even further before publishing the book.

The desirability of rethinking these matters is illustrated by Gerald Adler's 1985 monograph (based on a collaboration with Daniel Buie). Adler views so-called borderline psychopathology as a consequence of insufficient structuralization—in his terms, as a failure to form soothing introjects. Such maldevelopment leads to vulnerability in terms of self-cohesion and to the propensity to produce transferences of the kind described by Kohut. In other words, on the stage of everyday life, such people have to rely on selfobjects. Adler points out that the needs these persons must meet have little to do with self-esteem regulation, instead, they have to provide a "holding" (that is, soothing) function. In the context of self psychology, Adler's hypothesis is quite cogent, but it has not gained wide acceptance from orthodox Kohutians (cf. Goldberg, 1995, p. 1, where he decries the failure to expand the scope of Kohut's work).

Kohut consistently underemphasized the consequences of prior structuralization on the regulation of behavior. For example, he asserted that a pathological outcome of oedipal vicissitudes is invariably caused by the parents' unempathic responses to the child *in the present.* The same disregard for prior structuralization led to Kohut's excessive therapeutic optimism, his assumption that if the analyst provides "empathic acceptance" for patients, the development of psychic structure will resume (see also Kohut and Wolf 1978). Although he failed to cite the precedent, Kohut was espousing Balint's (1932) summation of Ferenczi's therapeutic views about analysis promoting a "new beginning" of growth. Such a happy outcome is to be expected only in cases of developmental arrest uncomplicated by characterological deformations. In the vast majority of cases, progress is contingent on painstakingly *undoing* maladaptive structuralizations (Gedo 1993b).

Of course, Kohut's optimism also reflected his redefinition of the appropriate goal of the psychoanalytic process, from the attainment of a maximal degree of self-knowledge to the restoration of a reasonable level of adaptation. This reduction in aim is the principal point of his 1977 book. As he put the matter, analytic termination is appropriate if, as a result of establishing a selfobject transference, the patient acquires "compensatory mental structures," that is, either idealized goals or stable ambitions (1977, chapter 1). The effects of this doctrine are well illustrated by the course of three analyses recently described by Goldberg (1995), in which, as I read his accounts, termination took place before various significant issues were clarified.

Kohut's entire theory was based on the premise that childhood development proceeds in the same manner as does the "repair" of a "fragmented" or "enfeebled" self in analytic treatment, as he had come to conceive that process. (For a critique of the assumption that early development can be conceptualized on the basis of adult psychopathology, see the chapter on the Theory of Development and the Yield of Infant Observation). Kohut explained "restoration of the self" on the basis of "transmuting internalization" that he believed to be the consequence of "optimal frustration." Another way he put the same point was that structuralization takes place through loss of the prestructural selfobject. In *Contexts of Being*, Stolorow and Atwood single out these assertions of Kohut's for criticism; Basch (1986) made the same point in a review of *How Does Analysis Cure?*: learning is *not* facilitated by frustration, even in manageable doses. Children learn not from losing their caretakers but through interactions with them. It should also be added that the concept "transmuting internalization" is a derivative of the metapsychological notion that mental structure is the product of the neutralization of some drive (in this context, presumably narcissistic libido), so that its retention within self psychology is both incongruous and anachronistic. Kohut had devised this concept when he still used Hartmann's metatheory: he wrote about the transformation of the energy of narcissistic libido into "a particle of inner psychological structure" (1968, p. 498; 1971, p. 66). $E=mc^2$! This is another instance of jargon covering over a gap in theory.

In his posthumous book, Kohut challenged Freud's concept that psychoanalytic cure is brought about through the mastery that insight makes possible. He insisted that change comes about not through reason or expanded cognition but only by way of optimal frustration. Hence he saw interpretation as epiphenomenal within the analytic process; he believed the crux of treatment to be the internalization of functions previously performed by the analyst—identifications promoted by frustration or loss. With some inconsistency, Kohut also stated that explanations about the analysand's need for selfobject functions are, however, essential steps in treatment.

Because Kohut believed that optimal frustration can occur only within an "empathic milieu" (see Kohut and Wolf 1978), he concluded that analysis must be conducted in an ambience of active empathic responsiveness. This requirement may lead the analyst to accede to unusual demands, to refrain from making interpretations if they cause trauma, and to accept reproaches within the transference as if they were realistically justified. Matters he singled out for mention because they require especially empathic responses are low anxiety tolerance and imperative needs for appetite satisfaction, external stimulation, or muted reactions from the environment. However, Kohut's cogent emphasis on the need for empathy ultimately became overly one-sided; he came to overlook the importance of making inferences about the analysand's mental functions (in an ethological mode), and he never alluded to the desirability of assisting the analysand's self-inquiry (Gardner 1983).

I trust I have made it clear that, despite the value of his manifold clinical discoveries, I look upon Kohut's theory as an excessively restrictive framework focused on a selected portion of human psychology. The theory of technique he derived from that clinical theory departs even further from the psychoanalytic ideal of exploration in depth. From the viewpoint of intellectual history, Kohut's evolving conceptualizations became increasingly radical in their dissent from the psychoanalytic consensus. As Goldberg has noted, Kohut's heirs have added little to his legacy, albeit this judgment slurs over the fact that some of them have tried but have failed to earn Goldberg's approval. Less than twenty years after the death of its founder, self psychology has splintered into a collection of contending factions.

Self psychologists have generally insisted that it makes no sense to pick and choose particular bits of various theoretical systems—that one must either accept or reject a system *in toto*. (For a detailed justification of this viewpoint, see Goldberg 1988, chapters 2 and 3.) Hence most tend to reject eclectic proposals such as those of Adler, despite his demonstrations of the usefulness of certain Kohutian concepts in conditions about which Kohut himself had written very little. It should be recalled that Kohut was interested only in the vicissitudes of a cohesive self, in "restoring" it if it is threatened with "fragmentation" and in dealing with the causes of regressive emergencies. He looked upon "borderline" states as psychotic forms of organization and schizoid withdrawal as a defense against potential traumatization; consequently, he recommended against attempting analysis with persons who suffer from these conditions (See Kohut 1971, chapter 1). Only in his 1984 book did Kohut mention that borderline states might be analyzable if the analyst succeeded in fitting their bewildering phenomenology into some cognitive schema; clearly, however, he had never tried to do so.

Adler's understanding of the psychopathology of borderline conditions modifies the schema of Otto Kernberg (1975), that of faulty introjection that results in a lack of integration; Adler suggests that this difficulty is preceded by an absolute insufficiency of introjects that leads to a sense of inner emptiness and a tendency for panic about potential annihilation. He proposes that, in the absence of a "holding" selfobject, such persons lose their sense of existential continuity, so that they are ever threatened with the experience of annihilation. In a treatment situation, if the selfobject therapist fails to provide adequate holding, there follows a crisis, filled with rage, and a regressive loss of functions, including that of self-cohesion. Adler believes that, if the therapist succeeds in providing holding, a new beginning of emotional growth will occur even with these patients, although he also lists a formidable array of potential obstacles in the way of such progressive developments. He points out that it is essential to repair splits in mental organization before dealing with self-esteem issues, in the manner Kohut recommended, that is, through "optimal disillusionment" (Gedo and Goldberg 1973). The independence of Adler's thinking is demonstrated by his view that grandiosity comes about as a reaction to loss of the holding experience; Kohut, in contrast, looked upon it as an expectable universal in infancy.

Probably the most significant intramural controversy in self psychology has been created by the effort of Robert Stolorow (and a series of coworkers) to introduce the "intersubjective" viewpoint within Kohut's legacy. The 1992 volume he co-authored with George Atwood tries to show that psychological life is ever a function of intersubjective transactions, so that all clinical material must be assessed from a relativistic perspective. This is the only feature of the book I intend to discuss, because this view contradicts Kohut's concept of "self" as a structure (or program of action) of some stability. Following in the footsteps of deconstructionist hermeneutics, Stolorow and Atwood espouse a postmodern epistemology based on the alleged hopelessness of attaining objectivity (see also D. B. Stern 1997).

Analysts have been aware, for some three generations, that the observer's subjectivity shapes and potentially distorts perception of the data; the dire effects of countertransference were already understood eighty years ago. The requirement of a preparatory analysis for would-be psychoanalysts was instituted to make them familiar with as many of their motivations as possible—in other words, to make them cognizant of the usual configurations of their subjectivity. Even so, most analysts are painfully aware that it is extremely difficult to reach valid conclusions in clinical work, and many realize that the range of transferences they are able to evoke in analysis is more or less limited by their personality attributes. Everyone agrees that clinical inferences must be presented non-dogmatically, as tentative conjectures to be evaluated on the basis of the analysand's subsequent associations. In other words, by working collaboratively with patients, analysts have hoped that they might reach valid conclusions. (These issues are discussed in further detail in the chapter on the Principles of Therapeutics.) In terms of this widely held opinion, the intersubjective viewpoint arbitrarily overstates the influence of the interpersonal field on adult behavior. As Muller (1996) has cogently argued, intersubjectivity does not provide psychoanalysis with a new paradigm; rather, it constitutes a reduction of the field.

The clinical vignettes Stolorow and Atwood present in *Contexts of Being* to illustrate their contentions show, instead, the extent of this exaggeration. For instance, in one case (pp. 64–83) they try to show that a patient's delusional viewpoint was adopted at age fourteen in response to her parents' wishes. However that may be, they also report that the therapist sensibly intervened to correct her disordered thinking—that is, in practical terms, objective conclusions about structured mental dispositions form part of the authors' clinical work, as they do for everyone else. In actual practice, Stolorow and Atwood merely attempt to discern the subjective viewpoint that originally led their patients to a particular notion by starting from the perceptual realities the latter report (cf. Schwaber 1983). In my experience, such tactics are often useful, but they can also be ineffective, and, whenever patients believe that certain risky behaviors are necessary, they can even be dangerous. There are other ways to get at the kernel of truth embedded in most distortions.

Beyond reconfirming that therapists' problems of countertransference or counteridentification lead to unfavorable results, Stolorow and Atwood fail to show that the intersubjective viewpoint is more advantageous than any other; as I have already indicated, they themselves seem to use it only for rhetorical convenience. As a matter of fact, whenever they deal with dream material, they make interpretations that to me seem highly arbitrary, in part because they pay insufficient attention to their own propensity to impose their views on others—an intersubjective issue of some moment!

As I read *Contexts of Being*, its ideological tilt justifies the judgment of Goldberg I have already cited that the productions of Kohut's epigoni (as Kohut himself was fond of calling them) have failed to develop self psychology beyond its state at the death of its founder.

13
The Relational Perspective: New Departures

- *The Ambiguity of Change.* E. Levenson.
- *Object Relations Theory and Clinical Psychoanalysis.* O. Kernberg.
- *Relational Concepts in Psychoanalysis: An Integration.* S. Mitchell.

Among the numerous contemporary contributions to object relations theory, none has had a greater impact on the American scene than Otto Kernberg's volume from 1976. Kernberg begins with an outline of the basic assumption of such theories, that of the accretion of mental structure as a result of the infant's dyadic experiences. It follows from this proposition that, whenever differing sets of these experiences have mutually contradictory characteristics, they produce different "ego states" that tend to alternate and thus lead to a lack of integration that is generally called splitting. Kernberg is careful to point out that the representations of early object relations cannot be construed, when they emerge in the form of transferences, as evidence for the historical truth, for what young children internalize is a version of their dyadic transactions that has been shaped by their own fantasies.

According to Kernberg, the foregoing internalizations lead to the structuralization of good and bad object representations, characterized respectively by predominantly libidinal and aggressive cathexes. He also describes this result as the learning of various human roles by the infant; the sum of these roles constitutes "ego identity." He attributes the integration of internalized object relations to a process of depersonification, meaning the generalization of transactional patterns with the original caretaker(s). It is fixation on these archaic patterns that constitutes psychopathology. Kernberg points out that these early transactions are characterized by overwhelming affect, and insofar as various sets of these experiences differ from each other, the resultant "ego nuclei" need later to be integrated. This is in part accomplished through the projection of representations that have negative connotations. Ego nuclei are also "fused" to produce idealized versions of both self and object(s). Their synthesis involves neutralization of both libido and aggression; alternatively, the occurrence of splitting produces "ego weakness." Consequently, in treatment, priority should be given to overcoming such splitting. Kernberg cautions, however, that primitive idealizations and "borderline" personality organization may be structured on the basis of constitutional anlagen.

Kernberg's theoretical position amounts to an attempt to make simultaneous use of Freud's traditional metapsychology and of object relations concepts. Because he uses theoretical terms from these incompatible paradigms without examining whether they are congruent or not, his work might be dismissed on the ground of illegitimate syncretism. To do so, however, risks throwing out the baby with the bathwater. Kernberg's basic idea about the structuralization of stable self and object representations as a process of integrating disparate nuclei (this part of his text was previously published as early as 1966) is, in my judgment, both sound and important (see Gedo and Goldberg 1973, chapter 5). When, however, he postulates that id, ego, and superego structures are made up of internalized object relations units, I am unable to grasp his meaning, for he is using words in a vague and confusing manner, as if they had no clear referents in the real world. Moreover, there is no justification for his assumption that psychosis is the consequence of those maldevelopments during the earliest phases of infancy that Mahler designated as autistic and symbiotic (see also the chapter on the Theory of Development and the Yield of Infant Observation).

On the positive side of the ledger, Kernberg makes legitimate use of data from brain science to underscore that the earliest memories concern (only) affective experiences. Even more important is the fact that his conception of development is properly hierarchical, although, regrettably, he is less explicit about this than he might have been. Yet he does make it clear that, in his schema, the attainment of differentiated self and object representations constitutes the start of a more differentiated (third ?) stage in development, that this as yet unstable mode of organization is what we call "borderline" when it is encountered in adults, and that such a state can be recaptured in every analysis if therapeutic regression is allowed to take place. The oedipal stage that is replicated in adult neuroses is one in which a stable "self-system" is available. This is the next (fourth ?) stage in Kernberg's model of development; with its onset, repression replaces splitting as the typical defensive operation. These propositions are fully congruent with those Goldberg and I put forward in *Models of the Mind*. Kernberg even agrees with our view that it is only when this stage of differentiation has been reached that it becomes possible to think of the functional distinctions Freud designated as ego and id. The fifth (and last) stage in this hierarchy begins with the consolidation of the superego.

When Kernberg does state that behavior is hierarchically regulated, he makes the unfortunate suggestion that "mind" is located over "brain" in that hierarchy, an inconsistent lapse on his part into Cartesian dualism (see the chapter on the Philosophy of Mind). That contention is also in conflict with Kernberg's belief that affects constitute the infant's earliest motivational system (see the chapter on the Theory of Motivation). In this, he bases himself on the neurological concept of the hierarchy of three physiological systems: those of pleasure/unpleasure, affectivity, and neocortical functioning. He also postulates that libido and aggression are organized as drives by the prior operation of affectivity, a notion difficult to understand without more detailed explanation. Moreover, Kernberg's definition of "affect" remains unclear, except for the suggestion that it refers to a "central state."

The success of Kernberg's book is probably attributable to his effort to provide a static (and therefore simple and lucid) classification of character pathology, based on the foregoing schema of structural development (chapter 5). In his view, a metapsychological classification requires consideration of the lines of development of the drives, defenses, object relations, and superego functions. Kernberg rightly states that when multiple developmental lines (portraying the history of an individual's developmental vicissitudes) are correlated, it becomes possible to diagnose that person's current level of organization. It is difficult to grasp, however, for what reason he believes that the nature of internalized object relations is the crucial variable in determining that organizational mode, especially in view of the fact that he claims that the degree of pregenital aggression also plays an important role in this regard. Kernberg adds another inconsistency when he proposes to classify character pathology in terms of putative structuralization (that is, a static model) yet concedes that an individual's organizational mode is subject to occasional spontaneous shifts.

I trust I have already made it clear that, despite its merits, I have serious reservations about Kernberg's work. I am most dissatisfied by his tendency to create a theoretical pastiche by borrowing popular terms from previous contributors without examining their conceptual status. I also see serious inconsistencies in *Object Relations Theory and Clinical Psychoanalysis*, like Kernberg's equivocation between a static and a dynamic view of current organization and his giving priority to object relations in some of his discussions of development but elsewhere conceding the priority of affectivity or of a self-system, without providing a rationale for such choices.

Steven Mitchell's 1988 monograph, like that of Kernberg, rests on the a priori assumption that the mind is "composed" of relational configurations.[1] In his judgment, the British object relations theorists, the American interpersonalists, and the self psychologists share this interactive viewpoint; he also believes that the "relational vision" of an interactive field adds a third alternative to previous concepts of intrapsychic conflict and developmental arrest. At the same time, he adopts the idea of self-organization, which, unaccountably, he tries to subsume under an object relational framework. From an observer's vantage point, such a structure is organized as a consequence of dyadic transactions, of course, but from that of the infant it is simply the result of the sum of remembered experiences. In other words, for structure formation it hardly matters whether experience occurs in a dyadic context or in solitude. Hence the relational assumption shared by Mitchell and Kernberg is unacceptably reductionist.

---

1. Such an exclusive focus on mental contents overlooks the crucial adaptive significance of issues of mental processing, such as the regulation of affectivity or cognitive apraxias.

Unlike Kernberg, Mitchell does not accept Mahler's postulated phase of autism; he rightly stresses that from the first infants have a constitutional propensity for attachment. Only this concept can be said to anchor Mitchell's viewpoint within any biological framework. In contrast to Kernberg's vagueness about the concepts of "ego identity" and "self system," Mitchell clearly asserts the centrality of the concept of "self" in his theory; for the most part, however, he uses the term as did Winnicott or Kohut (see the chapter on the Rise of the Relational Option and that on the Kohutian Legacy), so that he often loses sight of the fact that self is an intrapsychic entity, that is, a discrete structure. Consequently, he makes the unwarranted claim that self cannot be conceived in isolation. Contrast this with Modell's (1993) persuasive delineation of the "private self."

Mitchell strongly opposes the legitimacy of using mixed models of mental function, such as that of Kernberg. (It behooves me to mention that he dismisses my theoretical work under the erroneous impression that I advocate such a mixed model.) In his review of Freud's energetic model, Mitchell claims that the hypothesis that neuroses stemmed from seduction in childhood was a relational notion. He is correct in pointing out that the seduction hypothesis did not involve a concept of sexual drive, but he overlooks the fact that Freud's etiological formula depended on a concept of trauma, which involves only biological happenings and thus does not fit within a relational framework. This is a good illustration of the way Mitchell inadvertently slides into an outside observer's point of view. By contrast, he is persuasive in arguing that Freud's clinical theories were flawed, largely because they completely overlooked the (nonsexual) need for attachment.

Mitchell concedes that relational theories have been equally reductionist by *underemphasizing* sexuality. He devotes an entire chapter (chapter 4) to an examination of how sexuality could be understood if psychoanalysis abandoned drive concepts. He points out that sex has often been placed within a relational context as an instrument either for destruction or for reparation, and it has also been seen as a measure of self-affirmation or object-seeking. Mitchell is certainly persuasive in demonstrating that a drive concept is not necessary to understand many sexual behaviors; in my judgment, however, he fails to clinch this winnable argument, because he nowhere considers the significance of auto-erotic activities (for which drive concepts might seem to be tailor-made).

Mitchell is at pains to argue that the relational perspective is crucial throughout the life-span, a point hardly anyone is likely to dispute. I suspect that he may be defending the centrality of that perspective against our contention in *Models of the Mind* (Gedo and Goldberg 1973) that object relations theories are most useful to explicate mental organization in relatively early phases of development and the functional recurrence of such conditions in later life. I continue to believe that Mitchell's theoretical viewpoint is focused on epiphenomena. In spite of this, his clinical recommendations are generally perspicacious, for there is no denying that any emergence of analytic transference amounts to the recurrence of old relational patterns.

Mitchell is well aware, however, that (beyond transference) the relationship to the analyst also has novel features, albeit it is the infantile aspects that are generally subjected to interpretation. Mitchell is particularly good in his refutation of the common view that pathology is the result of passive victimization; he stresses that individual adaptation is always the outcome of a series of active choices. The ubiquitous subjective neediness experienced by analysands is, in his view, not necessarily infantile, however. Whenever a person's relational matrices are skewed, the pathology does not constitute a simple arrest in development; it is therefore magical to expect to correct these deformations in relatedness by providing something that was missed in childhood. For instance, "narcissism," according to Mitchell, is a learned response pattern that perpetuates such a skewed relational matrix by way of certain illusions. His therapeutic prescription is neither to attack nor to perpetuate these illusions.

Mitchell's salutary emphasis on the individual's freedom to make active choices entails the conclusion that personality is largely self-created, an instance of the universal self-organizing tendencies of complex systems. Mitchell properly understands that the establishment of self-organization thereafter limits the individual's flexibility.[2] He is also right to conclude that this theory calls into question previous psychoanalytic models of psychopathology (for my contemporaneous espousal

---

2. In his more clinically oriented book of 1997, Mitchell tends to overlook this important theoretical concept; there, he emphasizes seeming shifts in self-organization in response to interpersonal vicissitudes in adult life. Such flexibility is, of course, one possible mode of organizing the self.

of this view, see Gedo 1988). In view of these important and lucid insights, it is difficult to understand why Mitchell has clung to the centrality of object relations for psychoanalytic theory, particularly in light of the circumstance that his former collaborator (cf. Greenberg and Mitchell 1983), Jay Greenberg (1991) was shortly to repudiate the relational viewpoint as the sole explanatory system (see the chapter on Toward a New Technical Consensus).

In contrast to such doctrinaire adherence to former positions, Edgar Levenson's *The Ambiguity of Change* is a rare example of originality. Levenson starts with the finding that the sharply differing interpretive schemata of various schools of psychoanalysis can all be effective, and he proposes a brilliant explanation for this anomaly: all psychoanalytic schools share commonalities in their therapeutic procedures. It follows from this that it is not the content of the analytic dialogue that determines outcome but the very *process* of communication. Levenson postulates that the semiotic rules of psychoanalysis constitute the tools of its influence. (Because this factor has been overlooked in all theories of technique, in the terms used by Grünbaum [1993], the curative effects of psychoanalysis would have to be attributed to their influence as "inadvertent placebos.") From the viewpoint of intellectual history, this implies that Freud's hypothesis that pathogenesis takes place by way of developing fantasies was in error; the better solution would have been to attribute neurosogenesis to the lack of psychological (semiotic) skills characteristic of childhood. In other words, the source of pathogenic ideas is the primitiveness of the child's linguistic and cognitive resources (cf. Weiss and Sampson 1986).

Levenson is undoubtedly correct in stressing that children are confused by adult semiosis, and that this is a primary source of potential helplessness and reactive rage. The fantasies of the oedipal child stem from an inability to decipher the mysteries of adult relationships—this in contrast to the triumph of the mythic Oedipus in solving the riddle of the Sphinx. Levenson reminds us that the acquisition of language and the organization of self are contemporaneous developments. Hence the "enemy within" is the confusion left in the wake of childhood vicissitudes, and the therapeutic task is to correct that confusion. Levenson goes on to delineate the common ground of (most) analytic praxis— the very basis of therapeutics that has remained independent of theory. He lists three areas of commonality: the framework of the analytic situation, the dynamics this sets in motion in the participants, and the transferences that inevitably ensue.

Levenson aptly compares the analytic framework to the rules that must be followed in organized games. Such a set-up is promoted by clarifying for the analysand the actual possibilities the treatment provides. It is also essential to intervene in a manner that keeps the pace of the transaction within appropriate boundaries. In this regard, Levenson rightly states that, whatever the analyst does (or fails to do), that activity constitutes an enactment in the nexus of countertransference: to interpret is to participate. The analyst must always choose between allowing free association to proceed and intervening to pursue some lacuna in the analysand's communications. Sooner or later, these will fit into various patterns that, in turn, fall into place as parts of an ordered whole. The focus of treatment should be on the here-and-now transactions of the participants; accordingly, analysis takes the form of an infinite regress of repeating structured patterns. In Levenson's judgment, such a process is contingent upon authentic emotional engagement on the part of the analyst, that is, a genuine encounter. He therefore believes that so-called analytic neutrality is illusory.

Although the analyst participates in the process mostly through the medium of language, Levenson rightly cautions that there is a continuum between actions and (mere) speech: he properly compares the analytic transaction to the "show and tell" behaviors of the young child. In other words, he broadens a restrictive (Lacanian) emphasis on language to a consideration of every form of semiosis (cf. Gedo 1996a). In this view, the therapeutic skill of the analyst crucially depends on semiotic competence. Much of this transcends the lexical meaning of communications, although metacommunications are most likely to be understood when their enactive components are isomorphic with their lexical content. Levenson is keenly aware of the intersubjective nature of such transactions, but he does not on that account doubt that, by enlarging the analysand's perspective, analysis can undo chronic confusion. He is also extremely skeptical about the possibility (espoused by many object relations theorists) of providing a direct corrective for inadequate nurture in the past, for such benign efforts are generally checkmated by various features of the analysand's character.

Levenson makes a vital distinction between a genuine cure and changes brought about by persuasion. In his view, if an analyst has some preconceptions of where the treatment ought to lead, the resultant process can only be one of persuasion. He defines psychoanalysis as a method to reach valid conclusions about the functions of mind. In the course of such an inquiry, we do not so much reveal hidden truths as we reach levels of greater complexity in understanding. This process permits the analysand to acquire hitherto missing cognitive and semiotic skills (see also Gedo 1988, chaps. 11–14 and Epilogue). For Levenson, symptom reduction is not enough; analysis must be able to fill the scotomata in the patient's psychological competence. This is a theory of technique novel enough to justify Levenson's conjecture that analytic success has hitherto depended on the analyst's skill in navigating against the current of the invalid theories espoused within his or her tradition. Levenson understands that his theory requires, in turn, a theory of mind congruent with how the central nervous system functions. As he conceives this, such a theory must therefore be hierarchical as well as holistic—that is, one that describes a network that may be enriched by the acquisition of new capacities.

Levenson's breakthrough to a view of psychoanalysis that transcends interpretation puts him beyond the purview of the relational perspective, although he never loses sight of the importance of object relations. Yet he characterizes the hopes of those object relations theorists who attempt cures through providing an opportunity to form new introjects as "exorcism." For him (as for me), genuine cure takes place by means of education that overcomes the analysand's apraxic handicaps.

14

The Kleinian Tradition

- *Introduction to the Work of Melanie Klein.* H. Segal.
- *The Kleinian Development.* D. Meltzer.
- *The Matrix of the Mind.* T. Ogden.

The neglect of Melanie Klein's (1984) valuable clinical contributions in America began to be overcome after the publication here of the second edition of Hanna Segal's summary of Klein's work. This authoritative monograph, rich in clinical illustrations, managed to convey that, despite adherence to Klein's strange (and often infelicitous) terminology, Kleinian analysts are often able to do skilled and empathic treatment with very difficult patients. From the clinical viewpoint, Segal reaffirmed that Kleinians practice in a classical manner, a fact that confirms Levenson's (1983) argument that most psychoanalysts actually share a clinical algorithm.

Segal wrote this book over a decade after Melanie Klein's death, but she remained uncompromising in her fidelity to Klein's ideas. Although, by 1974, most commentators acknowledged that Klein had the better of her controversies about child analysis with Anna Freud, and opinion was also tilting in her favor concerning her emphasis on the importance of the earliest phases of development for personality organization and pathogenesis, the majority view in America continued to reject her thinking. Segal acknowledged the speculative origin of Klein's theoretical edifice, but she categorically endorsed its validity and failed even to consider alternative viewpoints.

For American psychoanalysts, the most arbitrary feature of "the Kleinian development" was (and remains) its espousal and concretization of the notion of the death instinct (that is, an inborn force for entropy). To account for adequate adaptation despite such an inborn tendency for self-destruction, Klein of necessity had to postulate a countervailing force that is also inborn, an "ego" that is already functional at birth. The psychological functions that, in her view, overcome the effects of the death instinct are a capacity for "phantasy" in a way that permits splitting along a goodness/badness axis. This results in projection of badness into (internal) objects but may cause reacting to their goodness with destructive envy. Klein's judgment about the difficult nature of infantile development is the most pessimistic assessment of the human condition ever put forward within psychoanalysis. (For details, see Gedo 1986, chap. 6.)

Klein's critics have often construed her developmental propositions to entail an exclusive emphasis on constitutional dispositions for adaptation. Segal strives to refute these criticisms; she points out that Kleinians view good mothering as the essential precondition for overcoming the "paranoid/schizoid" position of infancy. One of the most unfortunate terminological choices made by Klein (and followed by Segal) is to label the anxieties stemming from these archaic issues "psychotic," thus needlessly confusing infantile conditions with the gravest psychiatric syndromes suffered by adults. Neither Klein nor Segal has hesitated to deduce ostensible psychic functioning in preverbal infants from that encountered in adult analysands (and, conversely, to assume that the etiology of various psychoses lies in unsatisfactory mastery of the developmental tasks of infancy).

According to Kleinian theory, the propensity for psychotic adaptation is surmounted by the attainment of the "depressive position," wherein the infant's aggression is counterbalanced by guilt and attempts at reparation. If, for whatever reason, the object seems endangered by the child's aggression, however, either regressive resort to the paranoid/schizoid position or a "manic defense" can be instituted as an adaptive measure. Unmindful of evidence from cognitive psychology, Segal endorses Klein's extraordinarily speeded-up developmental timetable, including the onset of oedipal conflicts, fantasies of omnipotence, and idealization, all within the first year of life. Moreover, Segal (like Klein) presents the foregoing speculative hypotheses as if they constituted validated biological truths.

Despite her tight adherence to Klein's ideas, Segal's book makes an original contribution through her attempt to systematize them. Even following the 1984 publication of the four volumes of Klein's collected works, Segal's summary remained the most concise and most reliable reference work for the Kleinian tradition, although it was soon complemented by Meltzer's exposition, which includes a detailed account of the contributions of Klein's student, Wilfred Bion. Meltzer states (in my judgment, correctly) that Klein's forte was not theoretical thinking but the description of clinical vicissitudes. Correctly, Meltzer concluded that the novel data Klein highlighted neither fit into Freud's structural model nor into the conceptual framework of his psychoeconomic (that is, energy) postulates. Consequently, Meltzer chooses to stress Klein's radicalism, instead of trying to defend her against charges of heresy, as other Kleinian partisans had done, by focusing on the continuity between her work and that of Freud. Specifically, he emphasizes Klein's twenty-year effort, after 1946, to articulate the implications of the concepts of splitting and of projective identification.

I am in complete agreement with Meltzer's judgment that Klein put forward a quasi-theological system, one in which "internal objects" assume the role of deities. He is also on the mark in characterizing Klein's therapeutic aim as the attempt to persuade analysands that good internal objects do exist. In other words, Meltzer does not try to cover over the flaws of Klein's work; he even criticizes a clinical report published late in her career, *Narrative of a Child Analysis* (1984), by pointing out that her early, deep interpretations were "theory driven." Moreover, Meltzer does not credit her with cogent theoretical innovations prior to 1946; he rightly calls her contribution until then the mere promulgation of a "semiotic system" (that is, a private vocabulary). In particular, he deems that Klein's correlation of archaic developmental positions with the psychoses had been wrong, and he also criticizes her early proposal (one she later modified) that the paranoid/schizoid and depressive positions constitute epigenetically related developmental phases. On this issue, I shall have more to say later.

In Meltzer's view, it was Klein's late work elaborating the crucial role of envy in determining the subsequent use of splitting and projective identification, as well as that of the manic defense or attempts at reparation, that finally differentiated the Kleinian tradition from others. In this system, the structural viewpoint is recognized in terms of defining various splits in the self. Yet Meltzer fails to acknowledge a more fundamental difference between Kleinian conceptualizations and those of other theoreticians: in her theory, the foregoing adaptive mechanisms are understood as mere unconscious fantasies. In other words, Klein would explain mental operations purely in terms of psychic content, the equivalent of viewing a computer exclusively in terms of its output; she does not differentiate between a fantasy of good versus bad internal objects from the inability to correlate varied memories of good and bad experiences described by Kernberg (1976). In *The Matrix of the Mind*, Ogden also points out that such a conflation of the dynamic and structural points of view has introduced confusion into Kleinian discourse.

Despite his occasionally critical stance, Meltzer does not doubt the validity and relevance of Klein's interpretive system, nor does he challenge the arbitrary hypotheses she promulgated about the development of cognition (see the chapter on the Input from Cognitive Science and Its Uses). He assumes that clinical improvement following an interpretation is caused by the impact of its lexical content and never considers the therapeutic effect of the omniscience implicit in offering arbitrary readings of unconscious fantasy life. Meltzer also seems comfortable with the extreme skepticism of the Kleinian view that human beings cannot transcend "psychic reality" and that at bottom omnipotence is never completely overcome, so that the outside world must remain unknowable and, consequently, relatively meaningless in comparison to that of internal objects (see the chapter on the Philosophy of Mind).

In Meltzer's judgment, Bion differed from Klein in proposing a psychoanalytic theory that would constitute a philosophical (rather than a religious) system. Bion was less concerned with any referents in the real world than with efforts to mathematize his theoretical ideas. Meltzer occasionally finds these formulas "nonsensical," but he continues to revere Bion's philosophical expertise. He concludes that late in his career Bion changed to an explicitly anti-scientific position that Meltzer characterizes as mystical; from then on, Bion saw the analyst as a kind of priest who engenders belief and thereby provides a corrective experience. Nonetheless, Meltzer remains admiring of his contribution.

In Meltzer's view, Bion explicitly repudiated Freud's "medical" (neurophysiological) model. Thus he looked upon schizophrenia as a purely psychic disorder, caused by an excess of destructiveness; in his view, preponderance of the death instinct and maternal failure to deal with the infant's projection (of badness) combine to create thought disorders, which often involve the formation of "bizarre" internal objects. According to Bion, the schizophrenic's destructiveness takes the form of attacking thinking itself, particularly the links between ideas. Meltzer makes no objection to this purely dynamic explanation for disordered mental processes—a position of mentalism run rampant.

On the positive side of the ledger, Meltzer calls attention to several contributions by Bion that seem eminently reasonable. For instance, Bion redefined the concept of "part object"; in lieu of Klein's "anatomical" terminology, he proposed that we try to devise a label that refers to a provider of missing functions. (This definition would make the term homologous with Kohut's "selfobject.") Bion also disagreed with the view that omnipotent or omniscient beliefs are ubiquitous; he regarded them as stigmata of pathology. Finally, he pointed out that when various skills have been securely mastered, they begin to be exercised unconsciously. Nonetheless, Meltzer has to concede that Bion's constructs are often simply confusing. As I read his account of Bion's work, its pragmatic yield has been the postulation of a set of prototypical "phantasies" even more complex than the one proposed by Klein. In Meltzer's view, Bion (like Klein) conceived of thinking exclusively in terms of the vicissitudes of fantasy contents; on the basis of the possible permutations of these putative building blocks of thought, Bion wanted to establish a "periodic table" of the mind, on the model of atomic chemistry. This effort constitutes a grandiose misuse of a rationalist epistemic position.

Writing from an American perspective and almost a decade later than Meltzer, Ogden presents a markedly different description of Kleinian developments. In contrast to both Segal and Meltzer, he rightly views Klein's exclusive focus on mental contents as insufficient for theoretical purposes. Ogden also points out, correctly, that Klein's tight coupling of instinct and "phantasy" amounts to an a priori commitment to the philosophical assumption of innate ideas. In his judgment, this presupposition is akin to Jung's notion of archetypes or, in a different domain, that of Chomsky of linguistic "deep structures." The innate "phantasies" Klein has postulated are putative, constitutionally available modes of organizing and interpreting experience. Ogden's review of these ideas betrays no hesitation about the theory of a death instinct, nor does he object to Klein's arbitrary invention of a developmental theory, or her failure to offer any evidence for her views.

Specifically, Ogden accepts Klein's conclusion (based on the unwarranted assumption that mentation in infancy is akin to the thinking of psychotics) that the newborn in a paranoid manner apprehends danger from a bad (internal) object. He acknowledges that Klein was incorrect in attributing subjectivity to infants (an error allegedly avoided by more recent Kleinian authors), but he fails to explain how, in the absence of words and even of images, the newborn could transform sensations and affects into "phantasies." It is also difficult to grasp how, in the absence of symbolic capacities, the infant could think in magical or omnipotent ways or experience envy. Indeed, in his less cautious moments (as on p. 33), Ogden slips into endowing infants with the putative capacity for symbolic thinking, such as the ability to suspect trickery. At the same time, Ogden hedges his bets about the expectable chronology of psychic development: he repeatedly fudges on the age levels at which the developmental positions hypothesized by Klein are either attained or transcended. In this manner, Ogden tries to foreclose the criticism that Kleinian theory is incompatible with evidence from cognitive psychology.

For the most part, Ogden avoids adultomorphizing the infant; he rightly states that the newborn is "lived by" its experience, that is, can only register it passively: thus favorable experiences "soften" the infant's paranoid attitude. Ogden puts forward the hypothesis that the good object is established through the use of projective identification; with this achievement, the child is allegedly protected from autism or psychosis. The foregoing developments ostensibly constitute a change from regulation on a biological level to psychological control. Yet Ogden has some doubts about the Kleinian view that the paranoid/schizoid position constitutes a normal phase of development; he leaves open the possibility that it might come about only as a result of a failure of the holding environment. However that may be, Ogden points out that either an inability to use splitting or the excessive use of such a defense will lead to the development of pathology. It is therefore a bit inconsistent that Ogden reverts to the Kleinian view of development by asserting that the optimal use of splitting results in integration of self and object and the onset of subjectivity—in Klein's vocabulary, the establishment of the depressive position. It is difficult to grasp what these assertions are supposed to refer to.

Ogden explicates Klein's concept of "positions" as entirely distinct modes of psychic organization that, once they are established, persist as human potentialities throughout life. In these terms, the depressive position is the state wherein the subjectivity of others is recognized, resulting in the capacity for concern and the onset of fear of object loss as well as guilt. In Ogden's opinion, the designation of this mode of organization as "depressive" is a misnomer; he proposes that the biological maturational step that makes it possible is the establishment of a system of memories organized in a sequential manner, so that the position might best be called "historical." Because, following this achievement, the child no longer lives exclusively in the present and, around the same time, subjectivity begins to prevail, Ogden makes the cogent point that henceforth life is normally experienced in an active mode, so that Schafer's "action language" (see the chapter on the Narrative Option and Social Constructivism) might thereafter be used to characterize behavior. (I am in agreement with Ogden's implication that Schafer's theory leaves out of account all human behavior more archaic than that organized in the mode of the "historical position.") At any rate, Ogden is persuasive on the point that everyone is potentially subject to psychopathology referable to each developmental position because of the persistence of the latter throughout the life span.

In the last three chapters of *The Matrix of the Mind*, Ogden reconsiders Kleinian theory from the perspective of Winnicott's contributions. (Oddly, he does not look upon this as a repudiation of Kleinian loyalties, for he regards Winnicott as a student of Klein.) Ogden apparently favors Winnicott's slower timetable of maturation over that of Klein, one in which subjectivity is established around the age of twelve months; he also concurs with Winnicott's more realistic view about the timing of the acquisition of the capacity to symbolize. In most respects, however, it is difficult clearly to discern Ogden's position on matters about which Klein and Winnicott disagree.

Ultimately, one gains the impression that Ogden has no real confidence in Klein's theory of development, but he shares her assumption that one can draw direct conclusions about infantile mental life from observations of archaic pathology. (He invariably illustrates developmental propositions through vignettes from the therapy of adult patients.) He seems to adhere to the Kleinian tradition because, in dealing with such psychopathology, he finds Kleinian constructs such as splitting and projective identification to be highly useful. He also looks upon Klein's emphasis on the role of aggression in mental life as an important advance beyond the earlier psychoanalytic overemphasis on the import of sexuality. He is willing to accept the Kleinian view of the role of internal objects, although he subtly redefines the concept—as a constituent of the self-organization the infant has created through the operations of splitting and projection.

In my opinion, Ogden has preserved far too much conceptual bathwater in order to make certain that he does not discard the Kleinian baby. At the same time, he has demonstrated that her baby is living and well.

15
French Psychoanalysis

- *Ecrits: A Selection*. J. Lacan, trans. A. Sheridan.
- *Lacan and Language: A Reader's Guide to Écrits*. J. Muller and W. Richardson.
- *A Plea for a Measure of Abnormality*. J. McDougall.

Psychoanalytic writings that originate beyond the boundaries of the English-speaking world generally do not have success in America. In our era, the outstanding exception to this rule has been the oeuvre of Jacques Lacan, which has infiltrated our intellectual life, largely by way of scholars of literature at our universities. This success preceded the 1977 publication in English of selections from Lacan's *Ecrits*. That volume proved to be so difficult to follow that a pair of American scholars, John Muller and William Richardson, prepared a book-length gloss that attempts to clarify Lacan's meaning. *Lacan and Language* apparently did this so successfully that, in 1987, a French translation was published, under Lacanian auspices. I believe this fact justifies a choice not to risk misrepresenting Lacan here by tackling *Ecrits* directly; instead, I shall consider his work through the mediation of that of Muller and Richardson.

It is worth noting that Lacan's writings in French are sufficiently obscure to make this American *explication du texte* useful even for his fellow countrymen; our difficulties with *Ecrits* are not to be blamed on its translator. Muller and Richardson repeatedly stress that Lacan claimed that he wanted his writings to mirror the murkiness of unconscious mentation, and they often concede defeat in their effort to illuminate his fog of metonyms and metaphors. *Lacan and Language* contains three separate clarifying tools: (1) a straightforward synopsis of Lacan's theses, (2) a linear outline of his text, and (3) a mass of editorial notes, keyed to both the English and French versions of *Ecrits*, where the authors comment extensively on particularly obscure points, including questions of precise translation. Muller and Richardson scrupulously avoid making any evaluation of Lacan's contributions, except for the message implicit in their laborious effort: that Lacan's ideas are sufficiently important to warrant the struggle to understand them.

The English version of *Ecrits* contains nine papers, with original publication dates ranging from 1949 to 1960. Muller and Richardson are thoroughly familiar with the evolution of Lacan's work in the subsequent 20 years of his life (he died in 1981), so that *Lacan and Language* will not mislead the reader about the message of *Ecrits*: Richardson is a Lacanian analyst, and Muller one of the few experts on semiotics in our field (see the chapter on the Narrative Option and Social Constructivism), and they are both at home with the French language. To put this differently: the work of Muller and Richardson shows that the selection of his writings for translation into English as *Ecrits* that Lacan made toward the end of his life does contain his most significant psychoanalytic contributions.

It has been widely understood that Lacan reconfigured psychoanalysis as a discipline based on linguistics, specifically the structural linguistics of Raymond de Saussure. *Lacan and Language* makes clear that this commitment simultaneously removes psychoanalysis from biological science. For Lacan, psychoanalytic theory is a doctrine, or, if you will, a philosophy of mind; he read Freud from the viewpoint of a rationalist epistemology and explicitly repudiated scientific empiricism (see Rapaport 1974). In other words, he tried to devise a coherent intellectual framework, based on those of previous thinkers such as Hegel, Heidegger, Lévy-Strauss—and Freud. Such a reading of Freud may strike Americans as a willful distortion, but, at the same time, it entails looking upon Lacan's version of the "master" (often called "the French Freud") as an ultimate authority.

The oldest paper included in the 1977 *Ecrits* articulates Lacan's theory of early development. This is a purely intellectual construct (that is, no evidence is offered for it, either from psychoanalysis or from infant observation); Lacan simply asserts that the mirror image the infant discerns of its physical gestalt is so different from the subjective experience it has previously felt that this image imposes an alienating identity on every individual. Hence, according to Lacan, acquisition of an imaging capacity initiates the inevitable miscognition of (inner) reality. Lacan insists that Freud's *Ich* refers to the foregoing representation of the whole self (not to a psychic structure, as Americans would have it); the construct with which I am familiar that comes closest to Lacan's notion is Winnicott's (1950) "false self." In Lacan's view, what this covers over is the child's actual state of subjective fragmentation; that state is understood in the most concrete terms imaginable, as experience of the body as a collection of bits—as if infancy constituted one continuous state of traumatization. In its pathographic assumptions, Lacan's developmental concept outdoes even that of Melanie Klein. In fact, we now know that infants have the capacity cross-modally to integrate their varied perceptions into one gestalt (see Bucci 1993, 1997), so that there can never be any possibility that they normally experience physical fragmentation: Lacan's developmental theory is mere science fiction.

Muller and Richardson specify that Lacan's entire theoretical edifice constitutes a (nonempirical) shift of psychoanalytic discourse into metapsychology. Thus the presumed dis-integration of the infant is inferred by direct deduction from the theory of a death instinct; the alienating love of the individual's own image is similarly deduced from that of narcissism. Because Lacan severs these Freudian concepts from their biological roots, his theoretical system is a mentalist one (see the chapter on the Philosophy of Mind). At the same time, for Lacan, the death instinct approximates Heidegger's notion of "finitude," and the young child's confrontation with his or her limits constitutes a primordial castration. This postulated loss of omnipotence is contemporary with the acquisition of language and the consequent ability to articulate desires, that is, entry into the symbolic order of human culture. In such a mentalist framework, even the genesis of psychosis is seen as exclusively psychological.

Muller and Richardson believe that the central idea of Lacanian theory is that the unconscious is structured like a language. In other words, Lacan assumed that all unconscious mentation, like the manifest content of dreams, is organized in accord with the primary process; for him, the domain of psychoanalysis therefore coincides with that of the symbolic. He expressed this idea through the aphorism that the unconscious is not "instinctual"—it is, rather, "lettered." Yet the authors advise caution about this, for, in his later work, Lacan's concept of the unconscious seemingly changed: thereafter he compared it to a cipher. This comes closer to Freud's repeated warnings that the nature of the unconscious is unknowable. Of course, if Lacan's assertions that the unconscious operates in accord with a "grammar" were meant to convey only that any system of information processing must operate in some lawful manner, he was merely paraphrasing a truism (see also Muller 1996).

Implicitly, at least most of the time, Lacan defined "thought" exclusively as a symbolic process (cf. Cavell 1993). Yet, when he criticized Kleinians for neglecting the symbolic order, he was clearly acknowledging that the acquisition of language alienates the child from a (thoughtless?) preverbal level of organization wherein one experiences boundlessness and what he termed *jouissance*. This alienation probably refers to the process Freud called primary repression. At any rate, Lacan saw the effect of successful psychoanalysis as the expansion of the domain of the symbolic order to previously uncomprehended repetitive behaviors. In his philosophical vocabulary, this was stated as the location of psychoanalytic action at the level of the analysand's "being." In this sense, for Lacan, transference should revive the analysand's unalienated experience with the primary caretaker(s).

To American readers, it may seem paradoxical that, while he insisted that analysis should deal with such archaic issues, Lacan explicitly opposed the pregenital focus of much of contemporary psychoanalysis. According to him, the Oedipus complex is crucial even in the genesis of the psychoses. I believe the apparent paradox disappears if we conclude that at this stage of his thinking Lacan conceived of development as an entirely linear process that invariably culminates in the retranscription of previous issues in an oedipal guise that then leads to a more or less permanent (and more or less satisfactory) solution. Thus Lacan could deal with archaic issues in his own, original, terms.

The theoretical system Lacan presented to his American readers is always arbitrary and often disproved by the empirical data he so despised. At the same time, in its metapsychological abstractness, it is excessively distant from the clinical arena. Perhaps the only direct consequence on clinical practice of Lacan's adoption of a linguistic basis for his theory of thinking is the careful attentiveness of Lacanian analysts to their analysands' precise choice of language, down to the details of its phonemic structure. In my judgment, such a focus may inadvertently lead to the neglect of other channels of communication (see Gedo 1996a), but if one avoids an exclusive concentration on the text of the analysand's verbalizations, Lacan's focus on language is a salutary one.

Lacan seems to be at his best when he deals with the therapeutic dialogue. He is certainly correct when he states that an analyst's most important qualification is the mastery of speech. Lacan wisely notes that the analyst should listen for "holes" in the analysand's discourse (that is, failures in adequate communication); he is equally right to recommend that the analyst's interventions should aim to evoke further subjective responses, rather than simply to provide information. His distinction between "empty" and "full" speech (meaning discourse devoid of subjectivity or expressive of it) is an important one. His recommendation not to respond to empty speech is generally sound, although (in my experience) it is sometimes preferable to challenge analysands about such blathering. I fully agree with Lacan's conception that the analytic dialogue should be seen as the equivalent of a musical score, although I do not grasp whether in *Ecrits* he understood that the lexical meaning of the words employed may not be the principal carriers of the affective message. (Yet it is the French who articulated that the heart of music is tone: "*C'est le ton qui fait la musique. . . .*") Concerning Lacan's contention that the analyst can punctuate the score of the transaction by varying the duration of sessions, I agree with his critics that such tyrannical power is best left in abeyance. Yet I believe Lacan was right in his claim that effective analysis is contingent on technical freedom, and that analytic cure in large measure depends on what kind of person the analyst is: in particular, whether authoritarian, or one to whom the analysand may speak freely—perhaps even blather? Thus, at the level of praxis, Lacan's recommendations are generally reasonable; as Levenson (1983) has pointed out, there is a wide measure of agreement about the psychoanalytic procedure as an algorithm, whatever the theories various practitioners may claim to be following.

Lacan gained a reputation as the *chef d'école* of a new dispensation because his writings are full of contempt for his putative rivals, particularly if they happen to be American. (The level of his prejudice about American society and intellectual life is both amazing and scandalous.) He accuses American psychoanalysts of trying to bully their patients into conformity with certain putative social expectations—this is Lacan's malicious misreading of Hartmann's (1939) concept of adequate adaptation. But his discussion of the views of other contributors (who are, in general, non-French!) seldom gives them the benefit of the doubt. One is tempted to respond in kind by labeling his work as a typical product of the nonconformist French intellectual who turns into a petty tyrant when he gains power (see Roustang 1990). As Hartmann might have pointed out, Lacan's was an excellent adaptation to the Paris intellectual milieu after the humiliations France suffered in the 1940s.

If Lacan's *Ecrits* strike the American reader as the responses of an oracle more ambiguous than that of Delphi, it should be stated that his provocative stance does not characterize all of French psychoanalysis. Among analysts in Paris who adhere to other traditions, the anglophone Joyce McDougall is probably best known in the English-speaking world, partly because her writings never seem "foreign" to us. Yet McDougall is very French in her psychoanalytic commitments: she adheres to Freud's metapsychology as if it were a convincing philosophical doctrine; she is a Cartesian dualist (for instance, she writes, "psyche grows out of the soma," p. 338); she tends to state her conclusions without offering empirical evidence and often collapses the realm of data with that of theory; finally, she implicitly endorses the inviolability of a traditional analytic technique. Like Lacan, she assumes an unwarranted certainty about the psychogenesis of psychoses and certain diseases she classifies as psychosomatic. In her illustrative case reports, her technique is consistently to focus on unconscious contents, to the neglect of defensive operations and even of affectivity.

A Plea for a Measure of Abnormality consists of a series of meditations on various syndromes more archaic than the neuroses: perversions, homosexuality, narcissistic problems, psychosomatic illness, and psychoses (which McDougall defines very loosely). In my judgment, her most important conclusion is that human beings have the "creative" ability to shift from one of these syndromes to another; I believe she is correct in her view that most people have neurotic, perverse, and psychotic features at the same time. McDougall does not use the concept of personality or character structure, so that she cannot explain the manner in which the differing functional modes available to one person are related or influence each other. Yet the title of her book reflects her attempt to delineate an important character type that she labels as the "anti-analysand." These are people who tend to view themselves as "normal"; in analysis they conform to our procedures like robots, but the process turns empty and static—interpretations are treated as irrelevancies. The thinking of anti-analysands is both concrete and banal, reflecting an inner "deadness," and their human relations are devoid of feeling, except for hostility. This is good observation, but this book leaves one wondering how such personalities are formed; it also raises questions about offering the same technical prescription to all comers.

McDougall asserts that pregenital vicissitudes are of crucial importance in pathogenesis. For instance, she believes that perverts pursue primitive desires, that they are ever threatened by a potential loss of individuality, that they suffer from "psychotic" anxieties, and that they are filled with infantile rage. She presents an extensive case report about such a person, through which she tries to show that a depressive structure underlies the grandiose sexual fantasies enacted in the perversion. She stresses that such enactments are obligatory and that they betoken a failure to attain symbolic thinking about certain matters, so that they cannot be contained in the realm of fantasy. She believes that the challenge of the Oedipus complex proves to be disorganizing for children made vulnerable by such preexisting conditions. The primary anxiety concerns disintegration, and the denial of sexual differences implicit in a perverse solution serves, at the same time, to ward off the more basic anxiety—caused, in McDougall's view, by some early failure in mothering. In other words, she regards perversions as attempts at self-cure through the creation of illusions, to compensate for some early derailment of development that affects areas of functioning broader than the domain of sexuality.

McDougall has had the opportunity to analyze an unusual number of female homosexuals and has come to conclusions about that syndrome parallel to those she articulated about perversions. In her view, homosexuality (in women) is a solution for a dilemma about identity.

She found that depression formed the basis of the problem in these cases, as it does in perversions; this is warded off through sexual behavior that McDougall characterizes as a "manic screen." These women have identified with their fathers and idealized their mothers—ultimately, women in general. They struggle against their own destructiveness; their childhood hostility toward mother had to be repressed. McDougall lists the manifold parental failures that lead to such conditions, but her basic explanation for the problem is resort to the Kleinian notion of the fantasy of the "persecuting breast." She views these patients as persons running the risk of psychotic developments, from which they are protected by their partners' acceptance of their masculine identification as well as the neutralization of their self-hate by these love affairs. Hence disappointments in love often lead these patients to become disorganized.

It appears that McDougall is an astute clinical observer, but her efforts to differentiate various archaic syndromes from each other are unsatisfactory because they are confined to the dynamic and genetic determinants that may be at work, to the exclusion of structural considerations. (It is no coincidence that French psychoanalysts do not call Freud's theoretical proposals of 1923 a "structural theory" but the "second topographic" one!) Moreover, her text betrays a theoretical eclecticism that indiscriminately mixes concepts from a wide variety of analytic traditions. What I found most disturbing in her work, however, is a consequence of her mentalist viewpoint: for instance, she believes that the capacity to symbolize is wholly the product of appropriate nurture, that psychosomatic conditions result from certain vicissitudes of narcissistic libido, and that creativity is the outcome of the sublimation of drives. For American empiricists, her speculations about pathophysiology or the nature of infantile perceptions also seem too arbitrary, not to say uninformed about data in cognate disciplines. Yet McDougall's book, firmly centered on clinical observations, presents a refreshing contrast to Lacan's discourse, with its mixture of abstract theory and dogmatic prescription.

Beyond the marked differences in manner of discourse, Lacan and McDougall clearly belong to a tradition of psychoanalysis peculiar to France. Lacan's influence on the French cultural scene has been so overwhelming that even his psychoanalytic opponents have been largely preoccupied with his ideas, which tend to find their way into their writings. (For example, McDougall uses the Lacanian notion that the idealized phallus is the "essential signifier.") Her explicit disagreements with Lacan concern her willingness to use the analyst's countertransference as evidence for those aspects of the analysand's mentation that have never been verbally encoded, a procedure Lacan explicitly condemned.

McDougall's stress on the importance on semiosis beyond language challenges Lacan on his home ground, so to speak. Where he refers to "empty speech," she understands the analysand's verbalization as an *action* rather than consensual communication. In such circumstances, the message is encoded nonlexically; from the analysand's viewpoint, there are gaps in thinking and feeling. McDougall rightly stresses that this contingency renders patients unable to use interpretations or to tolerate the analyst's silence. It is therefore essential to establish a link with them through a communion mediated through signs (see Muller 1996).

I believe that McDougall's position on this matter is the most fruitful one available, but I am puzzled by her inconsistency in thinking of these archaic manifestations as resistances. She understands that such a clinical impasse demands that the analyst exert some benign influence, but she appears to preclude such success when she prescribes that it is "not [our] role to teach the analysand how to perceive the world and how to react to it" (p. 294). Her equivocation betrays an unresolved conflict between submission to tradition and the original technical conclusions suggested by a set of novel observational data.

The Future of Psychoanalysis

16
The Principles of Therapeutics

- *Analysis of Transference*. M. Gill.
- *The Anatomy of Psychotherapy*. L. Friedman.
- *Drive, Ego, Object, and Self*. F. Pine.
- *Self Inquiry*. R. Gardner.

Whatever the theoretical controversies of the past generation have produced in the conceptual arena, at the level of practical clinical application (in terms of micro-technique within individual analytic sessions) there has been little change. As a result, relatively few monographs have been devoted to this subject, but those few have put forward proposals with profound implications that a conservative profession has treated with great caution. Perhaps the most wide-ranging of these reconsiderations of basic therapeutics was Lawrence Friedman's book of 1988, the title of which—*The Anatomy of Psychotherapy*—is slightly misleading. Friedman wishes to consider all forms of psychological treatment based on psychoanalytic principles, but he rightly approaches this task by placing psychoanalysis proper at the center of his inquiry.

Friedman's work includes long sections on the evolution of Freud's theory of mind and on that of alternatives proposed by some of his successors. These are matters germane to his therapeutic concerns,

159

because Friedman is trying to counter the growing tendency of practitioners to adhere to various psychoanalytic traditions without regard for theoretical considerations but purely on the basis of personal preferences of an affective nature, a self-indulgence Friedman believes can only lead to intellectual anarchy. His excellent surveys of intellectual history, enriched by sophisticated epistemological analyses, will not be considered here (the issues have been considered in the chapter on the Philosophy of Mind); for our present purpose, only sections I, II, and V of the book are relevant.

Friedman starts with the premise that it is impossible to approach the task of psychological treatment without theoretical presuppositions. Among extant theories, that of psychoanalysis is the most coherent, especially in its original Freudian version, but even this account leaves out a great deal of what transpires in a therapeutic transaction. Consequently, the literature on psychoanalytic technique had tended to be unrealistic, particularly on the matter of the analyst's own subjectivity, but to some extent on that of the analysand's motivation for treatment as well. This gap has been papered over through various metaphors suggesting an alliance between the participants.

Freud (1912) articulated the foregoing dilemma through the paradox that transference on the one hand serves as the motor propelling the analysis, while, on the other, it constitutes the principal resistance to it. In Friedman's judgment, later efforts to attribute motivation for treatment to the ego were based on illusion. (Insofar as the only source of motives in Freud's theoretical system is a set of drives, Friedman's point is well taken. See also the chapter on the Theory of Motivation.) He concedes, however, that the transference of early expectations for maternal care onto the analyst, as postulated by Loewald (1960), Gitelson (1962), and Stone (1965), does arouse hope in the patient. To safeguard the alliance, the analyst must avoid moralizing or in any way reproaching the analysand. Friedman also stresses that any attempt to promote the alliance risks provoking a negativistic response. Nonetheless, it is essential to forge a positive bond if analysis is to succeed.

In the 1960s, the notion that analysands have the power through their emotional requirements to govern the process of treatment aroused strong opposition on the part of most commentators. (In my judgment, they were unwilling to concede the intersubjective components of the transaction.) Friedman points out that, at the same time, a school of object relations gained strength which postulated that analytic cure occurs as a result of the treatment relationship, albeit none of the transactions required to achieve such an outcome were specified in these writings. In other words, certain object relations theories arbitrarily assumed that a new relationship can automatically promote growth (see Balint 1932).

More recently, a greater number of contributors have been willing to grant that analysis can succeed only if certain needs of the analysand are gratified. From another perspective, it is now agreed that the analytic process is predicated on attachment to the analyst, and that this tie is inevitably gratifying. Friedman notes that such a relationship constitutes the emotional ambience in which *learning* optimally takes place. The change in majority opinion is dramatically evident through consensus of the fact that even the analyst's interpretations must be seen as reactions to the analysand's initiatives. Most of us have also stopped pretending that one can make interpretations without producing interpersonal complications. In other words, even when the analyst's interpretations are truly meant to be purely descriptive, they are bound to have effects on the analysand's future performance; consequently, they provoke strong reactions. In retrospect, Friedman sees the rigidity of the technical prescriptions prevalent in the period after World War II as the use of theory in the role of a chaperone who makes sure that the analyst does not succumb to sentimentality.

In parallel with the idea of a therapeutic alliance, there arose that of the analyst's "work ego," a concept that minimized the anxiety aroused by a view of treatment as mutual seduction. In order to deal with the ever-present risk of exploiting analysands to gratify the analyst's unstated (probably unconscious) wishes, these have generally remained concealed by being rationalized on the basis of some respectable theory. (In my judgment, this tendency was best described in Grossman's incisive examination of certain dissident movements [1976, 1986; see also Gedo 1986, for further examples]). Of course, one of these illegitimate wishes is often that of confirming some pet theory and thereby reaching closure on the ubiquitous ambiguities of the analytic role.

One of the irreducible ambiguities is whether any particular action is a mere technical operation (something required for therapeutic purposes alone) or, to a greater extent, part of the simultaneous social reality. As a consequence, *whatever* the analyst does can be legitimately criticized from one of these incompatible points of view. Greater or lesser consensus has developed about three roles that the analyst always has to play in performing the treatment, those Friedman calls Reader, Historian, and Operator. The most congenial of these roles is that of the empathic reader of the analysand's narrative—including the fictions constituting the latter's fantasies—because the therapeutic modality that corresponds to this activity is that of interpreting. It is the categorization of the patient's narratives in terms of familiar models (such as the Oedipus drama) that permits "personal recognition," individual understanding that is not feasible at the level of theoretical abstractions. Such recognition makes possible analytic interventions that reflect the analysand's own "voice."

Friedman strongly disagrees with theoreticians who slight the analyst's role as historian by claiming that historical reconstruction can only yield fictions (see the chapter on the Narrative Option and Social Constructivism). In his view, the analytic dialogue actualizes the past; the analysand's associations not only possess significance in the present, they also indicate the causation of the speaker's situation in the world. Hermeneuticists, such as Schafer (1976), have been unable to explain why their rhetorical interventions are effective without making use of terms that denote causal connections. Starting with those of Freud, psychoanalytic explanations have included inferences about psychic activities that are not verbalizable, thereby locating themselves within natural science. In other words, psychoanalysis aims to apprehend reality, past and present. The link between current significance and history is established by the process of reconstruction. Humans live in a world of non-motivated, impersonal constraints, both environmental and phylogenetic, that govern their subjectivity; these non-mental (biological) forces place humankind in the realm of causality, that is, historicism. As an illustration, Friedman cites the biological concept of maturation, used by every psychoanalytic school.

The analyst as historian, in the process of making reconstructions, tries to recontextualize the past. Although past realities are difficult to ascertain, this does not mean that the truth about them is relative. All analysts use extra-analytic knowledge to apprehend past history (for instance, by fitting the data into certain model sagas espoused by particular analytic schools), but the assertion of this kind of expertise does not amount to bullying, as certain criticis of psychoanalysis have charged—particularly not if the reconstructive work is carried out collaboratively (see also Wallace 1985).

The analyst's role as operator has provoked even more unease than the necessity for historicism. Because activities designed to influence patients can easily degenerate into manipulations, there has been a strong tendency to deny that we engage in them. Such denial, in turn, leads to an atheoretical stance that reduces analytic practice to a program of concrete procedures. Friedman points out that analysts cannot avoid taking responsibility for the outcome of their clinical work; they are *conducting* the treatment even if they just "clear off" resistances or operate by means of inaction. In his last statement about analysis as treatment, Freud (1937), outlining the operative roles of model, educator, and object of attachment, acknowledged that the analyst is no mere reader and historian. Also in 1937, at the Marienbad Symposium, most speakers agreed that the analyst teaches both tolerance and the ways of self-inquiry. Friedman suggests that these propositions may once again find wide acceptance, but he points out that we lack consensus about how far to change the basic procedures of psychoanalysis when we deal with "difficult" patients.

In my judgment, the greatest contribution of Friedman's book is his detailed demonstration of the fact that, in order to develop better ways to assist a wider spectrum of patients, one must base novel therapeutic strategies on an explicit theory of mental functioning. Moreover, he correctly points out that even the contributors who deny the need for a metatheory (beyond clinical generalizations) must covertly use *some* hypothesis about human mentation, even when carrying out relatively simple operations, such as an effort to console a friend. Finally, Friedman makes clear the necessity to assess competing theories as integral entities, for it is never legitimate to make use of isolated fragments of these coherent schemata out of the original context that gave them meaning.

One of the most influential authors who made do without a theory of mind was Merton Gill. His 1982 monograph, *Analysis of Transference*, allows him to manage this by focusing exclusively on mental contents verbalized as associations; as one might expect, most of the material he considers is referable to developmental phases in which the child had already mastered a consensual language. The book is intended to focus on the importance of giving priority to interpreting transference in the here-and-now of the analytic encounter. Gill's use of the term "transference" dispenses with the metapsychological implications of Freud's definition of this process, that is, the energic implications of the term, but he fails to clarify this difference in meaning. (It is also conceivable that he did not really tear the concept out of its theoretical context, but, by using it, was covertly introducing Freud's metapsychology into a work allegedly free of it.)

Gill rightly credits Samuel Lipton, who already taught some of us the same lesson in the 1950s, for the insight that *everything* that occurs in the consulting room (even inactivity) has meaning for the analysand, so that the notion that one can avoid "contaminating" the transference by keeping analyst–patient interactions to a minimum is an illusion. This error led to unproductive policies of nonresponsiveness that often interfered with establishing a workable analytic process. An assessment of transference in the here-and-now must always consider the actualities of the analyst's prior behavior.

Gill believes that analysis is facilitated by a transference attachment; he disagrees with that majority of authors who deny that a therapeutic alliance constitutes a transference. He advocates vigorous (albeit "nonmilitant") interpretation not only of transference-as-resistance, but also of any resistance to becoming aware of transference. As I read him, Gill denies that overcoming resistances involves making use of the irrational component of the "facilitating" transference. Through his conception of effective transference interpretation as the triumph of the voice of reason, he appears to imply that the facilitating transference does not operate in the manner of infantile mentation. (Such are the incoherent consequences of refusing to consider *how* people think at various developmental stages.) At any rate, Gill's position illustrates Friedman's contention that many analysts deny their operational activities and mislabel these as interpretations of meanings.

In explicit agreement with Strachey's (1934) concept of "mutative interpretation," Gill contends that interpretation of the transference is the heart of analysis. Consequently, he recommends that the analyst search for indirect references to transference in the stream of associations; he also believes that the most frequent cause of therapeutic impasse is the failure to detect and then to interpret transferences. Another way Gill puts this is that resistances do not disappear spontaneously, and inaction in the face of persisting resistance does not amount to

"neutrality." These are sound clinical principles, as is Gill's fearless-
ness about the possibility of making incorrect interpretations and his
skepticism about any predetermined technical policy. I am also in agreement with his recommendation to address attitudes and characteristics
that are ego syntonic but maladaptive in order to mobilize patients to
look into their psychological significance. I am not certain, however,
whether Gill would have conceded that this abandons the analytic role
of reader for that of operator.

In Lipton's view, the actual transactions in the analytic situation
have a role in evoking transferences parallel to that of the day resi-
due in encoding dreams. Transference interpretations will gain in
plausibility whenever they can be correlated with the realities of prior
analyst–patient transactions. Gill points out, however, that in addition to irrational responses, analysands may also react realistically to
the behaviors of analysts. For this reason, Lipton urged analysts to
"act human," as did Freud, whenever technical requirements do not
preclude this. For example, a persistently silent stance on the part of
the analyst is needlessly provocative. Gill is aware of the fact that it
is considerations of this kind that led to the acceptance of "alliance"
concepts; he warns, however, that the wish to create an alliance may
lead to manipulations in lieu of appropriate interpretation of the
meanings of resistance.

Gill sees transference interpretations as mutative because it is easier
for the participants in analysis to differentiate the patient's fantasies
from reality in the immediate situation than it is in extra-analytic ones.
Hence it is not even desirable for the analyst to aspire to become a
"blank screen." It is most effective to give priority to the elucidation
of transference in the here-and-now, although, of course, the interpretation should ideally be completed by including the genetic determinants of the current transference.

Gill conceives of the psychoanalytic process as a progressive reve-
lation of transferences, so that he believes it is desirable to encourage
the development of these. At the same time, nowhere does he consider
the process of working through (see Gedo 1995a, b) or the affective
dimensions of analytic cure. The only concession he makes to the need
for any therapeutic tool beyond interpretation is the acknowledgment
that analysis must also provide patients with a new relationship. (In
this connection, he leans on Loewald 1960.) In my view, however, this

concession completely contradicts Gill's main thesis, that transference interpretation is *the* crucial therapeutic tool of psychoanalysis.

In my judgment, transference interpretation is only *one* of our crucial therapeutic modalities, important in helping not only to resolve intrapsychic conflicts but also to eliminate the resistances that make it impossible for analysands to learn from the analyst how to deal with maladaptive dispositions (both dyspraxic and apraxic) that stem from developmental levels other than the "defense transference" in question. In this sense, every transference constellation serves as a defense against the emergence of every other. We should never forget that Freud devised transference interpretation as the solution to his discovery of (transference) resistance precisely because the latter stood in his way when he attempted to repair psychopathology—traumata and their sequelae—without a detour through a transference neurosis.

In contrast to Gill's seeming lack of concern for epistemic issues, Fred Pine wrote *Drive, Ego, Object, and Self* as if to produce a manifesto to proclaim that psychoanalysis has no need for a unitary theory of mind. In this sense, his book (published only two years after that of Friedman) implicitly disputes every methodological principle espoused in *The Anatomy of Psychotherapy*. Pine starts from the finding that unprejudiced attention to clinical material demonstrates that the four clusters of issues alluded to in the title of his monograph can play independent roles in pathogenesis, albeit in varying proportions in specific instances. Correctly, he notes that excessive emphasis on one of these clusters (sometimes on a combination of two of them) characterizes most of the ideological factions within psychoanalysis. In other words, whatever credit these schools deserve for highlighting the importance of one or another issue, Pine rightly condemns them all for excessive reductionism. Commendably, his own program for psychoanalysis is one of ecumenicism.

Pine calls his chosen clusters the four "psychologies" within psychoanalysis, and his work has been widely described as an attempt to use multiple models (see *Psychoanalytic Inquiry*, vol. 14, no. 2, pp. 159–234). In a later commentary on critiques of his book, Pine (1994) shows that he was quite aware of the fact that it is focused on categories of mental content, which he named by borrowing familiar conceptual terms without regard for their exact meaning within the broad theoretical schemata to which they belong. To put this in more precise terms,

Pine's usage amounts to the phenomenological classification of clinical material into the categories of wishes, adaptive mechanisms, patterned transactions with others, and subjective experience. Because these phenomena are all continuously present in everyone, I cannot agree that they represent distinct models of psychic function; in my view, Pine's "psychologies" are encompassed within a single clinical model that remains vague about mental operations as such—or worse, switches inconsistently among a number of previously proposed models of mind that are incompatible with each other. Pine defends this evisceration of psychoanalytic theory when he writes, "there is nothing at all to keep in mind in an analysis except what the patient is saying, all the rest [that is, our theoretical baggage] is clutter (until such point as theory helps clarification)" (1990, p. 258). In Friedman's view, and mine, theory is essential for clarification as soon as analyst and analysand meet; without it, everything that happens remains clutter.

Of course, in actual practice Pine was not as atheoretical as all that: he consciously borrowed clinical theories from several schools of psychoanalysis (ego psychology, object relations, self psychology), and in his 1994 rebuttal of his critics, he stated his willingness to borrow from the Kleinians as well. (He also acknowledged that there are more than four "psychologies" at our disposal. For instance, we also possess a psychology of superego issues.) Pine is aware of the fact, almost universally proclaimed by the adherents of various schools, that these theories are incompatible with each other, but he claims the privilege of scavenging useful fragments from them to be used in whatever manner suits his convenience, even if that means that their original sense is discarded. (Anarchy!)

The consequences of Pine's methodological flexibility have to be assessed on the basis of their clinical results. Hence it is appropriate that narratives of clinical work form the core of his book. In addition to two cases he culls from the literature, he provides a dozen fresh illustrations, ranging from relatively brief vignettes to fuller accounts of completed analyses. Whatever the purpose of a particular case example, Pine's accounts are clear, coherent, and lifelike; they convey the extent of the human complexity analysts have to deal with. Pine always provides sufficient detail to permit the reader to grasp the rationale of his conclusions. In the few places where his reasoning outruns the evidence cited, he shows awareness that he might be challenged. The case material reveals a resourceful and empathic clinician who appears to perform effective, even superior, analytic work, often with difficult patients. These virtues undoubtedly justify the positive response to Pine's book.

What Pine fails to show through his clinical illustrations is his rationale at any particular juncture for the specific choice of focus on one of his four clusters. This does not mean that he did not have good reasons for his choices, only that he does not specify the advantages of giving priority to one of the clusters. For instance, in the case of "Mr. C.," Pine demonstrates that all four "psychologies" were in evidence in the course of a single session. Pine chose to focus on the significance of the analysand's behavior in the here-and-now of the transference (in the manner recommended by Gill), and this strategy produced analytic progress. Yet we cannot judge whether Pine's was the optimal choice of focus. To confront the patient's delinquency in withholding associations (that is, the superego issues Pine fails to consider in his discussion) might have yielded even better results.

Pine's failure to articulate rules of clinical transition among his "psychologies" reduces his version of psychoanalytic technique to an art that cannot be verbally transmitted to other practitioners. Because Pine himself is seemingly able to make the necessary shifts of focus, he must be operating in accord with a set of rational criteria, but to codify these it would be essential to articulate a theory of mind. In this book, Pine keeps the secrets of his art to himself; he implies that the analyst simply needs to do what comes naturally. As one of the Surrealists put it, "Let's phosphoresce by intellection!"

The analytic dilemma that almost any intervention (especially one inspired by the accumulated experience of the profession) is more likely to interfere with the analysand's pursuit of self-knowledge than to promote it is the central topic of Robert Gardner's *Self Inquiry*. Gardner's solution for this dilemma was to redefine the analytic process as one of "assisted self-inquiry," a felicitous term that found its way into print only in a later paper (Gardner 1993), although its conceptual meaning was spelled out in the 1983 book. Gardner views clinical psychoanalysis primarily as a method of inquiry, and he judges the mastery of the method to be much more important than is dealing with particular mental contents. This radical change of focus leads him to see effective analytic work as the result of parallel self-inquiries by both participants that eventuate in a degree of mutuality. Gardner postulates that successful treatment is based on the biological principle that cooperating individuals achieve mutuality and synergy through automatic accommodations that lead to functional synchronies. (A well-known illustration of this process might be the tendency of women who live in the same quarters to menstruate in synchrony.)

Gardner believes that the crucial technical problem in psychoanalysis is that of finding the issues about which the analysand is currently prepared to expand his or her understanding—in other words, to focus on questions tolerable for both participants. The analyst can help only by assisting in the exploration of these matters, through attention not only to the content but also to the form of the patient's communications. Connections are made between various aspects of the associative flow until one or both of the participants arrives at a novel gestalt. Gardner has found that, to participate constructively in this process, it is desirable to become consciously aware about the ways in which the analysand's expanding self-knowledge overlaps that of the analyst. Another way he puts this is that the analytic process is inevitably one of matching the subjectivities of the participants about the universal problems of humanity: what one finds is likely to be whatever one has privately been looking for.

In describing the parallel self-inquiries of analyst and analysand, Gardner is specifying the manner in which transference may be identified through recognition of the analyst's counteridentification. He dramatically illustrates this process by incidents wherein he experienced visual imagery that replicated that of a patient's dream the latter had not as yet reported. Gardner stresses that such a result may more easily come about when the analyst's thought makes use of a nonverbal code. Because, in the experience of many analysts, the non-verbal code that produces mutuality has more often been music than visual imagery, I believe the choice is a matter of the analyst's cognitive style. At any rate, Gardner points out that transference repetitions are more likely to obstruct self-inquiry than to renew it. In this regard, he is diametrically opposed to the views of Gill, who advocates *promoting* transference reactions.

In more general terms, Gardner tries to provide a counterweight to the customary psychoanalytic emphasis on interpretation and insight; as he puts this, when the words are right but the tune is wrong, only "pseudo-inquiry" will follow. The implication of his work is that the end-point of a successful analysis has been reached when the analysand can perform self-inquiry without assistance. In other words, analytic treatment is in principle terminable, but there can be no end to the need for self-inquiry. Gardner views the human condition as a dialectical oscillation between the need for mutuality in attachment and the inevitability of solitude—and the opportunity for mastery and creativity that solitude provides.

Self Inquiry demonstrates that the dyadic format of psychoanalysis imposes unbreakable epistemic constraints on our endeavors: on the one hand, we can discover in our patients only whatever we are capable of apprehending in ourselves; on the other, the psychoanalytic situation automatically steers analysands into the realm of mutuality. In those conditions, experiences that occur in solitude can be recollected only dimly, and their elucidation usually has to await the analysand's post-termination self-inquiry, a process of self-creation that inevitably takes on the qualities of play (see especially Gardner 1993). These matters are likely to be encoded so idiosyncratically that even the most empathic analyst can hardly form any judgment about them. One's solitary experiences are likely to seem a bit autistic to the uninitiated.

Gardner has not articulated a complete new theory of mind, but he has postulated one biological given on which such a theory should be based: the predominant effect of attachment motivations in the psychoanalytic situation (see the chapter on the Theory of Motivation). His conceptual work has carried the theory of technique into new territory; in the process, Gardner has redefined the basic goals of treatment and its fundamental tools.

17
Toward a
New Technical Consensus

- *Impasse and Interpretation.* H. Rosenfeld.
- *The Intimate Edge.* D. Ehrenberg.
- *My Work with Borderline Patients.* H. Searles.
- *Other Times, Other Realities.* A. Modell.
- *The Use of the Self.* T. Jacobs.

In the past decade, a succession of contributions, from a wide spectrum of traditions within psychoanalysis, has opened new avenues in analytic therapeutics. Although most of these proposals differ from each other in numerous respects, some of the most thoughtful among them are in sufficient agreement to constitute the beginning of a new consensus about certain requirements of effective psychoanalytic technique. Among the authors I have chosen to feature in this segment, there are representatives of the Freudian mainstream (Jacobs), the Kleinian school (Rosenfeld), the interpersonalists (Ehrenberg), object relations theorists (Searles), and a new biological orientation (Modell). It must, however, be acknowledged that the clinical procedures of these contributors appear to resemble each other precisely because, for the most part, they do not have any direct relationship to those theoretical matters about which their respective psychoanalytic traditions are in sharp disagreement. These controversial issues are hardly mentioned in the books under consideration here, although none of the authors makes any effort to arrive at an ecumenical position. On the contrary, some of them write, ingenuously, as if the innovations they espouse have been made possible only by the prior contributions of their own school of thought.[1]

Alone among these contributors, Modell is explicit about his aim to develop a new theory of psychoanalytic treatment, to propose a hypothesis about the mode of action of psychoanalysis that is applicable in the full range of maladaptation to the amelioration of which analytic methods are appropriate. Modell's past theoretical orientation was to follow in the footsteps of Winnicott; in his prior work (Modell 1968, 1976, 1984) he emphasized the necessity of providing a "holding environment" for analysands, a locus of safety where the earliest attachments to caretakers may be relived in the transference. If this basic therapeutic *sine qua non* is present, he notes that improvement may take place even if the analysand does not gain new access to his or her inner life—and this may happen in the absence of further constructive transactions with the analyst.

In Modell's view, it is the invariable features of the analytic setting (the physical environment, the schedule, financial arrangements, etc.) that constitute a facilitating environment in the context of which past traumata may safely be reexperienced. In cases properly classified as neuroses, these matters of setting generally do not consciously impinge on the analysand's associations; because they remain silent, the role of the setting in promoting such reliving has received little notice. Leaning on the understanding of memory proposed by the neurobiologist Gerald Edelman (1987), Modell focuses his hypothesis about the mode of action of psychoanalysis on the opportunity to retranscribe the transference repetition of traumatic experiences in terms of new meanings. Such recontextualization may eliminate defensive splits in self-organization, and this change is one factor that leads to adaptive improvements. (Parenthetically, it should be noted that Modell's hypothesis eliminates the false dichotomy of differentiating types of psy-

---

1. In his survey of these developments, Mitchell (1997) notes this rapprochement in views about the art of psychoanalysis but attributes it to the spreading influence of the relational perspective.

chopathology that are putatively based on conflict from others attributed to some kind of structural deficit. These conditions invariably coexist; one implies the other and vice versa.)

From the foregoing perspective, the analytic relationship may be conceived as a frame within which multiple levels of reality are allowed to coexist. From the viewpoint of the participants, these are the subjective experiences we classify as transference and countertransference. In the "potential space" of the analytic situation, it is often possible to establish a shared reality. If this occurs, it becomes both irrelevant and difficult to establish with which participant a specific insight originated (see also Gardner 1983). In Modell's terms, the phenomena previously called resistances are the inevitable reactions of analysands whenever the analyst's alien view of reality impinges upon them. The issue of resistance takes center place in treatment with patients who are unable consistently to accept the analytic situation as a framework that delimits a unique experience with its own particular ground rules.

Contrary to some recent voices in the analytic literature that espouse a radical relativism, Modell believes that it is the analyst's responsibility to "conduct" the treatment—and that this inevitably occurs, whatever the analyst's intentions in this regard may be. Because of this therapeutic responsibility, the role of the analyst's personality cannot be eliminated from therapeutic consideration. The aspect of the ground rules that produces this circumstance is the asymmetrical roles assigned to the participants with regard to communication (free association versus freely hovering attention) as well as to affective experiences. This is a second aspect of the analytic situation that promotes recapitulation of early phases of the parent–child relationship. Modell calls the process of reliving these "symbolic actualization," in other words, he implies that the conviction of analysands that the analytic holding environment is actually protective is an illusion. It remains unclear whether he believes that such an illusion of safety is sufficient to carry the analysis of most patients to a successful conclusion. In my experience (see Gedo 1988, chapters 11–14; Gedo and Gehrie 1993), severely impaired analysands, with limited adaptive resources, often need concrete assistance, formerly called "ego support," to patch over their apraxic deficits, at least temporarily making the treatment relationship serve a prosthetic function.

Be that as it may, Modell sees the crux of analytic success as affective retraining, mastery of hitherto traumatic situations through repetition and recontextualization. This theory of therapeutic action is congruent with Modell's view that what is specifically repeated within the transference (and naturally evokes a congruent countertransference) is a mosaic of affect categories. Consequently, the repetition may easily take place in the form of the reversal of the roles played out by the participants in the childhood transactions relived in the transference. These are the circumstances Kleinians explain on the basis of the mechanism of projective identification. Modell rightly cautions that either self-hatred or self-idealization may be projected in this manner. At any rate, because Modell views all psychopathology as a result of some degree of affect intolerance, his theory lays emphasis on the biological deficit involved in this, in contrast to the usual stress on the importance of mental contents. Consequently, he explicitly rejects the hermeneutic viewpoint in psychoanalysis (see the chapter on the Narrative Option and Social Constructivism).

The logical conclusion follows that the therapeutic role of interpretations of mental contents is limited to certain specific tasks. The biological deficit can be overcome only through learning new psychological skills (for instance, through acquiring an "analytic attitude" by way of identification with the analyst). Modell is explicit in characterizing his position as a revival of some of Ferenczi's views in the controversies *circa* 1930. At the same time, in disagreement with (most) self psychologists, Modell believes that, in order to establish a shared reality in the analytic dyad, it is always essential to make transference interpretations, and he insists that, in terms of current dynamics, these interpretations must be veridical. He also points out the importance of applying the same ground rule by meticulously attending to the personal significance of the analyst's affective reactions.

Darlene Ehrenberg's account of her clinical procedures may well serve as a practical guide to the application of many aspects of Modell's theory of technique in the consulting room. The principal components of these clinical recommendations might be listed as follows:

1) Do not confine attention to verbal associations alone; carefully monitor the affectivity of both participants as well as their wordless activities, particularly their reactions to each other.

2) Give priority to analyst–patient interactions in the here-and-now.

3) Take responsibility for devising a solution specifically tailored to fit the circumstances whenever any obstacle in the way of analytic progress arises.

4) Use your subjective reactions in the course of the work as clues about the analysand's attitudes within the transference.

5) Be alert to the danger of repetitively engaging in covert enactments by overlooking the countertransference significance of your subjective reactions.

6) Instead of defending against such feelings, identify them and use them as data by tactfully affirming their function as reliable signals about the analysand's role in the ongoing transaction.

7) Do not hesitate to communicate in an affectively charged manner and through all your rhetorical resources.

8) Never allow yourself to be abused; take action to stop destructive enactments.

These conclusions were already implicit in the results of Ferenczi's technical experiments (see Dupont 1988), although Ehrenberg explicitly relies on more recent contributors, such as Heinrich Racker (1968). Her book is written from a purely pragmatic viewpoint, without reference to theories of any kind. Thus it deals with clinical psychoanalysis as an art rather than as applied science; or one might say, in Levenson's (1983) terms, that she provides an algorithm. Consequently, she does not explain the rationales of her recommendations and is therefore unable to specify the limits of their applicability. Sound as I believe them to be in general, they are not universal prescriptions: for instance, a countertransference reaction may *not* be a reliable indicator of what a particular analysand is experiencing. Ehrenberg herself provides illustrations of contingencies when she disregarded one of her own therapeutic recommendations: "attending to the [analyst–patient] interaction can itself become a form of resistance" (see pp. 46–47). Yes, indeed!

It is heartening to compare Ehrenberg's viewpoint with one published almost simultaneously, that of Theodore Jacobs, a respected member of the American psychoanalytic "mainstream." Jacobs also credits Racker with pioneering the developments in technique he espouses, and he is explicit in stating that in certain quarters these needed innovations may have been accepted too slowly because of political struggles against the "interpersonal" school (that is, Ehrenberg's cohorts). The other contributor he singles out for mention is Merton Gill (1982), whose emphasis on the powerful effects of *all* therapist behaviors (including inactivity!) Jacobs endorses.

Where Modell uses the concept of a holding environment, Jacobs writes about establishing a therapeutic alliance; the particular measure he recommends to accomplish this is to devise a specific manner of responding to the individual requirements of each analysand in forming such an alliance. He conceives of the psychoanalytic process as a sequence of (partially nonverbal) enactments in which both members of the therapeutic dyad are automatically embroiled; in accord with Gill's contention about the effects of whatever the analyst chooses to do, a refusal to play a part in the analysand's scenario is merely to take on the role of a frustrator.

Jacobs gives several (painfully self-revealing) illustrative examples of missing the significance of certain transactions because they had a bearing on some issues the *analyst* did not wish to face (see also Gardner 1983). In such a circumstance, the material is unlikely to emerge in the form of the analysand's verbal associations. Transactions of this kind echo the need in childhood never to mention family secrets, so that their occurrence also tends to repeat a certain type of past experience. Incidentally, Jacobs' clinical vignettes demonstrate that, in analytic work, to follow any widely accepted technical rule of thumb may backfire if, inadvertently, the analyst's unthinking choice duplicates a pattern of parental behavior and thus completes a dyadic reenactment. One can never predict the historical meaning for a specific analysand of any of one's actions, however routine they may seem to us. As Modell put it, multiple levels of reality coexist in the frame of analysis. Thus a therapeutic sequence of idealization, disillusionment, and a reaction formation to the latter is likely to constitute a repetition of an analogous sequence in the course of a childhood relationship. Yet the appropriate reconstruction of the past can be made only if the analyst avoids the twin pitfalls of accepting the analysand's version of reality or insisting on the exclusive validity of his own.

Like Ehrenberg, Jacobs stresses that the analyst's persona *qua* analytic instrument functions through simultaneous use of every conceivable communicative channel. He gives excellent examples of his own tendency to use gestural communications before he is able to encode the same information in words; monitoring such actions is an important avenue for understanding one's countertransference reactions. Jacobs correctly points out that automatic adherence to "standard" technical procedures serves to conceal one's countertransference reactions, for these tend to be relatively subtle, that is, unlikely to betray themselves by any gross behavior. It is much more probable that these covert attitudes will manifest themselves as some "routine" performance, such as keeping silent or repeating oneself, or, for that matter, in the form of focused attention to the analysand's transferences, in the manner Gill (1982) seems to have advocated. Another type of countertransference resistance identified by Jacobs is the tendency to allow oneself to be abused—for instance, by passively listening to pointless and unending narratives.

Although Ehrenberg and Jacobs do not cover exactly the same ground (and the literature they cite hardly overlaps, because both authors focus too narrowly on contributors of their own persuasion, even those from their own geographic area), I have the impression that, on the matters I have summarized, they are essentially in agreement. Their minor differences are probably matters of temperament. Ehrenberg portrays herself as unusually emotional and expressive; Jacobs comes across as quiet and reserved. She cries; he makes a gesture. (Some analysts tell jokes; others whistle. . .) .

In his writings, Herbert Rosenfeld used a vocabulary more or less unfamiliar to American psychoanalysts, so that his posthumous book may at first seem difficult to follow. In actuality, Rosenfeld's text is straightforward and well argued; the effort to translate his language into our customary one is highly worthwhile. One of the most distinguished London Kleinians (albeit with the reputation of a maverick), he pioneered the analytic treatment of the most difficult clinical problems (including that of psychotics who needed periodic hospitalization). *Impasse and Interpretation* was clearly intended to distill the clinical experience of fifty years into a guide for analysts perplexed by therapeutic difficulties. Rosenfeld's book is refreshingly free of a priori theoretical commitments.

In his Conclusion, the author asserts that therapeutic impasse in psychoanalysis is generally caused by a combination of factors. He dismisses the facile notion, popular with Kleinians, that analyses fail because of analysands' excessive envy of their therapists' potential effectiveness: Rosenfeld points out that such envy tends to disappear if the treatment becomes truly helpful. Hence he advises against frequent confrontations about the analysand's putative destructiveness in relation to the joint effort, recommending, instead, acknowledgment of the fact that the handicaps necessitating analysis are inevitably humiliating. Bravo!

Rosenfeld believes that the greatest threat to therapeutic cooperation is an analysand's need for omnipotent self-sufficiency. He also states that the destructiveness of patients is most likely to be turned against themselves, and that it is the analyst's responsibility to devise some kind of protection for the analysand who has these dangerous propensities. In other words, Rosenfeld is ever alert to the analyst's contribution to treatment failures through such grievous errors as being provoked by patients' negativism, premature interference with their need to idealize the therapist, rigidity, detachment, or lack of emotional expressiveness. He advocates the use of countertransference reactions as essential information about the nature of the transference; in particular, he stresses their importance as indicators of the patient's confusional state or the reliving of childhood misunderstandings with parents, especially whenever the analyst feels confused or the therapeutic dialogue is derailed. (Unlike many Kleinians, Rosenfeld insists on the need to scrutinize carefully past and current family transactions as sources of transference developments.)

If there is anything specifically Kleinian in Rosenfeld's prescriptions, it is his continuous emphasis on the importance of projective mechanisms in regressed patients. He assumes that such behaviors are always defensively motivated, although he also makes clear that the ability to differentiate one's own volition from that of caretakers is a developmental achievement, preceded by conditions in which misattribution of some motive is apraxic rather than defensive—in other words, such misattributions may emerge as mere transference developments.

Rosenfeld was one of the earliest contributors to discuss transference psychoses, that is, conditions wherein a psychotic core becomes manifest only in the analytic transference, while the patient's customary adaptation continues to prevail everywhere else. He was also instrumental in bringing to our attention forms of transference in which the analyst is assigned the role of the analysand's childhood persona and the analysand plays the part of one of the early caretakers. In the book, he continues to refer to such role reversals as consequences of projection, although they are more likely (I believe) to indicate that these early experiences were encoded merely in terms of their affective parameters, without distinction of subject and object.

At any rate, Rosenfeld points out that the analyst should not "accept" these "projections"; he or she has to think for both participants and thus "contain" the transaction. Thereupon the analyst's counterreactions become understandable as responses to primitive communications and can be translated into consensual language. Unless this is accomplished, the analyst will yield to the emotional pressure (for instance, by accepting depreciation or getting sleepy) and an impasse will ensue. Rosenfeld believes that, to create the requisite "containing environment," the analyst must be able to participate in the transaction in an emotional manner, thereby becoming a sane but experiencing participant in the analysand's inner life. The therapeutic task then becomes that of integrating and organizing the various uncoordinated islands of the patient's psychic functions. Rosenfeld correctly points out that, at these levels of regression, much of the essential communication in analysis takes place through nonverbal channels.

Again and again, Rosenfeld returns to the issue that the *manner* of therapeutic interventions is just as important as is their lexical content. Because of their communicative apraxias, many analysands tend best to grasp lively and dramatic messages, provided these are not overdone. The analyst's reliance on words may create excessive distance from a patient regressed to a primarily preverbal mode, although the appropriate words will, naturally, buttress the holding function of the treatment. Ultimately, of course, the analyst is responsible for encoding the entire transaction in words. Hence our interventions should not be vague or repetitive, and they must take into account the tendency of regressed patients to concretize. In sum, it is ever the analyst's responsibility to avoid breakdowns in communication.

In the work of Harold Searles, the kinds of clinical contingencies described by Rosenfeld are called "borderline psychotic transferences." The title of the Searles's book is somewhat misleading, because he has concluded that every analysand has the potential to develop such a transference, from which it ought to follow that it makes no sense to classify any particular person as "borderline." Searles has found that such regressive states are evoked in analysis by the analyst's willingness to comply with the analysand's pressure to establish a symbiosis. He believes that many analysts forestall such regressions because they need to defend themselves against anxieties concerning issues of separation. Of course, the best defense of all is avoidance of the psychoanalytic method: if patients are not seen on an intensive schedule, borderline transferences do not ordinarily emerge. Searles is aware of the fact that with regressed patients an interpretive technique is largely inappropriate; he therefore vacillates about whether to call the optimal form of treatment for them "psychoanalysis."

Searles prefers to use a nonintrusive technique, in which he remains largely silent. (Modell [1984] also recommends that we allow patients to remain within a "cocoon" if they feel the need to do so.) The usefulness of interpretation is confined to the late stages of these analyses, after the symbiotic transference has emerged and the analyst has come to serve as a transitional object for the patient. Searles is cognizant of the fact that his tactical recommendations place unusual burdens on the analyst, not only because of the passivity they enforce, but also because they lead to a situation in which all of his or her behaviors (even markers of physiological states) become highly meaningful for the analysand.

Because of the impairment of patients' communicative abilities in states of regression, Searles has found that he can best convey his meaning if he honors both the analysand's rhetorical habits and the *tone* of the latter's speech. Although experienced clinicians tend to make these adjustments automatically, Searles points out that it is best to be continuously aware of these aspects of our performance. In agreement with the other authors considered here, Searles believes that monitoring one's countertransference reactions—what he calls empathy with oneself—is the optimal way to understand profound regressions. To succeed in this, the analyst must be able to tolerate experiencing regressive levels of self-organization, including that of a "countertransference borderline psychosis," without mistaking such reactions for an unmanageable reality. Generally, these responses echo aspects of the patient's childhood transactions with caretakers, often with the roles reversed.

In order to be able to use countertransference signals constructively, the analyst must have a stable sense of identity, which then permits the recognition of unaccustomed reactions as analytic data. Searles asserts that borderline transferences reproduce conditions that originally prevailed in the preverbal era—at the latest, when the child was barely learning to communicate verbally. Hence in these states verbal statements may be confused with the actions they symbolize. If the transference does not involve a whole person, this state reproduces a (sometimes bizarre) childhood misperception of an important figure, in some cases of oneself. Unstable relationships in early childhood may be relived in the form of frequently shifting transference constellations. Fragmented inner states are reexperienced as unintegrated affective reactions or mutually contradictory attitudes about which the analysand feels no conflict. Some of these mental contents may be projected onto the analyst, who must be able to perceive that the resultant experience is an intrusion of alien motives; such an insight makes it possible to integrate these with the patient's self-experience.

Searles rightly concludes that in such circumstances the interpretation of childhood *conflicts* (which are necessarily of later origin) is irrelevant. What is appropriate is reconstruction of the childhood actualities on the basis of their recurrence within the transference, and, even more crucially, as countertransference reactions. Patients tend to confuse the repetition of the past with interpersonal realities in the present, and it is the analyst's task to undo this kind of denial of the therapeutic frame.

Searles has encoded his presentation in the conceptual vocabulary of object relations theory. This is an appropriate choice for conditions prevalent just before and just after the establishment of a cohesive self, but when transferences referable to other phases of development are in the forefront, other models of the mind become more relevant. Suffice it to say here that in this book Searles narrows his focus to a specific segment of the analytic process, but this is the phase of treatment when the crucial curative steps postulated by Modell must take place: those of mastering the propensity for trauma and of healing splits in mental dispositions. Rosenfeld extends the focus to other modalities of treatment I consider to be equally indispensable: optimal disillusionment (overcoming grandiosity and unrealistic idealizations) and the repair of apraxic deficits (Gedo 1988). Modell does not explicitly write about these matters, but his emphasis on the need to reconcile the disparate realities of the analyst and analysand clearly refers to the issue

I have discussed under the rubric of "illusions," and he does refer to the importance of helping analysands to acquire new procedural skills.

Although the books of Ehrenberg and Jacobs are ambiguous about the range of transference developments within which their therapeutic prescriptions are applicable, their recommendations are entirely congruent with those of Rosenfeld and Searles, and all four authors espouse techniques called for by the theory of therapeutic action put forward by Modell. That is my rationale for bracketing these contributions as components of the developing consensus about a new technical paradigm that I wholeheartedly endorse.

18
Toward a Paradigm of Self-Organization

- *Clinical Interaction and the Analysis of Meaning.* T. Dorpat and M. Miller.
- *Oedipus and Beyond.* J. Greenberg.
- *The Private Self.* A. Modell.

The regulation of human behavior is increasingly understood as one of those complex systems the operation of which is a matter of self-organization. It is in parallel with the ascendancy of systems theory in science in general (and biology in particular), that psychoanalytic theories have begun to pay more and more attention to the centrality of a concept of self (Lichtenstein 1977; see also G. Klein 1976; Kohut 1977; Gedo 1979a). As I have reviewed in the chapter on the Rise of the Relational Option, several historians contend that even object relations theories are mere stepping stones that lead in the direction of theories potentially centered on a self-concept. The books I consider in this final chapter go a long way toward the achievement of this goal.

Perhaps it is most interesting that Jay Greenberg, one of the co-authors of *Object Relations in Psychoanalytic Theory* (Greenberg and Mitchell 1983), a book that did not endorse the foregoing view of conceptual progression, a few years later became the sole author of a monograph in which he crossed this conceptual Rubicon. Although he calls the model of mentation he endorses "representational" rather than one of mental organization, he is explicit that it is self-representations (rather than those of objects) that have a decisive influence on a person's subsequent wishes. Dorpat and Miller, who approach theoretical issues from a cognitive point of vantage, borrow the vocabulary of that branch of psychology and give an operational definition of "character" as an organization of schemata that comes about through self-organization. In their view, the earliest operational schemata are those that record the infant's actions in the course of various experiences; in other words, initially schemata are not focused on the subject/object differentiation. In my judgment, this implies that the transactions observers see as interpersonal are for some time encoded by infants only as procedural memories (or, in the terms used by Dorpat and Miller, as "performance memories"). Hence the core of the self-schema is *not* relational; it is merely the experiences the felt *consequences* of which are remembered that take place in the context of what an observer would call an object relationship. The very title of Modell's book conveys the same idea, and he concludes *The Private Self* with the statement that the maintenance of self-organization is a vital biological urge.

Beyond this emerging consensus, these volumes represent widely different conceptions of psychoanalysis. Greenberg is exclusively concerned with mental contents; this reduction of the purview of psychoanalysis permits him to claim that he is a pure empiricist. He disapproves of a rationalist epistemology that would, he believes, infer a theory of motivation from nonpsychological data (see the chapter on the Philosophy of Mind). He is unembarrassed about espousing mentalism; in his model, the basic motivational impetus is a wish. By contrast, the other books embrace evidence from neurobiology. Dorpat and Miller introduce their thesis with the claim that clinical theories are always impregnated by extra-clinical assumptions, that is, by what Greenberg decries as rationalism. They go on to cite those findings of brain science that have rendered Freud's views on perception, cognition, and consciousness untenable. Modell makes repeated use of the theories about consciousness and memory of the eminent neurobiologist Gerald Edelman.

Greenberg is a skilled polemicist; his criticisms of previous theories are generally cogent and telling, and these broadsides constitute a large part of his book. (A couple of misdirected shots are aimed at my work, in ways that may have made it difficult for me to remain a fair judge of Greenberg's.) Although he is on the mark in his conviction that Freud's metapsychological errors occurred through resort to a rationalist method, Greenberg overstates the case against such procedures. As Grünbaum (1984) has noted, Freud's biological hypotheses lent themselves to refutation by empirical means, so that his conceptual work ultimately met scientific requirements. *Pace* Greenberg, it is not possible to launch any scientific enterprise without a priori postulates, and one does not always get these right the first time around. But Greenberg is surely correct in pointing out that commitment to a motivational theory exclusively based on drives entails the inescapable corollary that mentation is ever conflictual. With the exception of Brenner (1982), subsequent theoreticians have not followed Freud in the view that intrapsychic conflict is ubiquitous.

Greenberg goes on to examine the motivational underpinnings of the relational theories in psychoanalysis (chapter 3). All such theories give priority to the human need for attachment. In view of his prior ideological commitments, Greenberg deserves great credit for pointing out that relational theories also share the false assumption that attachments are formed without the operation of some pre-experiential force. In other words, in some covert way every object relations theory arbitrarily postulates some biological process; in Kohut's system, for instance, it is the concept of selfobject need that corresponds to Freud's concept of *Trieb*. Such a priori assumptions then illegitimately prescribe some therapeutic response that in given circumstances the theory deems appropriate. Greenberg concludes that psychoanalysis cannot dispense with a motivational theory, that by itself a focus on the nature of attachments is insufficient, and that we cannot avoid postulating the operation of drive-like mechanisms. Finally, he makes explicit that relational theories necessarily underplay the role of intrapsychic conflict and cannot explain the need of children to "separate" from their caretakers.

Despite his mentalist outlook, Greenberg realizes that he should articulate how psyche and soma are related, for he is committed to the (biological) proposition that endogenous motivations are constitutional givens. Although he acknowledges that his theory needs a "psychosomatic bridge," he continues incongruously to assert that "mental activity is by definition not organic" or that the "somatic is external to the mind" (p. 117). In my judgment, these statements contain a category error: as Miller points out (Dorpat and Miller, p. 105), "mind" refers to those information processing functions of the nervous system that generate meaning. Because Greenberg defines "drive" as a characteristic of human nature, without any explanation of its somatic origin, his theory is not merely mentalist: his drives are nonmaterial vital forces. Nor is this the only example of scientifically unacceptable vitalism in Greenberg's theory. For example, although he allegedly eschews the use of biological concepts, he continues to accept Freud's hypothesis of a "repression barrier."

Although he is cognizant of the complex motivational hypotheses proposed by G. Klein (1976) and Lichtenberg (1989)—here discussed in the chapter on the Theory of Motivation—Greenberg arbitrarily rejects them because he believes that such complexity will confuse clinicians (see chapter 5), and he fails to acknowledge that only extraclinical evidence can decide the adequacy of any motivational proposition. He suggests reducing endogenous motivations to two categories, a solution that will satisfy the most simple-minded among us: the need for safety, and the need for effectance. It is difficult to grasp how this system could account either for play or for sexuality, to cite only the most obvious examples.

On the positive side of the ledger, Greenberg is persuasive about the shortcomings of Freud's structural theory. He points out that defenses are made necessary by threats to the sense of self, and yet the tripartite model of mind is applicable only in case of structural conflict. The model can neither account for altruism nor deal with intrasystemic conflicts. In conclusion, Greenberg declares that the structural theory has become "irrelevant." In place of the intersystemic conflicts Freud highlighted in the tripartite model, Greenberg proposes that we focus on conflicts among representations, particularly those of disparate feeling states. This proposal is the logical reflection of his hypothesis that human wishes are derivatives of various self-representations. Such a hypothesis might be adequate if Greenberg had a satisfactory explanation of how wishes can become unconscious. But all he has to say about this is that certain mental contents are "banished" from consciousness. For him, the unconscious is a locus he regards as a "container" for the unacceptable. These are metaphors that fail to clarify the processes in question; moreover, Greenberg makes no distinctions among defenses (that is, repression, disavowal, and projection, for example).

In my judgment, *Oedipus and Beyond* is a thoughtful work of criticism that demonstrates that the existing paradigms—both those of drive/structure and those of relation/structure, discussed in Greenberg's 1983 collaboration with Mitchell—are exhausted. Although Greenberg's own effort to find a third way is not entirely satisfactory (mostly because of his refusal to adopt any explicit neurological assumptions), his abandonment of a purely relational perspective in favor of one centered on "self" is a major positive development on the contemporary psychoanalytic scene.

Dorpat and Miller divided the labor on their monograph: Dorpat wrote the critique of traditional theory and Miller articulated their proposed substitute. (A third section that outlines a number of applications need not concern us here.) Dorpat's criticism is focused on two biological assumptions Freud made about early mentation that have been refuted: that unconscious thoughts must undergo distortion to reach consciousness, and that primary processes are cut off from reality. Dorpat believes that Freud's conception of "unconscious [wishful] fantasy" was a deductive inference based on a mistaken understanding of perception, that of some veridical representation of reality, a *Vorstellung*. Erroneously, that hypothesis equated perception and consciousness and held that correct percepts are "stored" in memory. Currently, neuroscientists understand that both perception and memory are constructed and repeatedly reconstructed. To cite only one finding that invalidates Freud's hypothesis, visual perception has been demonstrated to be possible without consciousness. At any rate, Freud conceived the mental apparatus as passive unless activated by a drive; hence he postulated that the unconscious entirely consists of wishes (drive derivatives) that therefore cannot be admitted to consciousness without disguise. This would mean that the *Vorstellungen* used to express them must be distorted. Dorpat holds that the postulate of psychic energy is untenable, and that the hypotheses of hallucinatory wish-fulfillment and the censoring functions of "dream work" have been refuted. The infant has no evocative memory; percepts cannot be dreamed or hallucinated until late in the second year of life.

The earliest memories involve only action patterns that are then organized into action schemata. It is action schemata that permit the child actively to repeat previous experiences. Hallucinations are mere neural events and, in terms of their genesis, so are dreams, for they are the common biological property of all viviparous mammals. In other words, dreams merely *happen*; they are not *caused* by unconscious wishes, albeit their symbolic content does reflect the dreamer's personal goals. These neurobiological findings have invalidated Freud's hypotheses about the nature of early mentation—in my view, they have also invalidated the developmental postulates of every school within psychoanalysis as well as the elaborate interpretive systems based on them, be they Freudian, Kleinian, Winnicottian, Mahlerian, Lacanian, Kohutian, and so on.

According to Dorpat, the primary process (one of the cardinal Freudian empirical discoveries substantiated by subsequent findings) should not be assigned to an id. It is a cognitive system that analyzes the individual's interaction with the milieu; it does not distort rationally ordered thoughts. It is a code natural to the right brain, nonverbal and nonsyntactical; through affects and imagery it provides a system suited for processing certain types of information. Primary process thinking is a procedural skill that, like all others, has to be learned and, through mastery, becomes automatized. Hence this skill may undergo maturation and come to subserve creativity. Conversely, if mental functions undergo splitting, primary process skills may remain unaltered by experience, hence archaic. In any case, primary and secondary process thinking coexist, and both may be either conscious or unconscious. Contrary to Freud's assumptions, the primary process is essential for the proper assessment of reality: humankind needs both kinds of semiosis for optimal adaptation (see also the chapter on the Input from Cognitive Science and Its Uses). In summary, Dorpat states that unconscious thinking involves not fantasies of wish fulfillment but the analysis of the meanings of the individual's real situation.

Miller attempts to construct a psychoanalytic theory on the basis of such an understanding of perception and cognition. Thinking makes use of established cognitive structures that serve as cues for appropriate action. These structures are organized, starting in infancy, from memories of action and experience that become schemata of self and of interactions with the milieu. Thus it is problem solving in action that increases cognitive capacity. These processes take place preconsciously, and the schemata that organize experience are also preconscious. With the acquisition of the capacity for episodic memory, the infant is enabled to experience a sense of self. Various schemata are gradually organized into more complex units, particularly once language development permits the addition of conceptual schemata to the earlier affectomotor ones. In this manner, the child learns a system of rules and beliefs. In Miller's view, this developmental line enables psychoanalytic theory to encompass both issues stemming from the vicissitudes of self-organization and those stemming from later intrapsychic conflicts.

The maturation of affectomotor (also called "operational") schemata leads to the elaboration of primary process mentation; that of conceptual schemata develops the secondary process. As I understand this, Miller means that thinking effectively is a result of procedural learning, whichever semiotic code is in question. What psychoanalysts call transference is the preconscious organization of current experience in terms of existing schemata. Should subsequent events disrupt such a match, an alternative schema will be mobilized. This is the mode of operation of psychological therapy. In case further processing is needed to effect a match, it becomes necessary to resort to conscious reflection. Miller notes, however, that the capacity for conscious thinking is limited, and this is one of the constraints on the human capacity for change. "Resistance" in treatment therefore amounts to an effort to conserve existing schemata; the same tendency constitutes the greatest pitfall for introspective efforts.

Miller assumes that the nidus of psychopathology is trauma, and that even the threat of its repetition will mobilize defensive avoidances. Consequently, humans always find it essential to assess the meaning of environmental circumstances. The occurrence of trauma leads to the organization of a conceptual schema, often of a kind called a "pathogenic belief" (see also Weiss and Sampson 1986). These schemata remain active even if they are disavowed. Any denial of subjective experience increases the likelihood that schemata of the self will become disorganized, "fragmented," as Miller puts this. From the perspective of adaptation, post-traumatic schemata are apt to prove dyspraxic. Because every phase of development is likely to produce particular types of maladaptive schemata, Miller postulates a sequence of expectable pathologies referable to particular phases (see also Gedo and Goldberg 1973).

Miller correctly stresses that for effective psychoanalytic treatment it is essential to use a valid theory of mental function—to paraphrase Bettelheim, empathy is not enough. He believes that, to affect the core of pathogenic schemata, it is necessary to understand and to make use of nonverbal semiotic codes (see also Gedo 1996a; Bucci 1997). In practical terms, this requires the use of multiple noninterpretive interventions. Such technical measures do *not* mean that the analyst takes the role of a parent, for the enactment of such parental transactions would only reinforce childhood schemata. It does mean that, in order to choose appropriate interventions, the analyst must correctly gauge the developmental level of the schema currently in operation. Before old dyspraxic schemata can be altered (through conscious reflection), it may be necessary, if their developmental level is archaic enough, to assist in regulating the analysand's behavior. I believe Miller is right to deny that such interventions are designed to provide a corrective emotional experience. I would note, in addition, that they are not efforts to remedy matters through the wholesale internalization of a novel relationship, either, but they allow for the construction of new schemata in areas of former defect (Gedo 1988).

Unlike Greenberg's effort, this attempt to find a third way, beyond ego psychology or object relations theory, is both scientifically unflawed and coherent. Yet, in my judgment, it remains incomplete, for Miller's exclusive reliance on cognitive science makes it impossible to explain what he means by one of his central constructs, that of trauma. In the Freudian system, this is a psychoeconomic concept, and there is nothing to replace that in Dorpat and Miller's. As I read their work, such a term has no conceptual meaning in their psychology. (It could be rendered meaningful in neurobiological terms, but that is an avenue these authors leave unexplored.) Nor do they consider the crucial issue of the reasons for an inability to alter dyspraxic schemata on the basis of ordinary life experience, although such an inability to change is the only factor that makes any inconvenient schema "pathogenic." Some people are able to learn and to assimilate novelty; what makes others unable to do so? Although Dorpat and Miller realize that "pathogenic beliefs" are merely potential sequelae of certain unfortunate experiences, they have no explanation of why and when they do or do not come about.

Despite these shortcomings, this new theory centered on the self-organization constitutes a promising beginning. I am naturally very pleased that Dorpat and Miller draw many of the same therapeutic conclusions from their theory of mind that I have advocated for many years. In that regard, I demur only about their counsel that it is sufficient in analysis to focus on interactions in the here-and-now to the exclusion of genetic explanations. In my experience, unless analysands discover the original reasons for having stuck to dyspraxic schemata, they are generally unable to master a compulsion to repeat. Of course, such phenomena are not even considered in *Clinical Interaction and the Analysis of Meaning*.

In *The Private Self*, Modell takes arms against the increasing tendency among psychoanalysts to think of mind as disembodied. He particularly condemns the theories of Kohut, Lacan, and Schafer on this score. If our discipline is to remain one of the life sciences, however, it must follow the rest of the biological community in abandoning the concept of instinct. To do so, Freud's "id" must be replaced by the concept of the "embodied self." In Modell's view, this is a choice fraught with difficulty, because of the apparent paradox that self-experience both endures and continuously changes. He begins to resolve this conundrum by differentiating the "social self" from a "private self" that constitutes a map of the individual's inner states. He quotes Edelman about the adaptive advantages of the human capacity for "higher consciousness," that is, the ability to conceive current, past, and future experience in such symbolic terms. The construction of a private self allows the child to disengage from caretakers; it sustains the individual in solitude.

A biological conception of the private self is that it is a system of value-laden memories. In this sense, this schema is necessarily self-generated, although such an achievement is possible only if the primary caretaker is sufficiently in synchrony with the child. Such "self-actualization" constitutes a biological priority. (Note the congruence of these statements with the general principle about the self-organizing propensity of complex systems.) The self-schema is initially organized around the body image by means of signals from the homeostatic mechanisms of the central nervous system. Modell concludes that the troubling paradox of continuous change and simultaneous continuity is resolved on the neurobiological level by the realization that higher-order consciousness of self requires continuous contact with current perceptions. Through self-organization, each brain becomes unique.

Self-experience consists of *activity* that should lead to mastery and therefore to joy. It seems that such results are most likely to occur when the child is provided open space, that is, manageable intervals of solitude—a vital consideration overlooked in most analytic theories of development (but see D. Stern 1985). In the absence of sufficient experience of effectance, the child will develop a sense of futility and depression. Once the private self is established, the child will defend this private space against intrusions. Ideally, the private space is preserved with the cooperation of the caretakers. Of course, psychoanalytic treatment inevitably intrudes on the analysand's private self. As Modell has long advocated, it may be advisable with certain patients to postpone such contingencies, allowing them respite to dwell in their "cocoon." Some analysands fend off intrusion by replacing free associations with Lacan's "empty talk"; others *feel* empty because they are themselves alienated from their private self: this is the circumstance Winnicott called the false self.

Modell cautions against the naïveté of many object relations theories that falsely assume that object representations are veridical; on the contrary, the child's schemata are self-created. For instance, various people may be unrealistically idealized, and the child may then identify with that fantastic representation. At the same time, Modell returns to his previous concept of "separation guilt" (1965) as one of the vectors in opposition to the need to protect the private self against intrusion. This need is explained by the fact that the development of intersubjectivity between mother and child may give rise to wishes for psychological merger. In other words, Mahler's developmental hypothesis puts things in reverse order: in actuality, neonates perceive the me/non-me distinction; if a sense of merger supervenes, this is a relatively late occurrence and it is always illusory. The propensity for idealization and the risk of disillusionment and its unfavorable sequelae also supervene relatively late.

Modell stresses that the capacity for solitude is a self-created achievement that does *not* depend on internal objects that sustain the person but on memories of (successful) experience. Solitude can replenish people; it does not imply any loneliness. In this sense, the child's early interests become the resources of the private self. For certain analysands, the analytic situation provides an opportunity to experience companionable solitude. But the aim of psychoanalysis must be to create new meanings through recategorization of percepts and memories, thereby extending the effective range of the self-organization; these new meanings replenish the person. Pathology always involves a failure to retranscribe the past.

Although the self-organization is largely unconscious and functions on a nonexperiential level, the memory systems that constitute it may be objectively described. Fairbairn (1954) first drew attention to the possibility that the self-organization may not be integrated. In such circumstances, some unconscious schemata of self may be disavowed through projective identification. The self-organization may also be impaired as a result of splitting or "decentering" wherein the person loses touch with the private self. A complete cessation of the continuity of the sense of self is, of course, a psychological catastrophe. And so on.

As my summary of *The Private Self* surely conveys, I am fully in agreement with its theoretical proposals as well as with the therapeutic implications Modell draws from them. In my judgment, the contributions of Modell, those of Dorpat and Miller, and my own writings on these matters complement each other and have very few features that cannot be reconciled with the views of the other contributors to this consensus. Moreover, I believe that the emerging pragmatic consensus about optimal therapeutic techniques (see the chapter on Toward a New Technical Consensus) calls for exactly the kind of theory of mind developing in these works.

II

HISTORICAL SUMMARY

19
A History of
Theoretical Innovation

The intellectual history of psychoanalysis over the past generation can equally well be described either as a chronicle about a discipline breaking into irreconcilable fragments under the impact of underlying philosophical differences or one about the emergence of a new paradigm that transcends the differences of opinion that characterized the discourse of the preceding era. Both alternatives constitute narratives that must highlight the emergence of unprecedented attention, both within psychoanalysis and on the part of scholars from other disciplines, to epistemic issues. The most divisive of these still unresolved questions concerns the very nature of psychoanalysis as an intellectual discipline, a matter most frequently addressed in terms of asking whether it should be classified as a natural science. The answer to this question depends, in turn, on another philosophical issue—that is, one that cannot be decided on purely empirical grounds—that is commonly called the mind/body problem.

One set of psychoanalyts feel free to disregard the dependence of mental functions on a somatic substrate and therefore contend that psychoanalysis should not be regarded as a branch of biological science. Among them, Gill (1994) may have been alone in continuing to believe that we can create a *scientific* psychology entirely based on the understanding of mental contents. The great majority of this mentalist camp has accepted a purely hermeneutic viewpoint, first advocated by certain continental European philosophers, that would place psychoanalysis among the *Geisteswissenschaften*, that is, scholarly disciplines wherein the standards and constraints of natural science do not apply. Implicitly, by claiming that psychoanalysis can arrive only at some "narrative truth" (rather than at a valid reconstruction of personal history), Spence (1982) has lent support to such a retreat from Freud's scientific ambitions. The acknowledged *chef d'école* of American hermeneuticists has been Schafer (1976, 1978, 1992), who attributes the therapeutic efficacy of psychoanalysis to the process of reformulating the analysand's life story in accord with various "master narratives."

The response to the challenge from such a hermeneutic option has been two-fold. Epistemologists such as Grünbaum (1984, 1993) and Strenger (1991) have rejected the goal of mere narrative coherence as too easy, for it is attainable even on the basis of fundamentally absurd accounts. If no interpretation can be shown to be invalid, the choice among rival psychoanalytic viewpoints cannot be made on rational grounds, and intellectual chaos is bound to follow. These critics, seconded by the psychoanalyts Rubinstein (1997) and Edelson (1988), have also shown that the hermeneuticists' effort to deny that psychoanalysis provides causal explanations for the phenomena it observes is an unjustified attempt to avoid the obligation scientifically to validate such causal hypotheses. A second objection to a purely hermeneutic option, in my judgment even more decisive than the foregoing, is the fact stressed by several authors that none of these theories has managed to avoid postulating various covert biological assumptions. For example, in asserting that all mental phenomena are consequences of some active choice, Schafer has postulated a biological hypothesis—a fact he has failed to acknowledge.

Because of the (often deliberate) ambiguity of Lacan's (1977) texts, it is difficult to determine whether his position is merely one of mentalism or whether it is also hermeneuticist. At any rate, Lacan's contempt for empiricism clearly places his version of psychoanalysis beyond the boundaries of natural science. His explicit use of the work of certain philosophers as an armature for his theorizing is, moreover, analogous to the hermeneuticists' resort to such a framework: even if different philosophical ideas are involved, the theoretical systems are both based on a purely rationalist foundation. Be it noted that in principle such a priori philosophical commitments preclude the modification of theory as a result of contrary empirical evidence. In practice, psychoanalysts of a mentalist persuasion tend to avoid theoretical discourse, in favor of a pragmatic focus on the practice of psychoanalysis. It is in this sense that unbridgeable fissures have developed within the psychoanalytic community, and I see no possibility of reconciling the mentalist viewpoint with those that aspire to the status of biological science.

The adherents of the natural science view of psychoanalysis have, of course, borne the brunt of the epistemological critique of the scientificity of the discipline. Grünbaum (1984) has carefully demonstrated that philosophers who read psychoanalysis as a set of propositions not subject to refutation through empirical testing were misrepresenting existing psychoanalytic theory, but he has also pointed out that Freud's most important hypotheses have never been validated. In particular, he challenged the unwarranted assumption that the detection of any particular mental content can validate any causal proposition within psychoanalytic theory, a point no subsequent commentator has contradicted. This stunning critique from a partisan of psychoanalysis has played an important role in facilitating the rethinking of its theoretical edifice.

Grünbaum's contentions have been supported by epistemologically sophisticated analysts such as Rubinstein (1997) and Strenger (1991). The latter added the important point that as long as psychoanalysis constitutes a fruitful research program, the need for validation is properly relegated to a position of lesser urgency. Strenger's judgment is in accord with the views of the eminent philosopher of science Michael Polányi (1974). The latter has demonstrated that scientific progress seldom takes place as a result of validation studies. Rather, new hypotheses gradually replace older ones because they have gained credence with a majority within a discipline as the best explanation currently available for some set of phenomena. In this regard, the intellectual history of psychoanalysis is fundamentally no different from that of other scientific disciplines.

It was the meticulous work of Rubinstein (belatedly collected in 1997) that initiated the theoretical rethinking that has characterized the recent history of psychoanalysis. Without declaring Cartesian dualism to be untenable, he demonstrated that its correlate of mentalism is indeed incompatible with natural science, for the propositions of mentalism are ultimately untestable. Consequently, Rubinstein espoused the monist view of the mind/body problem, that of the brain as an information processor. This commitment entails the obligation to articulate psychoanalytic propositions that simultaneously fit the observational data collected in the psychoanalytic situation and conform to neurophysiological knowledge. (In other words, Rubinstein implicitly agreed with Grünbaum's contention that psychoanalytic hypotheses need extraclinical validation.) Another way to state this position is that psychoanalysis must simultaneously explicate a world of personal reasons and one of organismic causes.

Although brain science still does not provide sufficient evidence fully to carry out the program of validation Rubinstein deemed desirable, it is already able to *invalidate* many of the biological assumptions Freud made in erecting his metapsychology. Most important in this regard is that the principle of constancy he postulated is untenable. Rubinstein demonstrated that it follows from this conclusion that "psychic energy" is not a valid biological concept; its use in psychoanalytic theory thus amounts to resort to a vitalist notion, contrary to Freud's absolute commitment against the postulation of non-material entities. Further, the abandonment of the energy construct deprives drive theory of its rationale and thus also hollows out Freud's structural theory of 1923.

Holt (1989) amplified this critique of Freud's metapsychology; he pointed out that the Freudian attempt to link clinical findings to biology was based on the erroneous assumption that the central nervous system is passive. Holt also showed that Freud never abandoned the untenable biological hypotheses he had borrowed from his neurological predecessors, such as the purely quantitative explanations for pleasure and unpleasure that persisted in his theories. Yet most psychoanalytic authors have dealt with metapsychology as if it had no connection to human physiology, so that the evidence that refuted Freud's biological assumptions was long disregarded.

The challenge to Freud's metapsychology presented by Rubinstein and Holt has never been answered; in the course of the 1970s, a succession of contributors (G. Klein 1976; Schafer 1976; Rosenblatt and Thickstun 1977) joined them in repudiating these discredited assumptions. This collapse of the metapsychological consensus led to the split between those who chose to deny the need for any basis for psychoanalysis in natural science and those, like Rubinstein, who sought a valid neurophysiological foundation for it. George Klein made an abortive attempt to achieve a compromise solution, that of developing a purely "clinical theory" for psychoanalysis, but he failed to eliminate all biological assumptions from his proposals, as Rubinstein soon pointed out in a critique of Klein's work.

Rosenblatt and Thickstun articulated the outlines of a new metapsychology centered on the concept that mental functions consist of the communication of information. The input of information activates various subsystems of the mind/brain (generally without the attainment of consciousness). Brain activity takes place by way of cybernetic (feedback) mechanisms that are organized into sets and, further, into integrated programs. These constitute a stable hierarchy of personal aims; at the same time, when faced with adaptive failure, the hierarchic system is capable of alternative choices at a lower level of integration. Rosenblatt and Thickstun's model is essentially congruent with the hierarchical schema proposed some years earlier by Gedo and Goldberg (1973) on the basis of clinical considerations.

The invalidation of Freud's drive theory has made it necessary to supply psychoanalysis with a new theory of motivation, a requirement already recognized by G. Klein. Rosenblatt and Thickstun were the first to propose that motivational theory should conform to a cybernetic model; in their view, affects constitute crucial components of the feedback loops that organize the gamut of motivations into a behavioral system. The establishment of a hierarchy of priorities produces a supraordinate control system that Rosenblatt and Thickstun call the "self." (See also Gedo and Goldberg 1973; G. Klein 1976.) Lichtenberg (1989) adopted these proposals and made an attempt to specify the various categories of inborn human motivation. It is noteworthy that this effort followed Rubinstein's insistence on the need to consider both psychoanalytic and neurophysiological evidence in theory formation. Lichtenberg postulated the operation of five independent subsystems of inborn motivation: the regulation of physiological requirements, attachment/affiliation, exploration/assertion, aversion, and sexuality/ sensuality. (According to Hadley [1992], neurophysiological evidence suggests that sexuality and sensuality constitute separate motivational systems.) Further categories of motivation undoubtedly come "on line" later in the course of development.

The development of a new, biologically sound metatheory has also been pursued by means of a sequence of studies that attempted to correlate recent advances in brain science with psychoanalytic data. Levin (1991) has suggested that the domains of communication and cognition are the intermediate fields of study where the findings of psychoanalysis and neurophysiology intersect. He has emphasized that the acquisition of language has an organizing role for the development of the brain. That insight implies that pre- and proto-linguistic modes of functioning potentially remain available throughout the lifespan, as lower levels of integration within the functional hierarchy. Such aspects of the adaptive repertory operate automatically and unconsciously, on a level best understood in physiological terms. (Hadley [1989] has explained the phenomena of the repetition compulsion in such terms.)

Levin has also pointed out that the hierarchical organization of the developing brain signifies that the psychoanalytic model of mental functioning should also follow hierarchical principles, in Levin's view, a requirement first satisfied by the work of Gedo and Goldberg (1973). The feature of the hierarchy Levin concentrates on is that of the individual's "self-in-the-world-potentials," a core map of which is initially established in the cerebellum and is later retranscribed in the basal ganglia and the central parietal cortex. With that retranscription, this representation becomes a long-term memory; this means that self-cohesion has also been established.

Recent brain research has demonstrated the role of infantile experience in influencing the structuralization of the central nervous system. Schore (1994) has given a detailed account of these developments, particularly with regard to the prefrontal structures crucial for emotional experience and regulation of the autonomic nervous system. Through neuroendocrine mechanisms, these structures activate the centers for pleasure and pain. Feedback loops from these centers and further structures laid down as a result of maternal prohibitions establish increasing autonomy in the self-regulation of behavior. In this sense, Schore is able to show that neurochemistry underlies psychology.

Schore endorses the hierarchical view of neural—and consequently of psychic—organization. In his schema, self-organization is established by around eighteen months, when significant symbolic capacities become available, the left cerebral hemisphere acquires predominance, and affects begin to operate as signals. This reorganization is by no means the final one: Levin postulates that increased interhemispheric integration as a result of myelinization of the corpus callosum (around the age of 3 ½) constitutes the next nodal point in the development of the central nervous system. Reiser (1984) concurs with these views of neural (and psychic) organization as a hierarchy of multiple modes wherein abrupt changes of state are expectable.

According to Bucci (1997), the domains of psychoanalysis and neuroscience can best be integrated on the middle ground of cognitive psychology. Bucci has proposed a model of cognitive development congruent with contemporary brain science, precisely the kind of hypothesis Rubinstein insisted psychoanalysis must propose. In this hierarchy, the earliest mode is that of subsymbolic processing, consisting of parallel perceptual channels that subsequently may or may not become linked to language. A second mode, one of symbolic processing by means of images and words, supervenes in toddlerhood. A third mode is established when connections between subsymbolic and symbolic processing are set up, a process Bucci calls "referential activity."

Bucci's revision of cognitive psychology calls into question the cognitive model implicit in previous psychoanalytic theories, that of a single basic common code, comparable to language—the theory explicitly endorsed by Lacan (1977). The neurophysiological evidence supports Bucci's position: there are separate systems of memory for symbolic and subsymbolic processing, the declarative and procedural systems, respectively. (This explains why behavioral change is contingent on enhancing procedural skills through measures that must go beyond dealing with verbalizable mental contents. This consideration is the most significant objection to a mentalist approach in psychoanalysis. For details, see Gedo 1995a, 1997a.)

Bucci understands emotion as a response system that serves as a guide for action, even if it does not necessarily attain consciousness. She points out that our affective core is linked to nonverbal perceptual schemata, early memories that constitute the basis of our sense of self. Hence she views the task of psychoanalysis to be the enhancement of referential activity in order to make such nonverbal memories available for verbal processing. The standard technique of psychoanalysis has overlooked the need to devise different modalities of intervention for each mode of the cognitive hierarchy. In cases of cognitive apraxia, it may be necessary to assist analysands for the first time to acquire a symbolic code to deal with certain matters (see also Gedo 1988).

In Bucci's view, symptoms, enactments, and dreams all constitute attempts to process the meaning of human experience on a nonverbal level. She postulates that dream imagery simply represents subsymbolic emotional schemata activated during sleep. What Freud called "dream work" is merely the standard way of subsymbolic processing; in other words, Bucci denies that verbally encoded "latent thoughts" have been transformed into dream imagery (see also Bollas 1987).

Dorpat and Miller (1992) have also concluded that evidence from brain science has refuted Freud's assumptions about perception, cognition, and consciousness—particularly the *equation* of perception with consciousness. It is now understood that both perception and memory are constructed and continually reconstructed. Dreams and hallucinations are neural events; they are not caused by unconscious wishes. The primary process, according to Dorpat and Miller, is one of Freud's cardinal discoveries that *has* been substantiated by neurobiology: it is a cognitive system that analyzes the individual's interactions with the environment. In other words, they agree with Bucci that primary process mentation does not distort rationally ordered thoughts: it is simply the natural code of the right brain. It is a procedural skill that is gradually learned and, with mastery, may become automatized; with maturation, it may subserve creativity. If, as a result of being split off, primary processes remain unaltered by experience, they will persist in an archaic form.

It is worthy of note that observational data on infancy collected by investigators uncommitted to any analytic viewpoint are entirely congruent with the evidence from brain science and cognitive psychology. Lichtenberg's (1983) synopsis of these studies portrays human infants as continuously active, object oriented, and stimulus-seeking. They have capacities for adaptation in concert with whatever their caretakers are able to offer them. In neonates, processes in the central nervous system produce the states of alertness, crying, quiescence, and sleep. The ability to plan behavior develops well before the acquisition of symbolic capacities and reflection. These signs of organization on a biological level are sufficient to refute previous developmental hypotheses, such as those of Winnicott, Mahler, or Melanie Klein, that

adultomorphized the infant. Lichtenberg concludes that psychoanalytic treatment must be redesigned to deal with derivatives of the
presymbolic stages of development, such as basic regulatory deficits,
cognitive deficits, and so on.

Stern (1985) uses the yield of infant observations to construct an
epigenetic, hierarchical schema of the development of the sense of self.
(This refers to the subjective aspect of the self-organization highlighted
by most of the other contributors whose works have been mentioned.)
Stern also concludes that all previous developmental schemata in psychoanalysis are untenable because they attribute symbolic capacities
(the capacity for fantasy) to infants. Stern describes several stages of
development through the first eighteen months of life that precede the
acquisition of language, derivatives of which are important components
of adult functioning. Along the same lines, Freedman (1997) has called
attention to the fact that neonates have no object relations; they do have
experiences involving human beings. These produce changes in the
brain that, in turn, function as unconscious mentation. As Freedman
puts it, the only Freudian idea about early development that has found
support in biology is that of bisexuality!

Let me briefly review the history of the theoretical revolution I
have surveyed thus far. It arose as a consequence of the insight that
the central nervous system is primarily a processor of information, a
function that does not involve significant transfers of energy. Details
of the biological discoveries about brain function then invalidated some
of Freud's principal metapsychological assumptions. In North America,
the psychoanalytic community (to its credit) promptly responded with
the abandonment of the metapsychology that, for close to a century,
had held together the theoretical structure of its discipline.

It is the problem of finding a replacement for the biological framework Freud established in the 1890s that has produced the recent fissures within American psychoanalysis. The simplest way to characterize
these is to differentiate efforts to develop a tenable biological substitute for metapsychology from mentalist solutions that would confine
psychoanalysis to the study of psychic contents. Among the latter, I
have thus far dealt only with the hermeneutic option, because its
advocates have made explicit their epistemic assumptions; there are further mentalist alternatives that simply avoid these basic theoretical
issues and can therefore only be discussed in terms of their clinical

consequences. The exclusively hermeneutic version of psychoanalysis has been extensively examined by a series of psychoanalytically informed epistemologists, and there is general agreement among them that its rejection of natural science would lead psychoanalysis into intellectual anarchy—to mention only the most telling of their criticisms.

In order to place psychoanalysis on a currently viable biological foundation, it is necessary to bring its hypotheses into conformity with contemporary knowledge in brain science, cognitive psychology, and the direct observation of (preverbal) children. It is both remarkable and highly encouraging that the relevant evidence from each of these disciplines is entirely congruent with that from the others. For psychoanalytic theory, it is most important that all three have organized their data in accord with hierarchical and epigenetic developmental principles; consequently, it would be most useful to conceptualize mental functions in the same manner.

Such an epigenetic view highlights the continuing availability throughout life of archaic modes of the organization of behavior on presymbolic levels. Because, in the expectable course of favorable development, this biopsychological core of the personality achieves structuralization when it is retranscribed in symbolic form (once the cerebral cortex becomes sufficiently mature), all the authors who have worked to integrate psychoanalysis with other biological disciplines have focused on this process of self-organization as the crux of a viable psychoanalytic theory of personality development. To put this matter differently, we have reached consensus on the conclusion that evidence from cognate disciplines has invalidated all previous psychoanalytic hypotheses about early childhood on the grounds that these have been excessively adultomorphic and pathomorphic: preverbal children turn out not to be comparable to maladapted adults.

I shall discuss the implications of the foregoing theoretical conclusions for clinical theory and the theory of technique after a review of recent contributions focused on these subjects.

20
Recent Clinical Discourse

In comparison to the rapidity of change in the basic theory of psychoanalysis, its clinical propositions (and the theory of technique focused on interpreting mental contents) have remained relatively stable.[1] This is particularly apparent if one chooses to focus on the distinct schools of thought that have been contending for preeminence in the psychoanalytic arena. Some of the most authoritative monographs recently published by representatives of these inward-looking groups have simply restated the orthodoxy that has long prevailed within their tradition. This is especially notable about the revised edition of Segal's (1974) primer of Kleinian psychoanalysis and about the contents of Lacan's (1977) selection of his writings for translation into English.

One could make the same judgment about Brenner's (1982) exposition of contemporary ego psychology, except for the fact that Brenner has taken cognizance of the epistemological objections to Freudian metapsychology. Consequently, he elaborates a clinical theory that does not postulate psychic energies and reduces his purview to the intrapsychic conflicts provoked by (infantile) wishes of a sexual or aggressive variety. Without quite denying the import of pregenital vicissitudes, Brenner's version of ego psychology is, *de facto*, entirely focused

---

1. The traditional technique of Freudian psychoanalysis focused on unconscious mental contents because it was based on a theory of pathogenesis centered on the significance of putative early childhood fantasies.

on derivatives of the oedipal period. In other words, this monograph attempts to maintain the traditional clinical positions of the American psychoanalytic mainstream by refusing to pay attention to any contingency to which those positions are poorly applicable.

The fact that, in practice, such reductionism can only lead to disastrous consequences has been extensively documented by a distinguished series of publications reporting the results of carefully designed followup studies (Firestein 1978; Schlessinger and Robbins 1983; Wallerstein 1986). These books present the outcomes of analyses, conducted in the traditional manner (within an ego psychological framework), in three different localities (New York, Chicago, and Topeka). All three demonstrate a great deal of overoptimism about prognosis on the part of the clinicians who performed these analyses. Wallerstein, whose sample included the largest proportion of patients with obviously severe difficulties, comes to the conclusion that the use of "classical" psychoanalysis (that is, analysis confined to an interpretive technique) in cases with "heroic indications" is unwise, to say the least.

Even with analysands who were less clearly impaired, the detailed case material presented in these books documents only disappointing results—modest therapeutic improvements at best. Schlessinger and Robbins show that, at follow up, unresolved pregenital issues continued to interfere with the adaptation of analysands whose oedipal conflicts had formed the exclusive focus of treatment. In other words, the widely held assumption that a new solution for oedipal problems could simultaneously deal with their pregenital *Anlagen* has been refuted. These authors conclude that characterological attributes crucial for adaptation have their genesis earlier in development than the oedipal period. Wallerstein also attributes some of the disappointing outcomes of treatment to insufficient attention to more archaic issues.

It is therefore scarcely surprising that, in response to its therapeutic disappointment, the past generation has been characterized by the appearance and/or growth of a number of dissident movements within American psychoanalysis. Among these, the most influential have been those of self psychology and of the relational viewpoint. The latter combines the object relations framework imported from Britain with our indigenous interpersonal orientation. Historians of these developments (Greenberg and Mitchell 1983; Bacal and Newman 1990; Summers 1994) contend that Kohut's self psychology is also best understood as a special form of object relations theory, one that postulates crucial relations with objects who perform functions essential for the individual's adaptation and further development.

Be that as it may, self psychology as a comprehensive psychoanalytic system was not articulated in Kohut's lifetime but only in a (1984) posthumous book. In that work, Kohut belatedly joined the list of contributors who had repudiated Freud's metapsychology before him, but he failed to specify whether he subscribed to any alternative set of biological assumptions. As a result, his followers seem to have adopted a mentalist framework and a position attributing personal destiny entirely to the effects of nurture. In this system, the only source of maladaptation is some disturbance in self–selfobject relations. This notion led to an assumption that providing analysands with "empathic acceptance" is sufficient to restart the development of psychic structure and, further, it led to redefinition of the aim of treatment in terms of mere adaptive improvements, effected through identification with the analyst.

All of that scarcely adds up to a psychoanalytic theory; it is at best a more or less coherent list of pragmatic guidelines for conducting treatment in a humane atmosphere and hoping for the best. Its very simplicity has probably made this system popular, particularly with practitioners of psychotherapy. Insofar as self psychologists still conduct analyses in the manner described in the casebook edited by Goldberg (1978), however incomplete these may be by our usual criteria, they certainly never do harm, and, by focusing on issues of self-esteem, they may achieve significant adaptive gains. Kohut's single-minded focus on the subjective aspect of mental life has also had a salutary effect on the attention clinicians pay to the consequences of their interactions with patients, a perspective on psychoanalytic transactions that has been popularized as the "intersubjective" viewpoint (see Stolorow and Atwood 1990).

The kind of indeterminacy that characterizes Kohut's epistemic position is by no means unusual among adherents of the relational option. None of the major contributors to this viewpoint has articulated a general hypothesis about the nature of mental operations. Almost by default, most of them seem to fall into a mentalist position; as Summers (1994) put this, they resort to a "pure psychology." Winnicott was particularly unwilling to systematize his ideas, many of which have become the common currency of clinical discourse. As Summers recounts these contributions, they actually transcend the realm of object relations. In this regard, Bacal and Newman (1990) point to Winnicott's emphasis on the development of a "sense of self," on the importance of a concept of "me-ness," and on the possibility of a split between a "true self" and a "false self." (I would add his postulation of "transitional experiences" that often involve only the infant's own body as another instance of structure formation beyond a relational context.)

These considerations call into doubt the historical validity of the attempt of Greenberg and Mitchell (1983) to dichotomize psychoanalytic theories into those based on drive/structure and those they called "relational." Their thesis obviously disregarded the main thrust of theoretical innovation in the 1970s (which I reviewed in the preceding chapter), the construction of theories of mentation based on the biological concept of self-organization. Although I cannot endorse the historical view of Summers, according to which object relations theories were stepping stones toward understanding structuralization of "the self," I believe that his very misjudgment indicates that the relational paradigm has now outlived its usefulness. Even Mitchell (1988), co-inventor of the "relational" label, has begun to use the concept of self-organization, although he tries (in my view, wrongly) to subsume it under the rubric of object relations. He does understand, however, that the establishment of self-organization thereafter limits the individual's flexibility—in other words, structuralization diminishes the current influence of object relations.

Greenberg (1991) has gone even further than his former collaborator in repudiating the centrality of a relational option: he has realized that relational theories share the false assumption that attachments can be established without the operation of inborn, pre-experiential vectors. Greenberg points out that such an assumption amounts to the illegitimate postulation of a biological prcess: Kohut's "selfobject need" corresponds to the Freudian notion of *Trieb*. In other words, psychoanalysis must have a theory of endogeneous motivations as constitutional givens (see Lichtenberg 1989).

Departures from received ideas have also taken place within the Kleinian tradition of psychoanalysis. As early as 1978, Meltzer acknowledged that Klein had erred in trying to force her novel clinical observations into Freud's theoretical framework, and he characterized much of her theoretical activity as the promulgation of an esoteric vocabulary. In his view, her clinical conclusions about splitting, projective identification, manic defenses, and making reparation constitute the valid core of her contributions. Following Bion, Meltzer criticized Klein's "anatomical" choice of terminology in her hypothesis that infants relate to "part objects"; in their view, what is at issue is the provision of functions the infant does not possess. Again in agreement with Bion, Meltzer cast doubt on the universality of omnipotent and omniscient attitudes.

Ogden's (1986) critique of Klein as a theoretician is even more radical. He rightly concludes that Klein's exclusive focus on mental contents is insufficient for theoretical purposes (cf. Rubinstein 1997). Further, he points out that Klein introduced confusion into her system by conflating the dynamic and structural points of view. He also expresses doubts about Klein's speeded-up chronology of psychic development, and (in a muted way) about her a priori commitment to the assumption of innate ideas. Ogden acknowledges that, before the era of psychological control, infants live through a period characterized by the purely biological regulation of behavior. Finally, he entertains the possibility that Klein's "paranoid/schizoid position" may crystallize only as a result of pathological developments, and he proposes that the mode of organization Klein called the "depressive position" is made possible by the establishment of a memory system organized in a sequential manner; hence he prefers to call this position "historical." Clearly, Ogden's version of Kleinian psychoanalysis does not amount to a sectarian enterprise.

Such willingness to reconsider outworn orthodoxies has manifested itself among a few authors from many schools of psychoanalysis, at least in the English-speaking world. That is my reason for asserting that, despite the disruptive consequences of varying epistemic commitments, a strong ecumenical tendency may gain the upper hand in contemporary psychoanalysis. Probably the most cogent statement of the rationale behind this movement is that of Levenson (1983). Starting from the observation that the differing interpretive schemata of the various psychoanalytic schools can be equally effective, Levenson concludes that theories of technique that attribute change to the influence of the information conveyed to the analysand cannot be valid.

Levenson proposes an alternative explanation, that the curative factor is inherent in some procedure that all psychoanalytic schools carry out in common—namely, that the semiotic rules of psychoanalysis (that is, the very process of communication in the analytic situation) constitute the tools of its influence. This implies, at the same time, that pathogenesis takes place as a result of the lack of semiotic and cognitive skills in childhood; hence, the therapeutic task of psychoanalysis is to correct the confusion left in the wake of childhood vicissitudes. Levenson rightly defines psychoanalysis as a method whereby we reach valid conclusions about the functions of mind (and not about mental contents). As a result, analysands acquire hitherto missing cognitive and semiotic skills (see also Gedo 1988). From this it follows that, until now, analytic success has depended on the analyst's skill in overcoming the influence of the invalid theories that were allegedly guiding him or her.

Views like these have gradually come to permeate the psychoanalytic literature on basic therapeutics. For instance, Friedman (1988) has decried the unrealistic qualities of past theories of technique, gaps he believes to have been papered over through metaphors suggesting some "alliance" between the participants. Friedman points out that these notions find some justification in the fact that learning optimally occurs in the context of a positive relationship. His own theory of technique gives equal cognizance to three therapeutic roles for the analyst: those of reader, historian, and operator. As reader, one grasps the gestalt of the analysand's narratives (cf. Schafer 1992); as historian, one recontextualizes the significance of past events through reconstructions (see also Wallace 1983); as operator, one serves as model, educator, and object of attachment. It is the analyst's role as operator that has been disavowed in previous theories of technique, and it is the delineation of the appropriate parameters of that role that constitutes the most pressing task for clinical psychoanalysis.

In a work intended to advocate the technical primacy of the interpretation of transference (in the here-and-now), Gill (1982) actually demonstrates the senselessness of policies of nonresponsiveness, rationalized on the illusory ground that they minimize the risk of "contaminating" the transference. He shows that, because *anything* that occurs in the analytic situation has transference significance for the analysand, there is no hope of avoiding such reactions through a refusal to engage in operational activities. In other words, Gill persuasively argues that inaction does not amount to neutrality; there is no hope that the analyst can be transformed into a blank screen. Gill concludes that the best policy, therefore, is simply to act human.

I have provided a set of rationales for various operational interventions commonly used in psychoanalysis (Gedo 1988, 1993a). Pine (1990) has joined me in repudiating the traditional viewpoint prevalent in American psychoanalysis, but he continued to advocate only those interventions Friedman characterized as broadening the choice of master narratives we ought to be attentive to. (Pine cogently notes that an exclusive focus on one, possibly two of these has characterized most of the ideological factions within our field.) But he endorses no measures beyond interpretation, nor does he indicate any rules of transition concerning the need to switch therapeutic focus from one master narrative to another.

In my judgment, the best argument for a change of technical focus has been provided by Gardner (1983), who redefines the ideal analytic process as one of "assisted self-inquiry." He means that it is helping the analysand to master methods of self-inquiry that is central for effective analysis, not the elucidation of any particular mental content. Success is contingent, however, on focusing on content issues tolerable for both participants. The analyst may help to explore these matters by attending not only to these contents, but to the form of the communicative interchange as well. According to Gardner, the analytic process is inevitably one of matching the subjectivities of the participants. (In my view, this is the best exposition of the actual import of intersubjectivity in the psychoanalytic literature.) The implication of this change of focus for the goal of treatment is that termination is appropriate when the analysand has learned to perform self-inquiry without assistance.

Gardner has also pointed out the epistemic constraints imposed on psychoanalysis by virtue of its dyadic format: on the one hand, analysts are only able to assist patients to discover whatever the analysts have the ability to apprehend about themselves; on the other, the analytic relationship inevitably brings into focus the analysand's functional state in a situation characterized by mutuality. In other words, analysis is less suited for the elucidation of conditions in states of solitude. Thus the acquisition of the capacity for self-inquiry is particularly crucial in order to enable analysands to deal with these matters on their own, generally after termination.

In parallel with these shifts of viewpoint about basic therapeutics, a series of more radical contributions (Ehrenberg 1992; Gedo 1979a, 1993a; Jacobs 1991; Modell 1990; Rosenfeld 1987; Searles 1986) has marked a movement toward consensus about a new theory of technique. Even Gray's (1994) restatement of the theory traditional within ego psychology makes it explicit that such an approach is appropriate only in dealing with "neuroses" (defined as narrowly as possible), or—better put—with oedipal transferences alone. Influenced by Gardner's work, Gray points out that resistances should be not overridden but functionally analyzed, in the service of learning how the analysand's mind operates. He advocates systematic efforts to promote patients' self-observing abilities, in a frankly educative manner, including demonstrations of such operations on the part of the analyst.

In contrast to Gray, the other authors under discussion do not believe that analysts can often succeed if attention is narrowly focused on oedipal vicissitudes. For instance, Searles documents that all of his analysands responded to (his specific manner of conducting) analytic treatment with archaic transferences that he calls "borderline." When these regressive states supervene, communication in the analytic situation cannot take place successfully as long as it is confined to the language of secondary process. Because of such complications, Ehrenberg, whose monograph confines itself to pragmatic issues, outlines a series of rules of thumb applicable to analytic work across the board. Her algorithm (cf. Levenson 1983) includes careful attention to nonverbal semiosis, monitoring the analyst's subjectivity and using countertransference reactions as data that signal the analysand's reciprocal expectations, communicating in an affectively charged manner, stopping enactments destructive toward either participant, and taking responsibility for devising solutions for any therapeutic impasse.[2]

I find it most heartening that the developing technical consensus includes contributions from analysts trained in most of the traditions prevalent in psychoanalysis before the period under review. Thus

---

2. Ehrenberg's sound clinical recommendations demonstrate that a mentalist viewpoint does not preclude effective analytic work—it does, however, make it impossible to articulate a rationale for the clinical decisions in question.

Jacobs (formerly an ego psychologist) echoes many of the recommendations of Ehrenberg (an interpersonalist), and both have a large measure of agreement with Rosenfeld (a Kleinian). In addition, the theory of technique I have proposed in my own writings is entirely congruent with that of Modell. The latter defines the mode of action of psychoanalysis as the retranscription of the transference repetition of traumatic experiences in terms of new meanings and the elimination of splits in the self-organization. Modell sees the crux of treatment as affective retraining, leading to mastery through repetition and recontextualization. In other words, he lays stress on biological issues, rather than on mental contents, in explaining psychopathology. Hence the therapeutic task consists in the acquisition of new psychological skills.

Conclusion

The foregoing survey of a large sample of the most significant psychoanalytic monographs of the past generation suggests that current theoretical differences in the field are actually based on fundamental disagreements about appropriate methods for the attainment of knowledge. The most intractable of these epistemic disputes is one between those who emphasize the need for empiricism and those who follow a predominantly rationalist path. The first group conceive psychoanalysis to be a branch of natural science; those in the second either explicitly repudiate that commitment or merely pay lip service to it while they give priority to various philosophical doctrines. In contrast to natural science, disciplines that employ a rationalist epistemology lack agreed-upon standards of validation; consequently, schools of psychoanalysis that adhere to rationalism can maintain their a priori viewpoints, no matter what kind of empirical evidence may come to light.

Such imperviousness to fresh data (especially evidence from extra-clinical sources) has characterized a number of psychoanalytic traditions that construe Freud's century-old metapsychology not as a scientific theory that has been refuted but as a reliable philosophy of mind. This viewpoint is particularly clear in the case of Lacan, whose innovations were explicitly based on the work of philosophers, such as Hegel and Heidegger. In my judgment, it also explains the continuing adherence of most Kleinians and Mahlerians to the metapsychology of the 1890s, although they have not provided any philosophical justification for their commitment.

It is more difficult to understand the recent emergence of an (exclusively) hermeneutic school of thought within psychoanalysis, for this development was undoubtedly precipitated by the invalidation of Freud's metapsychology by data from neuroscience. Yet this led a number of contributors to decide that psychoanalysis is not a natural science; by adopting a purely hermeneutic viewpoint, these authors thereupon tried to abandon the obligation to pay heed to further empirical evidence. As a number of epistemologists have pointed out, such a philosophical decision can only lead to intellectual anarchy, because it does not provide a rationale for making choices among competing explanations.

Among active contributors to psychoanalytic discourse, a great majority have opted for natural science and the empiricist method also endorsed by most epistemologists interested in psychoanalysis. Within this camp, however, there is a further split about the mind/body problem between monists and dualists. None of the epistemologists of psychoanalysis adheres to a dualist position, nor has any psychoanalyst openly advocated such an unfashionable view, but many analytic proposals utterly disregard anything beyond mental contents—in other words, de facto they make use of purely mentalist presuppositions. Among the books surveyed in this guide, it is the work of most contributors in the relational school (including the self psychologists) that I classify as mentalist.

My own convictions follow the predominant view, that is, the monist position on the mind/body question and the classification of psychoanalysis as one of the biological sciences. Although I prefer not to condemn alternative positions as untenable, I believe the majority have chosen the best option available, because it is the only one through which psychoanalysis as a body of knowledge can progress by making use of empirical evidence from both clinical and extraclinical sources. The necessary flow of information can best be described by means of the accompanying diagram (Figure 1). In contrast to this rich input of information from cognate sciences, a mentalist viewpoint isolates psychoanalysis from neurobiology, and the schools committed to rationalist epistemologies disregard the potential input of all other disciplines.

As a component of biological science, contemporary psychoanalysis was bound to take advantage of the evolution of theoretical biology, just as Freud was prompt to incorporate Hughlings Jackson's con-

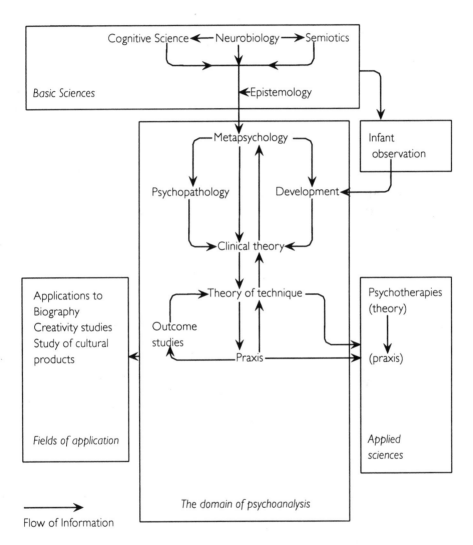

Figure 1. Psychoanalysis as a Natural Science

cept of the hierarchic organization of the brain into psychoanalysis. The most recent concept from biology to have entered analytic discourse is that of the self-organizing property of complex systems (see Gedo 1979a; Dorpat and Miller 1992; Modell 1993). Modell has rightly stated that the maintenance of self-organization is a vital biological priority; this is the functional explanation for the phenomena psychoanalysis has seen as the repetition compulsion. Thus self-organization constitutes a paradigmatic concept for a biological view of mental functioning. Such a structure is gradually established on the basis of memories of early experience—action schemata, rather than representations of objects—and it reaches completion with the addition of conceptual schemata of self-in-the-world. Weiss and Sampson (1986) propose to call dyspraxic schemata "pathogenic beliefs." Dorpat and Miller understand transference as the organization of current experience in terms of preexisting schemata; in parallel, resistance is the tendency to conserve the self-organization, and trauma is the disorganization that follows the inability to do so.[1]

Modell stresses that it is by means of self-organization that each brain becomes unique. To put this differently, the schemata that are organized into "self" are themselves self-created. This is a cogent argument against transforming psychoanalytic theory into a "two-person psychology" (Mitchell 1997); it is echoed in Modell's emphasis on the *privacy* of self and the importance of solitary experiences for autonomous development. It is memories of successful activity (rather than benign internal objects) that enable children to manage on their own. From this it follows that the curative factor in psychoanalysis must be the acquisition of new procedural schemata by means of the actions performed in the analytic situation.

Finally, Levenson (1983) rightly states that a theory based on the concept of self-organization can simultaneously satisfy the three basic requirements for an adequate psychoanalytic framework: it can accurately reflect the organization of the central nervous system, it can

---

1. It is the persistence of dyspraxic action schemata that interferes with the ability to learn, to overcome false beliefs, and successfully to adapt to novelty.

accommodate a hierarchical view of behavioral regulation, and it can map mental functions as a holistic network.

*   *   *

I trust that the foregoing summary has made clear my reasons for believing that psychoanalysis is in the midst of a veritable metamorphosis: the intellectual vanguard of our profession has, in the last quarter century, altered psychoanalysis as drastically as chemistry was transformed when it progressed from the molecular to the atomic level of conceptualization. (I use the analogy advisedly: psychoanalysis has a long way to go to approximate the scientific maturity of contemporary chemistry!) At the same time, it must be admitted that the great majority of analytic practitioners have paid scant attention to the avant garde but have continued to do clinical work in the manner they learned during their training. And this state of affairs is perfectly natural— such a contrast between academics and clinicians characterizes most health specialties.

It is the next generation of psychoanalysts who should be able to put the lessons of the recent past into practice. For the moment, however, most students have great difficulty in separating the wheat from the chaff of our ever expanding literature; consequently, they are likely to confine their reading to authors within a single tradition or, even worse, to be carried away by current fashions. Hence thoughtful assessments of the widest possible array of contributions are urgently needed. Because every historian is inevitably somewhat biased, alternative versions of the intellectual history of the past generation should be developed. This book is offered as a reader's guide organized by a commitment to view psychoanalysis as a biological science, a vantage point recommended by every epistemologist familiar with the field.

It is this commitment to scientific standards that alone can make possible the articulation of a theory of technique rationally related to what is known about mental functions (adaptive and maladaptive), both on the basis of clinical observations and from the findings of cognate disciplines. The most difficult task facing the next generation of psychoanalysts will be to abandon those of our traditional procedures the (largely forgotten) rationales of which have been invalidated by fresh evidence from these sources.

References*

*Items marked with an asterisk are discussed in detail.

*Adler, G. (1985). *Borderline Psychopathology and Its Treatment*. New York: Jason Aronson.
*Bacal, H. and Newman, K. (1990). *Theories of Object Relations: Bridges to Self Psychology*. New York: Columbia University Press.
Balint, M. (1932). Character analysis and new beginnings. In *Primary Love and Psychoanalytic Technique*, pp. 151–164. London: Maresfield Library, 1985.
——— (1985). *Primary Love and Psychoanalytic Technique*. London: Maresfield Library.
Basch, M. F. (1975a). Perception, consciousness, and Freud's "Project." *The Annual of Psychoanalysis*. 3:3–19.
——— (1975b). Psychic determinism and freedom of will. Paper presented at the Institute for Psychoanalysis, Chicago, March.
——— (1975c). Toward a theory that encompasses depression: a revision of existing causal hypotheses in psychoanalysis. In *Depression and Human Existence*, ed. E. Anthony and T. Benedek, pp. 483–534. Boston: Little Brown.
——— (1976a). The concept of affect: a re-examination. *Journal of the American Psychoanalytic Association* 24:759–777.
——— (1976b). Psychoanalysis and communication science. *The Annual of Psychoanalysis* 4:385–422.
——— (1976c). Theory formation in Chapter VII: a critique. *Journal of the American Psychoanalytic Association* 24:61–100.

————— (1977). Developmental psychology and explanatory theory in psycho-analysis. *The Annual of Psychoanalysis* 5:229–263.

————— (1983). The perception of reality and the disavowal of meaning. *The Annual of Psychoanalysis* 11:125–154.

————— (1986). "How does analysis cure?": an appreciation. *Psychoanaytic Inquiry* 6:403–428.

*Bollas, C. (1987). *The Shadow of the Object*. New York: Columbia University Press.

Bowlby, J. (1969). *Attachment and Loss*, vol. 1. New York: Basic Books.

*Brenner, C. (1982). *The Mind in Conflict*. New York: International Universities Press.

Bucci, W. (1993). The development of emotional meaning in free association: a multiple code theory. In *Hierarchical Concepts in Psychoanalysis*, ed. A. Wilson and J. Gedo, pp. 3–47. New York: Guilford.

*————— (1997). *Psychoanalysis and Cognitive Science*. New York: Guilford.

*Cavell, M. (1993). *The Psychoanalytic Mind*. Cambridge, MA: Harvard University Press.

*Dorpat, T. and Miller, M. (1992). *Clinical Interaction and the Analysis of Meaning*. Hillsdale, NJ: Analytic Press.

Dupont, J., ed. (1988). *The Clinical Diary of Sándor Ferenczi*. Cambridge, MA: Harvard University Press.

Edelman, G. (1987). *Neural Darwinism*. New York: Basic Books.

*Edelson, M. (1988). *Psychoanalysis: A Theory in Crisis*. Chicago: University of Chicago Press.

*Ehrenberg, D. (1992). *The Intimate Edge*. New York: Norton.

Eissler, K. (1953). The effect of the structure of the ego on psychoanalytic technique. *Journal of the American Psychoanalytic Association* 1:104–143.

Erle, J. (1979). An approach to the study of analyzability and analysis: the course of forty consecutive cases selected for supervised analyses. *Psychoanalytic Quarterly* 48:198–228.

Erle, J. and Goldberg, D. (1984). Observations on assessment of analyzability by experienced analysts. *Journal of the American Psychoanalytic Association* 32:715–738.

Fairbairn, R. (1954). *An Object-Relations Theory of the Personality*. New York: Basic Books.

Ferenczi, S. and Rank, O. (1924). *The Development of Psychoanalysis*. New York: Nervous & Mental Disease Publishing.

*Firestein, S. (1978). *Termination in Psychoanalysis*. New York: International Universities Press.

Frank, A. (1969). The unrememberable and the unforgettable: passive primal repression. In *Psychoanalytic Study of the Child* 24:59–66. New York: International Universities Press.

Freedman, D. (1984). The origins of motivation. In *Psychoanalysis: The Vital Issues*, vol. 1, ed. J. Gedo and G. Pollock, pp. 17–38. New York: International Universities Press.

*———— (1997). *On Infancy and Toddlerhood*. Madison, CT: International Universities Press.

French, T. (1952). *The Integration of Behavior*, vol. 1. Chicago: University of Chicago Press.

Freud, S. (1891). Sketches for the "preliminary communication" of 1893. *Standard Edition* 1:147–154.

———— (1895). Project for a scientific psychology. *Standard Edition* 1:283–391.

———— (1900). The interpretation of dreams. *Standard Edition* 4/5: 1–626.

———— (1905). Three essays on the theory of sexuality. *Standard Edition* 7:130–243.

———— (1912). Recommendations to physicians practicing psycho-analysis. *Standard Edition* 12:110–120.

———— (1915a). Repression. *Standard Edition* 14:146–158.

———— (1915b). Instincts and their vicissitudes. *Standard Edition* 14:105–141.

———— (1920). Beyond the pleasure principle. *Standard Edition* 18:3–64.

———— (1923). The ego and the id. *Standard Edition* 19:3–66.

———— (1937). Analysis terminable and interminable. *Standard Edition* 23:216–253.

———— (1940). An outline of psycho-analysis. *Standard Edition* 23:141–208.

*Friedman, L. (1988). *The Anatomy of Psychotherapy*. Hillsdale, NJ: Analytic Press.

*Gardner, R. (1983). *Self Inquiry*. Hillsdale, NJ: Analytic Press, 1989.

———— (1993). On talking to ourselves: some self-analytic reflections on self-analysis. In *Self-Analysis*, ed. W. Barron, pp. 147–163. Hillsdale, NJ: Analytic Press.

Gedo, J. (1975). To Heinz Kohut: on his 60th birthday. *The Annual of Psychoanalysis* 3:313–322.

———— (1979a). *Beyond Interpretation*. New York: International Universities Press.

———— (1979b). A psychoanalyst reports at mid-career. *American Journal of Psychiatry* 136:646–649.

———— (1980). Reflections on some current controversies in psychoanalysis. *Journal of the American Psychoanalytic Association* 28:363–383.

———— (1981a). *Advances in Clinical Psychoanalysis*. New York: International Universities Press.

————(1981b). Measure for measure: a response. *Psychoanalytic Inquiry* 1:289–316.

————(1983). *Portraits of the Artist*. Hillsdale, NJ: Analytic Press, 1989.

————(1984). *Psychoanalysis and Its Discontents*. New York: Guilford.

————(1986). *Conceptual Issues in Psychoanalysis*. Hillsdale, NJ: Analytic Press.

————(1988). *The Mind in Disorder*. Hillsdale, NJ: Analytic Press.

————(1991). *The Biology of Clinical Encounters*. Hillsdale, NJ: Analytic Press.

————(1993a). *Beyond Interpretation*, revised edition. Hillsdale, NJ: Analytic Press.

————(1993b). Empathy, new beginnings, and analytic cure. *Psychoanalytic Review* 80:507–518.

————(1995a). Working through as metaphor and as a modality of treatment. *Journal of the American Psychoanalytic Association* 43:339–356.

————(1995b). Encore. *Journal of the American Psychoanalytic Association* 43:383–392.

————(1996a). *The Languages of Psychoanalysis*. Hillsdale, NJ: Analytic Press.

————(1996b). *The Artist and the Emotional World: Creativity and Personality*. New York: Columbia University Press.

————(1997a). Reflections on metapsychology, theoretical coherence, hermeneutics, and biology. *Journal of the American Psychoanalytic Association* 45:779–806.

————(1997b). *Spleen and Nostalgia: A Life and Work in Psychoanalysis*. Northvale, NJ: Jason Aronson.

————(in press). On inspiring confidence. In *The Person of the Analyst*, ed. E. Piccioli, P.-L. Rossi, and A. Semi, pp. 00–00. London: Karnac.

Gedo, J. and Gedo, M. (1992). *Perspectives on Creativity: The Biographical Method*. Norwood, NJ: Ablex.

Gedo, J. and Gehrie, M. (1993). *Impasse and Innovation in Psychoanalysis*. Hillsdale, NJ: Analytic Press.

Gedo, J. and Goldberg, A. (1973). *Models of the Mind*. Chicago: University of Chicago Press.

Gedo, P. (1988). The significant hour in psychoanalysis. Unpublished dissertation, University of Chicago.

Gill, M. (1976). Metapsychology is not psychology. In *Psychology versus Metapsychology*, ed. M. Gill and P. Holzman. *Psychological Issues*, Monograph 36, pp. 71–105. New York: International Universities Press.

*————(1982). *Analysis of Transference. Psychological Issues*, Monograph 53. New York: International Universities Press.

————(1994). *Psychoanalysis in Transition*. Hillsdale, NJ: Analytic Press.

Gill M. and Holzman, P., eds. (1976). *Psychology versus Metapsychology: Psychoanalytic Essays in Memory of George S. Klein. Psychological Issues* Monograph 36, pp. 71–105. New York: International Universities Press.

Gitelson, M. (1962). The curative factors in psychoanalysis. *International Journal of Psycho-Analysis* 43:194–205.

*Goldberg, A., ed. (1978). *The Psychology of the Self: A Casebook.* New York: International Universities Press.

——— (1988). *A Fresh Look at Psychoanalysis: The View from Self Psychology.* Hillsdale, NJ: Analytic Press.

——— (1995). *The Problem of Perversion.* New Haven, CT: Yale University Press.

Goldberg, A. and Stepansky, P., eds. (1984). *Kohut's Legacy.* Hillsdale, NJ: Analytic Press.

*Gray, P. (1994). *The Ego and the Analysis of Defense.* Northvale, NJ: Jason Aronson.

*Greenberg, J. (1991). *Oedipus and Beyond.* Cambridge, MA: Harvard University Press.

*Greenberg, J. and Mitchell, S. (1983). *Object Relations in Psychoanalytic Theory.* Cambridge, MA: Harvard University Press.

Grossman, W. (1976). Knightmare in armor: reflections on Wilhelm Reich's contributions to psychoanalysis. *Psychiatry* 39:376–385.

——— (1986). Freud and Horney: a study of psychoanalytic models via the analysis of a controversy. In *Psychoanalysis, the Science of Mental Conflict: Essays in Honor of Charles Brenner,* ed. A. Richards and M. Willick, pp. 65–87. Hillsdale, NJ: Analytic Press.

*Grünbaum, A. (1984). *The Foundations of Psychoanalysis.* Berkeley: University of California Press.

*——— (1993). *Validation in the Clinical Theory of Psychoanalysis. Psychological Issues,* Monograph 61. Madison, CT: International Universities Press.

Habermas, J. (1968). *Knowledge and Human Interests.* Boston: Beacon Press, 1971.

Hadley, J. (1983). The representational system: a bridging concept for psychoanalysis and neurophysiology. *International Review of Psycho-Analysis* 10:13–30.

——— (1985). Attention, affect, and attachment. *Psychoanalysis and Contemporary Thought* 8:529–550.

——— (1989). The neurobiology of motivational systems. In *Psychoanalysis and Motivation,* J. Lichtenberg, pp. 337–372. Hillsdale, NJ: Analytic Press.

——— (1992). The instincts revisited. *Psychoanalytic Inquiry* 12:396–418.

——— (in press). The self-organization and the autonomy system. *The Annual of Psychoanalysis.*

Hartmann, H. (1939). *Ego Psychology and the Problem of Adaptation*. New York: International Universities Press, 1958.

———— (1964). *Essays in Ego Psychology*. New York: International Universities Press.

Hayman, A. (1969). What do we mean by "id"? *Journal of the American Psychoanalytic Association* 17:353–380.

*Holt, R. (1989). *Freud Reappraised: A Fresh Look at Psychoanalytic Theory*. New York: Guilford.

*Jacobs, T. (1991). *The Use of the Self*. Madison, CT: International Universities Press.

Kantrowitz, J. (1987). Suitability for psychoanalysis. *Yearbook of Psychoanalytic Psychotherapy* 2:403–415.

Kernberg, O. (1975). *Borderline Conditions and Pathological Narcissism*. New York: Jason Aronson.

*———— (1976). *Object Relations Theory and Clinical Psychoanalysis*. New York: Jason Aronson.

*Klein, G. (1976). *Psychoanalytic Theory: An Exploration of Essentials*. New York: International Universities Press.

Klein, M. (1984). *Writings*, 4 vols. New York: Free Press.

Kohut, H. (1968). The psychoanalytic treatment of narcissistic personality disorders: outline of a systematic approach. In *The Search for the Self*, pp. 477–509. New York: International Universities Press, 1978.

———— (1971). *The Analysis of the Self*. New York: International Universities Press.

*———— (1977). *The Restoration of the Self*. New York: International Universities Press.

———— (1978). *The Search for the Self*, 2 vols. New York: International Universities Press.

*———— (1984). *How Does Analysis Cure?* Chicago: University of Chicago Press.

Kohut, H. and Wolf, E. (1978). The disorders of the self and their treatment: an outline. *International Journal of Psycho-Analysis* 59:413–426.

Krystal, H. (1988). *Integration and Self-healing: Affect–Trauma–Alexithymia*. Hillsdale, NJ: Analytic Press.

*Lacan, J. (1977). *Ecrits: A Selection*, trans. A. Sheridan. New York: Norton.

*Levenson, E. (1983). *The Ambiguity of Change*. New York: Basic Books.

*Levin, F. (1991). *Mapping the Mind*. Hillsdale, NJ: Analytic Press.

*Lichtenberg, J. (1983). *Psychoanalysis and Infant Research*. Hillsdale, NJ: Analytic Press.

*———— (1989). *Psychoanalysis and Motivation*. Hillsdale, NJ: Analytic Press.

Lichtenberg, J., Lachmann, F., and Fosshage, J. (1996). *The Clinical Exchange: Techniques Derived from Self and Motivational Systems*. Hillsdale, NJ: Analytic Press.

Lichtenstein, H. (1965). Towards a metapsychological definition of the concept of self. *International Journal of Psycho-Analysis* 46:117–128.

——— (1977). *The Dilemma of Human Identity*. New York: Jason Aronson.

Loewald, H. (1960). On the therapeutic action of psychoanalysis. *International Journal of Psycho-Analysis* 41:16–33.

Mahler, M. S. and Furer, M. (1968). *On Human Symbiosis and the Vicissitudes of Individuation*. New York: International Universities Press.

*Mahler, M. S., Pine, F., and Bergman, A. (1975). *The Psychological Birth of the Human Infant*. New York: Basic Books.

*McDougall, J. (1980). *A Plea for a Measure of Abnormality*. New York: International Universities Press.

*Meltzer, D. (1978). *The Kleinian Development*. Strathay, Scotland: Clunie Press.

Mitchell, J. (1974). *Psychoanalysis and Feminism*. London: Allen Lane.

*Mitchell, S. (1988). *Relational Concepts in Psychoanalysis: An Integration*. Cambridge, MA: Harvard University Press.

——— (1997). *Influence and Autonomy in Psychoanalysis*. Hillsdale, NJ: Analytic Press.

Modell, A. (1965). On having the right to a life: an aspect of the superego's development. *International Journal of Psycho-Analysis* 46:323–331.

——— (1968). *Object Love and Reality*. New York: International Universities Press.

——— (1976). "The holding environment" and the therapeutic action of psychoanalysis. *Journal of the American Psychoanalytic Association* 24:285–308.

——— (1984). *Psychoanalysis in a New Context*. New York: International Universities Press.

*——— (1990). *Other Times, Other Realities*. Cambridge, MA: Harvard University Press.

*——— (1993). *The Private Self*. Cambridge, MA: Harvard University Press.

*Muller, J. (1996). *Beyond the Psychoanalytic Dyad*. New York: Routledge.

*Muller, J. and Richardson, W. J. (1982). *Lacan and Language: A Reader's Guide to Écrits*. New York: International Universities Press.

Norman, H., Blacker, K., Oremland, J., and Barrett, W. (1976). The fate of the transference neurosis after termination of a satisfactory analysis. *Journal of the American Psychoanalytic Association* 24:471–498.

Noy, P. (1969). A revision of the psychoanalytic theory of the primary process. *International Journal of Psycho-Analysis* 50:155–178.

*Ogden, T. (1986). *The Matrix of the Mind*. Northvale, NJ: Jason Aronson.

Opatow, B. (1989). Drive theory and the metapsychology of experience. *International Journal of Psycho-Analysis* 70:645–660.

Oremland, J., Blacker, K., and Norman, H. (1975). Incompleteness in "successful" psychoanalyses: a follow-up study. *Journal of the American Psychoanalytic Association* 23:819–844.

Palombo, S. (1978). *Dreaming and Memory*. New York: Basic Books.

Parens, H. (1979). *The Development of Aggression in Early Childhood*. New York: Jason Aronson.

Pfeffer, A. (1959). A procedure for evaluating the results of psychoanalysis: a preliminary report. *Journal of the American Psychoanalytic Association* 7:418–444.

———(1961). Follow-up study of a satisfactory analysis. *Journal of the American Psychoanalytic Association* 9:698–718.

*Pine, F. (1990). *Drive, Ego, Object, and Self*. New York: Basic Books.

———(1994). Multiple models, clinical practice, and psychoanalytic theory. *Psychoanalytic Inquiry* 14:212–234.

*Polányi, M. (1974). *Scientific Thought and Social Reality*. *Psychological Issues*, Monograph 32, ed. F. Schwartz. New York: International Universities Press.

Racker, H. (1968). *Transference and Countertransference*. New York: International Universities Press.

*Rapaport, D. (1974). *The History of the Concept of Association of Ideas*. New York: International Universities Press.

*Reiser, M. (1984). *Mind, Brain, Body*. New York: Basic Books.

Ricoeur, P. (1970). *Freud and Philosophy*. New Haven: Yale University Press.

———(1981). *Hermeneutics and the Human Sciences*. Cambridge, UK: Cambridge University Press.

*Rosenblatt, A. and Thickstun, J. (1977). *Modern Psychoanalytic Concepts in a General Psychology*. *Psychoanalytic Issues*, Monograph 42/43. New York: International Universities Press.

*Rosenfeld, H. (1987). *Impasse and Interpretation*. London: Tavistock.

Rothstein, A. (1983). *Ego Psychology: An Evolutionary Perspective*. New York: International Universities Press.

Roustang, F. (1990). *Dire Mastery: Discipleship from Freud to Lacan*. Baltimore: Johns Hopkins University Press.

*Rubinstein, B. (1997). *Psychoanalysis and the Philosophy of Science*. *Psychological Issues*, Monograph 62/63, ed. R. Holt. Madison, CT: International Universities Press.

Sander, L. (1980). Investigation of the infant and its caregiving environment as a biological system. In *The Course of Life*, vol. 1, ed. S. Greenspan and G. Pollock, pp. 177–202. Rockville, MD: NIMH.

———(1983). To begin with—reflections on ontogeny. In *Reflections on Self Psychology*, ed. J. Lichtenberg and S. Kaplan, pp. 85–104. Hillsdale, NJ: Analytic Press.

———(1986). The inner experience of the infant: a framework for inference relevant to the development of the sense of self. Paper presented to the Mahler Symposium, Paris.

Schafer, R. (1976). *A New Language for Psychoanalysis*. New Haven, CT: Yale University Press.

———— (1978). *Language and Insight*. New Haven, CT: Yale University Press.

*———— (1992). *Retelling a Life*. New York: Basic Books.

*Schlessinger, N. and Robbins, F. (1983). *A Developmental View of the Psychoanalytic Process*. New York: International Universities Press.

*Schore, A. (1994). *Affect Regulation and the Origin of the Self*. Hillsdale, NJ: Lawrence Erlbaum.

Schwaber, E. (1983). Psychoanalytic listening and psychic reality. *International Journal of Psycho-Analysis* 10:379–392.

*Searles, H. (1986). *My Work with Borderline Patients*. Northvale, NJ: Jason Aronson.

*Segal, H. (1974). *Introduction to the Work of Melanie Klein*, 2nd edition. New York: Basic Books.

*Spence, D. (1982). *Narrative Truth and Historical Truth*. New York: Norton.

Spitz, R. (1946). Anaclitic depression. In *Psychoanalytic Study of the Child* 2:313–346. New York: International Universities Press.

———— (1962). Autoerotism reexamined. In *Psychoanalytic Study of the Child* 17:283–315. New York: International Universities Press.

Spitz, R. and Cobliner, W. (1965). *The First Year of Life*. New York: International Universities Press.

*Stern, D. (1985). *The Interpersonal World of the Infant*. New York: Basic Books.

Stern, D. B. (1997). *Unformulated Experience*. Hillsdale, NJ: Analytic Press.

*Stolorow, R. and Atwood, G. (1990). *Contexts of Being: The Intersubjective Foundations of Psychological Life*. Hillsdale, NJ: Analytic Press.

Stone, L. (1965). *The Psychoanalytic Situation*. New York: International Universities Press.

Strachey, J. (1934). The nature of the therapeutic action of psychoanalysis. *International Journal of Psycho-Analysis* 1969, 50:275–292.

*Strenger, C. (1991). *Between Hermeneutics and Science. Psychological Issues* Monograph 59. Madison, CT: International Universities Press.

*Summers, F. (1994). *Object Relations Theories and Psychopathology*. Hillsdale, NJ: Analytic Press.

Sulloway, F. (1979). *Freud, Biologist of the Mind*. New York: Basic Books.

Swanson, D. (1977). A critique of psychic energy as an explanatory concept. *Journal of the American Psychoanalytic Association* 25:603–633.

*Wallace, E. (1985). *Historiography and Causation in Psychoanalysis*. Hillsdale, NJ: Analytic Press.

*Wallerstein, R. (1986). *Forty Two Lives in Treatment*. New York: Guilford.

*Weiss, J., Sampson, H., and the Mt. Zion Psychotherapy Research Group (1986). *The Psychoanalytic Process*. New York: Guilford.

White, R. (1963). *Ego and Reality in Psychoanalytic Theory. Psychological Issues,* Monograph 11. New York: International Universities Press.

Winnicott, D. (1950). Aggression in relation to emotional development. In *Collected Papers,* pp. 204–218. London: Tavistock, 1958.

Wilson, A. and Gedo, J., eds. (1993). *Hierarchical Concepts in Psychoanalysis.* New York: Guilford.

Wolf, E. (1980). On the developmental line of selfobject relations. In *Advances in Self Psychology,* ed. A. Goldberg, pp. 117–132. New York: International Universities Press.

——— (1984). Disruptions in the psychoanalytic treatment of disorders of the self. In *Kohut's Legacy,* ed. P. Stepansky and A. Goldberg, pp. 143–156. Hillsdale, NJ: Analytic Press.

Name Index

Subject Index

Also of interest from Other Press . . .

OTHER

www.otherpress.com

toll free 877-THE OTHER (843-6843)